JESUS WITHIN JUDAISM

ABRL

THE ANCHOR BIBLE REFERENCE LIBRARY is designed to be a third major component of the Anchor Bible group, which includes the Anchor Bible commentaries on the books of the Old Testament, the New Testament, and the Apocrypha, and the Anchor Bible Dictionary. While the Anchor Bible commentaries and the Anchor Bible Dictionary are structurally defined by their subject matter, the Anchor Bible Reference Library will serve as a supplement on the cutting edge of the most recent scholarship. The new series will be open-ended; its scope and reach are nothing less than the biblical world in its totality, and its methods and techniques the most up-to-date available or devisable. Separate volumes will deal with one or more of the following topics relating to the Bible: anthropology, archaeology, ecology, economy, geography, history, languages and literatures, philosophy, religion(s), theology.

As with the Anchor Bible commentaries and the Anchor Bible Dictionary, the philosophy underlying the Anchor Bible Reference Library finds expression in the following: the approach is scholarly, the perspective is balanced and fair-minded, the methods are scientific, and the goal is to inform and enlighten. Contributors are chosen on the basis of their scholarly skills and achievements, and they come from a variety of religious backgrounds and communities. The books in the Anchor Bible Reference Library are intended for the broadest possible readership, ranging from world-class scholars, whose qualifications match those of the authors, to general readers, who may not have special training or skill in studying the Bible but are as enthusiastic as any dedicated professional in expanding their knowledge of the Bible and its world.

David Noel Freedman
GENERAL EDITOR

THE ANCHOR BIBLE REFERENCE LIBRARY

JESUS WITHIN JUDAISM

New Light from Exciting Archaeological Discoveries

JAMES H. CHARLESWORTH

DOUBLEDAY
NEW YORK LONDON TORONTO SYDNEY AUCKLAND

PUBLISHED BY DOUBLEDAY
a division of Bantam Doubleday Dell Publishing Group, Inc.
666 Fifth Avenue, New York, New York 10103

THE ANCHOR BIBLE REFERENCE LIBRARY, DOUBLEDAY, and the portrayal of
an anchor with the letters ABRL are trademarks of Doubleday, a division
of Bantam Doubleday Dell Publishing Group, Inc.

Library of Congress Cataloging in Publication Data
Charlesworth, James H.
Jesus Within Judaism.
(Anchor Bible Reference Library)
Bibliography: p. 223
Includes indexes.
1. Jesus Christ—Historicity. 2. Judaism—History—
Post-exilic period, 586 B.C.–210 B.C. A.D. 70
3. Bible—Antiquities. 4. Palestine—Antiquities.
5. Excavations (Archaeology)—Palestine.
6. Jesus Christ—Teachings. I. Title. II. Series.
BT303.2.C46   1988   232.9   87-13552
ISBN 0-385-23610-7

Dedicated to my colleagues in
New College,
the University of Edinburgh,
especially to the
principal, dean, and
heads of departments,
in remembrance of 1967 and 1968
and the gracious hospitality and great
honors received during May 1985

PREFACE

Jesus Within Judaism contains the Gunning (Victoria Jubilee) Lectures delivered in May 1985 in New College, the University of Edinburgh. In order to make these lectures more interesting and enjoyable for a wide audience, I have removed all technical language and supplied brief footnotes.

It is a distinct pleasure and honor to be allowed to share with all who are interested some of the exciting manuscript and archaeological discoveries that help inform us about Jesus' time and country. What is most significant is that they reveal some of the terms and concepts he inherited and, as far as we know, never explained or defined. The following chapters focus on Jesus in view of the light shone on him from the Old Testament Pseudepigrapha, the Dead Sea Scrolls, the Nag Hammadi Codices, an Arabic manuscript that contains a version of the testimony to Jesus by the Jewish historian Josephus, and archaeological excavations in Palestine, especially in Capernaum and Jerusalem.

Jesus Research has become captivatingly rewarding. Today we can peruse some Jewish documents roughly contemporaneous with him, hearing terms, concepts, and dreams that once were considered unique to, or at least typical of, Jesus. In a Jewish apocalypse probably written during the century in which Jesus lived, we read some strikingly familiar words; note the following:

> So, if there is no truth in human beings, then let them make an oath by means of the words, "Yes, Yes!" or, if it should be the other way around, "No, No!" (2En 49:1 [J])[1]
> . . . in the great age many shelters have been prepared for people. (2En 61:2 [A]; cf. 1En 39:4f., 41:2)

Many readers of these passages will immediately remember two sayings attributed to Jesus, namely the following:

But let your word (or oath, cf. 5:36) be "Yes, Yes!" (or) "No, No!" (Mt 5:37)[2]

In the house of my father are many (heavenly) dwellings (or shelters). (Jn 14:2)

I am convinced that 2 Enoch in the passages excerpted may not be edited and expanded by a Christian scribe; many scholars contend that here we confront early Jewish sayings that are impressively similar to those attributed to Jesus. What is now universally recognized seems clear: in the early Jewish pseudepigrapha and in the Dead Sea Scrolls we breathe the intellectual atmosphere that was once known only in and through the sayings of Jesus preserved by the evangelists.

The archaeological discoveries are no less spectacular. Israeli archaeologists digging south and west of the Temple area have unearthed paved first-century streets and the broken walls of first-century shops and dwellings. It is now much easier to feel Jerusalem as Jesus knew it, and to walk where first-century Jews hastened to observe the cultic activities in the Temple. Thanks to a series of spectacular discoveries, the Romans' destruction of the Temple, one of the greatest marvels of the ancient world, has also become increasingly more evident since I lived in Jerusalem, and only a few minutes walk from the excavations. One memorable moment was the time I let ashes and charred wood filter through my fingers. I had been scraping a layer of dirt and ash that dates from that fateful year, 70 C.E.

This book is an invitation to think about Jesus and his time. I invite you to consider with me why Jesus, like the founder of the Dead Sea Scrolls community, was rejected by the ruling priests in Jerusalem; and why and how Jesus' sayings and his self-understanding are now clearer, thanks to the recovery of a long "lost" gospel. As Bob Heller, the Executive Editor of the Religion Department at Doubleday, once said to me as we walked up Lexington Avenue in Manhattan on our way to a business lunch, Christians today need to be reminded that Christianity is a call to a great adventure. Here, in these pages, is an opportunity to think imaginatively about that time two thousand years ago, and yet—thanks to numerous momentous discoveries—today so movingly near and present, like the dirt and ash that slipped through my fingers.

During the past two centuries, hundreds of attempts have been made by brilliant scholars to place Jesus within the thoughts of the Church. Others, more historically inclined, have endeavored to discuss Jesus and Judaism. Now, I am convinced that the new discoveries, sensitivities, and methods compel us to strive to see Jesus within his contemporary Jewish environment. The thesis of this book is simple: Jesus of Nazareth as a historical man must be seen *within* Judaism.

As a Christian, I am also interested in the theological aspects of a scholarly study of the historical Jesus. But in this book I have focused on the historical questions and have edited out the faith-oriented comments that are presently intrusive. Hence, this book should help many readers—especially both Jews and Christians—better comprehend Jesus within Judaism.

My work is deeply indebted to so many. David Noel Freedman, the most gifted editor I know, has helped me improve this book. I am grateful to him. During the Gunning Lectures, I saw faces that reminded me of decades past and debts long overdue. By dedicating this book to my colleagues and former teachers in New College I am expressing my thanks to the many who have taught me, including those who have gone on ahead, and my gifted students who intermittently have been a little ahead.

J. H. CHARLESWORTH
Princeton
February 1986

NOTES

1. These quotations are taken from J. H. Charlesworth (ed.), *The Old Testament Pseudepigrapha,* 2 vols. (Garden City, N.Y., 1983, 1985). All translations of the Old Testament Pseudepigrapha are from the *OTP,* or they are my own.

2. All translations are my own, unless otherwise stated.

CONTENTS

LIST OF MAPS   XIV

LIST OF ILLUSTRATIONS   XV

INTRODUCTION   1

CHAPTER 1.   Research on the Historical Jesus in the Eighties   9

CHAPTER 2.   Jesus and the Old Testament Pseudepigrapha   30

CHAPTER 3.   Jesus and the Dead Sea Scrolls   54

CHAPTER 4.   Jesus, the Nag Hammadi Codices, and Josephus   77

CHAPTER 5.   The Jesus of History and the Archaeology of Palestine   103

CHAPTER 6.   Jesus' Concept of God and His Self-Understanding   131

CONCLUSION   165

APPENDIX 1.   List of Documents in the Old Testament Pseudepigrapha (With Abbreviations)   173

APPENDIX 2.   List of Documents in the Apocrypha and Pseudepigrapha of the New Testament (With Abbreviations)   176

APPENDIX 3.   List of Documents in the Nag Hammadi Codices (With Codex and Tractate Numbers)   182

APPENDIX 4.   List of the Dead Sea Scrolls (With Abbreviations)   184

APPENDIX 5.   A New Trend: Jesus Research (1980–84)   187

ABBREVIATIONS   209

SELECTED AND ANNOTATED BIBLIOGRAPHY   223

INDEX OF TEXTS QUOTED   245

INDEX OF NAMES   253

INDEX OF SUBJECTS   260

LIST OF MAPS

I.	Palestine; location of Qumran caves	76
II.	Plan of Old Jerusalem today	107
III.	Location of ancient synagogues in Israel	110
IV.	Outline of Jerusalem in various periods	113
V.	Jerusalem; 1st Century B.C.E.–1st Century C.E.	114

LIST OF ILLUSTRATIONS

following page 46

1. A letter from a leader at Qumran to the Wicked Priest
2. The Qumran Essene Monastery
3. An Aramaic fragment of so-called 1 Enoch
4. Qumran: the caves in the marl terrace
5. The famous leather scroll of Isaiah found in Qumran Cave I

following page 110

6. Capernaum: the commercial and fishing town to which Jesus moved from Nazareth
7. Herodium: the mountain constructed by Herod
8. Jerusalem: the family tomb of King Herod the Great
9. King Herod the Great's palace at Masada
10. The Latin inscription in which the name of Pontius Pilate appears
11. Jerusalem: the "Burnt House"
12. Jerusalem: the iron spear found in the "Burnt House"
13. Jerusalem: stone table and vessels from the "Burnt House"
14. The Temple of first-century Jerusalem
15. Jerusalem: the Temple Mount
16. Jerusalem: the Kedron Valley, David's City, the Temple Mount

following page 142

17. Sinai: St. Catherine's Monastery, at the foot of Mount Sinai
18. Jerusalem: Church of the Holy Sepulchre
19. Jerusalem: façade of the Church of the Holy Sepulchre
20. The name "Jesus" as written in Hebrew on an ossuary
21. The closing page of the Coptic Gospel of Thomas

JESUS WITHIN JUDAISM

ABRL

INTRODUCTION

Judging by its popularity in bestselling books and in box-office successes, World War II provides the perfect array of drama and conflicts for contemporary fiction. Irving Wallace, the popular novelist who has just completed *The Seventh Secret,* singles out the archvillain, Hitler, who is strangled in his capital city, and who dies like a trapped rat in an appropriate place, an underground retreat.

Another story, indeed a more powerful drama, judging again by its production of bestselling books and movies, occurred almost two thousand years earlier. In bold contrast, this story centers on the model of a perfect hero, Jesus of Nazareth. According to a popular celebration of his life, he was the perfect person, strangled by a rigid legalistic society, trapped in the Jews' sanhedrin, and murdered following diabolical outcries for his blood from the Jewish leaders and their followers in the Holy Land and in the Holy City. His death crowned his life; he was exalted above the earth on a cross. One of the purposes of this book is to disclose that this account does not derive from ancient history; it is medieval—even modern—fiction.

For most of the present century it has been judged unfashionable for a New Testament scholar, let alone a historian, to devote attention to research on the Jesus of history. A new beginning can be seen, at least in German-speaking circles, with E. Käsemann's famous lecture in 1953, which may be the date for the commencement of the so-called "New Quest for the Historical Jesus." The most successful attempt to synthesize what can be known about the historical Jesus is still G. Bornkamm's *Jesus of Nazareth,* which was translated from German into English in 1960. During the sixties and seventies, interest in the study of the Jesus of history waned. In the eighties, however, a marked shift is evident in scholars' opinions on Jesus Research (a better label than the "search" or "quest" for

Jesus). The contrast is perceived by juxtaposing two books on Jesus and two major studies on New Testament theology.

In the late twenties in a book titled *Jesus,* the internationally famous professor at the University of Marburg Rudolf Bultmann expressed the following highly influential judgment:

> I do indeed think that we can now know almost nothing concerning the life and personality of Jesus, since the early Christian sources show no interest in either, are moreover fragmentary and often legendary; and other sources about Jesus do not exist.[1]

In 1985, in *Jesus and Judaism,* the Dean Ireland's Professor of Exegesis of Holy Scripture at the University of Oxford, E. P. Sanders, reviewed the thrust of recent research and astutely and accurately stated what is basically the antithesis of Bultmann's judgment. Sanders expressed the following considered opinion:

> The dominant view today seems to be that we can know pretty well what Jesus was out to accomplish, that we can know a lot about what he said, and that those two things make sense within the world of first-century Judaism.[2]

To talk about the "dominant view today" as a return to considerable confidence in our knowledge about the historical Jesus is an exaggeration; what Sanders and I are observing is a marked turn in scholarly research, a paradigm shift in Jesus Research.

Two major studies on New Testament theology during this century help clarify this shift.[3] Again we turn to the work of the most influential New Testament scholar of this century, R. Bultmann. On the opening page of his *Theology of the New Testament* this brilliant scholar made a declaration that has been widely quoted and debated; his statement is bold and succinct:

> *The message of Jesus* is a presupposition for the theology of the New Testament rather than a part of that theology itself. . . . Thus, theological thinking—the theology of the New Testament—begins with the *kerygma* of the earliest Church and not before.[4]

As clear and unacceptable as this statement appears to me, it is contradicted by a following accurate judgment: "Jesus' message cannot be omitted from the delineation of New Testament theology" (vol. 1, p. 3). According to my own research, Jesus' life and thought cannot be reduced to one of the "historical presupposi- tions" of New Testament theology. The dreams, ideas, symbols, and terms of his earliest followers were inherited directly from Jesus. Thanks to fundamentally important discoveries and publications, these are now seen to be anchored deep within the world and thought of Early Judaism (c. 250 B.C.E. to 200 C.E.). In particular the title "Son of Man," so frequent in the sayings of Jesus, is not a Christian creation, as some scholars have maintained. It is now discovered in documents that are clearly Jewish and pre-70; that is, they date before the burning of Jerusalem by the Romans in 70 C.E.

The second major study is a posthumous work of the seventies, translated into English in the eighties, and titled, like Bultmann's masterpiece, *Theology of the New Testament.* In it, the Professor of New Testament at the Ludwig Maximilian University, in Munich, Leonhard Goppelt, decidedly broke with Bultmann on viewing the place of Jesus' life and thought for New Testament theology. Anti- thetical to Bultmann's whole approach to the beginning of New Testament theology are Goppelt's following insights:

> Of primary importance for the gospel tradition is the integration of the earthly ministry of Jesus and the kerygma so that the former becomes the supportive base for the latter. This "recollection" about Jesus re- mains, especially in the large Gospels, the primary intention. . . . If we desire to represent New Testament theology in keeping with its intrinsic structure, then we must begin with the question of the earthly Jesus.[5]

Goppelt rejected Bultmann's interpretation: "All that remains of Jesus is an eschatological call to decision; the picture of his person and work has disappeared" (vol. 1, p. 12). Hence, the subtitle of Goppelt's first volume of the *Theology of the New Testament* is *The Ministry of Jesus in Its Theological Significance.*

What has caused this momentous shift in New Testament re- search? Why is Jesus of Nazareth, the historical Jew of first-century Palestine, once again highlighted on center stage? One of the aims of the present book is to posit this paradigm shift and to try to clarify it in light of numerous phenomenal discoveries.

Some developments and advances in the seventies opened up the way followed by some leading scholars in the eighties. While my

attention is now drawn to an assessment of recent works and discoveries, I must acknowledge the pioneering contributions in the
seventies by such outstanding specialists as C. H. Dodd, E. Bammel, D. Catchpole, D. Dungan, M. Hengel, H. C. Kee, E. Schwei-
zer, N. Perrin, J. Jeremias, L. Keck, G. Vermes, H. Conzelmann,
N. A. Dahl, M. de Jonge, J. Bowker, G. Stanton, P. Winter, H.
Schürmann, A. Aalen, B. F. Meyer, H. Braun, M. Smith, and
J. D. G. Dunn.[6] Having expressed that indebtedness, I confess that
I was won over to the possibility and importance of Jesus Research
by three major works I read in the sixties, namely G. Bornkamm's
Jesus of Nazareth[7], H. Anderson's *Jesus and Christian Origins*[8], and
D. Flusser's *Jesus.*[9]

I have already made clear the main goal of the present book.
Seven distinct purposes may now be summarized. First, this work
introduces to a wide audience the exciting, even sensational, modern discoveries of the ancient world, and seeks to discern how and
in what ways these impinge upon our unabated curiosity regarding
Jesus and his contemporary world.

Second, the discussion attempts to disclose some weaknesses in
modern discussions on the centuries surrounding Jesus' time and to
expose the uninformed dimensions of some scholarly publications.
We scholars, of course, are human and not only make mistakes, but
are sometimes unaware of how much we may be influenced by the
spirit of our own time and the overreactions to acknowledged past
excesses. Our work is necessarily affected by our involvement in
present global or parochial crises and in theological claims made
upon us (or reactions to those claims).

Third, the chapters cumulatively contain an argument for the
importance of some discoveries made since World War II for Jesus
Research. The Old Testament Pseudepigrapha, the Dead Sea
Scrolls, the Nag Hammadi Codices, a rare copy of Josephus' testimony to Jesus, and numerous archaeological finds provide a fresh,
often startlingly different, view of the turn of the era and of Jesus
within Early Judaism.

Since those data lead to some new insights regarding Jesus' own
time and even help provide information regarding the reasons for
some of his actions and the meaning of some of his thoughts, the
present work intends to show how the new discoveries are impor-

tant in Jesus Research. On the one hand, we will see how the elusive background of Jesus' life is now much clearer than it was even twenty years ago, and, on the other hand, we will see how the amorphous concept "background" tends more and more to seep over into the preconceived foreground. The Judaism of Jesus' day was richer and more variegated than we had supposed; and Jesus himself had closer contacts with that Judaism than many New Testament specialists had previously presumed.

These insights lead us to a perception of how dangerous and indeed misleading are the caricatures that tend to *emphasize* Jesus' *uniqueness* in Early Judaism. Goppelt stressed Jesus' uniqueness, even to the extent of ripping away his Palestinian Jewishness.[10] Sanders, in his attempt to see Jesus as part of Palestinian Judaism, tends to downplay Jesus' uniqueness and must admit to being bothered by the concept of "uniqueness."[11] Only a historian can clarify to what extent "uniqueness" is conceivable and point out that a historical person cannot be totally unique. A historian can also make clear the perception that a powerful, influential, pioneering figure, like Jesus, must have been unique in some ways.

Fourth, this book is an attempt to demonstrate a more precise use of the so-called "criterion of dissimilarity." On the final page of his first section, "The Tradition of the Sayings of Jesus," of his wise and monumental *History of the Synoptic Tradition* (New York, London, 1963), Bultmann clarified his main criterion for discerning an authentic saying of Jesus:

> We can only count on possessing a genuine similitude of Jesus where, on the one hand, expression is given to the contrast between Jewish morality and piety and the distinctive eschatological temper which characterized the preaching of Jesus; and where on the other hand we find no specifically Christian features. (p. 205)

This criterion for authenticity demands a double contrast: Jesus' thought must be distinguishable from thoughts of contemporary Jews and it must be different from "specifically Christian features." This methodology, which was popularized by Norman Perrin, has the advantage of weeding out Jesus sayings that were incorrectly attributed to him from sayings in Early Judaism, and from highly edited or fabricated Jesus sayings that derive from the needs of Jesus' followers.

At this point I take a different course. I am convinced that we find our way to the greatest historical certainty by excluding (at least in the beginning) those Jesus sayings that can be attributed to the needs and concerns of the earliest "Christian" communities. But it seems unwise to tighten this criterion further by eliminating material that has its roots in Early Judaism. If a particular saying is discontinuous with the needs or motives of the earliest Christians, it does not necessarily render it inauthentic if it has points of contact with Early Judaism. Most specialists in Jesus Research would agree that Jesus' ideas were shaped by and composed of ideas inherited from ancient Israelite traditions and early Jewish theologies, and composed in a distinct fashion.

In the past, a preoccupation with the notion of "uniqueness" has caused many scholars to see this issue inaccurately. The historian's task is to sift through the accounts of those who wrote about Jesus to determine how much of their work may be reliably attributed to Jesus himself. My study of the Jesus tradition has led me to the conclusion that a considerable amount of that tradition which is discontinuous with the needs and concerns of the earliest Christians places Jesus squarely in the midst of Early Judaism, and that is precisely where one would expect to find a first-century Palestinian Jew. One of the goals of this book is to provide a number of case studies that illustrate this particular application of a more refined use of the criterion of dissimilarity.

Fifth, the present book attempts to demonstrate that we are not forced by dogma or theological concerns to initiate another *quest* for Jesus, but that floods of documentary and archaeological evidence raise questions about Jesus and his environment. Natural curiosity aroused by reading a scroll or document from his time, or the recovery of first-century walkways near the Temple, obviously prompts many to ask questions about Jesus and his time, and that leads to Jesus Research.

Sixth, the thrust of the chapters is carried on by the claim that our proper approach to Early Judaism and Jesus, and the attempt to compare and contrast Jesus with other Jews, does not need to be and must never again be anti-Semitic or anti-Jewish. Without becoming guilty of distorting philo-Semitism, we must struggle to see not Jesus *and* Judaism, as if we are confronted in some ways with an antithesis, but Jesus *within* Judaism. In other words, we must grasp that Jesus was a Jew who was obviously in some ways part of Judaism. This admission leads to two questions: What does it mean to say Jesus was a "Jew"? And can we talk representatively about Judaism, or are we forced to see only diversities and "Judaisms"?

Seventh, these pages contain some of my answers to the myriad of questions that have been asked me by laity, students, colleagues, and virtual strangers. Repeatedly I have been asked in what ways the discoveries since the Second World War help us better understand Jesus of Nazareth.

I am aware of the awesomeness of the task and the dangers it will entail. It would be presumptuous to suggest that the answers provided in the following pages are either my own insights or anything more than informed speculations. Yet it is time to speak to the questions being raised by the fresh sources.

NOTES

1. R. Bultmann, *Jesus* (Berlin, 1926, repr. frequently); the quotation is taken from the English translation by L. P. Smith and E. H. Lantero, *Jesus and the Word* (London, 1934, 1958) p. 14.

2. E. P. Sanders, *Jesus and Judaism* (Philadelphia, 1985) p. 2.

3. I have been influenced greatly by J. Jeremias' work, especially his *New Testament Theology: The Proclamation of Jesus,* transl. J. Bowden (New York, 1971). As the subtitle indicates, this work clearly rejects Bultmann's contention that Jesus Research is not proper in the study of New Testament theology. Unfortunately, Jeremias' untimely death left this series unfinished.

4. R. Bultmann, *Theology of the New Testament,* 2 vols., transl. K. Grobel (New York, 1951, 1955) vol. 1, p. 3; the italics are Bultmann's.

5. L. Goppelt, *Theology of the New Testament,* 2 vols., transl. J. Alsup, ed. J. Roloff (Grand Rapids, Mich., 1981, 1982) vol. 1, pp. 6–7.

6. For bibliographical information on the publications by these scholars, see the Selected and Annotated Bibliography on pp. 223–43.

7. G. Bornkamm, *Jesus of Nazareth,* transl. I. and F. McLuskey, with J. M. Robinson (New York, London, 1960).

8. H. Anderson, *Jesus and Christian Origins: A Commentary on Modern Viewpoints* (New York, 1964).

9. D. Flusser, *Jesus,* transl. R. Walls (New York, 1969).

10. Goppelt, out of an ignorance of Early Judaism, can make frequent assertions about the uniqueness of Jesus and his followers. For example, after discussing Jesus' understanding of the halakah (legal and moral teaching in an oral form), he can state, "Understandably so, Jesus thus stood alone in his environment" (*Theology of the New Testament,* vol. 1, p. 90). He can also make the following incredible statement: "It is historically certain that Jesus accomplished healings in significant proportion, and that not only upon demoniacs, but also upon other infirm people. This ministry was largely unique to Jesus in his Jewish environment." (vol. 1, p. 144; for other sweeping statements on "uniqueness" see vol. 2, pp. 13, 54, 99, 105, 204, 222) This judgment is misinformed. Jesus is not the only Jew who is famous for performing miraculous healings; for example, R. Ḥanina ben Dosa is reputed to have possessed this power (cf. m.Ber 5.5).

11. Sanders astutely raises a major question: "How can one argue historically that a certain attitude or conception is unique?" (*Jesus,* p. 138). Sanders rightly "must doubt many of the claims for Jesus' uniqueness" (p. 240); unfortunately his confession—"But I worry a bit about the word 'unique' " (p. 240)—reveals that he is too disdainful of theological concerns (p. 2 and *passim*) and approaches historical phenomena with too positivistic a perspective and bias (see esp. pp. 156, 167).

Chapter 1

Research on the Historical Jesus in the Eighties

INTRODUCTION

I am convinced that the single most important task of the New Testament scholar today is to take seriously the promise and problems of studying the historical Jesus. Research on Jesus and his time has been the primary preoccupation of New Testament specialists for the past two hundred years. The illusion that a moratorium on the quest has been in force is sustained only by looking at just one group of influential scholars.

I am dissatisfied with the popular phrase "the quest for the historical Jesus." It suggests we are in a dark room, fumbling about trying to find the door. A better analogy would be that we are in a dimly lit room and constantly bump into things that force us to bend down and examine what has confronted us. The data are what have jolted us.

The recovery of such documents as the Dead Sea Scrolls and the phenomenally significant archaeological discoveries cumulatively force us to ask questions about the Jesus who lived and died in Palestine before 70 C.E. We are not on a quest. We are compelled to raise historical questions because of what is now placed so graphically before us. We are not forcing historical issues and concerns upon theological texts. We are awakened to historical questions by facts and perceptions that have to do with pre-70 Judaism.

The Gospels are not merely confessions. Secular history and apparently irrelevant detail are embedded in them. For example, Pontius Pilate is a well-known name not because it has now been found chiseled on a stone at Caesarea (see Illus. 10), but because it is part of the passion narrative. Likewise, no confessional motive explains the account of the young man who followed distantly the band of men who had arrested Jesus and then ran away naked (Mk 14:51–52).

Origen was once asked what he did as a biblical scholar. He replied that his work was similar to that of a hunter who moved quietly through the woods until he saw something move and then went after it. Origen noted that he scrutinized the text until he saw something move, and then he pursued it (*Fragmenta in Evangelium John* 1:25–30).

For me, as a twentieth-century scholar who is preoccupied with the literature of Early Judaism and Early Christianity, the analogy is apt. We New Testament scholars are not seeking vainly for Jesus' footprints in the Gospels. We have begun to see more clearly that the Gospels were written to serve the needs of communities decades removed from Jesus; but they were constituted and empowered by older traditions, and some (perhaps many) of them derive ultimately and reliably from Jesus himself.

I am convinced that we cannot re-present the New Testament documents, their theologies, and their tendencies without ultimately focusing on the challenge of one single life. Jesus is the power paradigm for all the New Testament writers. We must acknowledge that New Testament—perhaps all Christian—theology develops out of the tension between tradition and addition, between remembered history and articulated faith.

In *Jesus and Christian Origins* (Oxford, 1964) Hugh Anderson contended: despite "all difficulties inherent in the nature of the sources in which history and 'kerygmatic' interpretation are indissolubly united, I do not think it is either theologically unjustifiable or critically hopeless to seek for historical knowledge" (p. 307). I am thoroughly convinced that Anderson has perceived the essential nature of our New Testament data and the need for historical questions that arise from them.

As James S. Stewart stated long ago in *The Life and Teaching of Jesus Christ* (Edinburgh, 1933, 1957², 1977 with amendments,

1981), the Gospels "are not biographies at all"; they are "a set of 'memoirs,' selected historical reminiscences" (p. 1). Indeed, two hundred years of intensive scientific historical research on Jesus has failed to produce a life of Jesus. The consensus among New Testament specialists is that a biography of Jesus is, and always will be, impossible. Our sources for Jesus' life are only meager. The evangelists are not primarily interested in Jesus as a person of the past.

Yet, talk about what cannot be said concerning the Jesus of history inevitably runs its course until doubts arise about such skepticism and the underlying perceptions and methods. Clearly the evangelists were not primarily interested in who Jesus had been and what he had said and done; but it is not representative of the New Testament authors to report that they were not interested in Jesus' words and deeds prior to Calvary. Certain specific aspects of Jesus' life were essential for the daily life and thought of his earliest followers. From his own life—as well as from ancient formative traditions—they learned how to think, preach, teach, and endure suffering, even martyrdom. Stories about what he had said and done were shared by eyewitnesses, who obviously embellished the account but who also had phenomenal *memories*. Today we scholars spend so much time reading sources and secondary literature that we do not possess the fertile memories of the ancients or of those who today in the Near East can recite verbatim the Torah, Koran, or Iliad. Due essentially to the Jewish and Christian belief regnant in the first century that the present was pregnant with future (eschatological) expectations—indeed the birth of the new and final age was at hand —these Jesus traditions remained at the oral stage for years.

Recently our attention has been drawn to the early Christian prophets who spoke in the name of the risen one. We are much more sensitive to this phenomenon in Christian origins thanks to the fruitful labors of such scholars as G. Theissen,[1] E. Cothenet, G. Dautzenberg, U. B. Müller, D. E. Aune, and D. Hill. These studies and the exegesis of the relevant New Testament passages, however, do not lead to the conclusion that the emotions and enthusiasms of the earliest Christian prophets went unbridled; they were *at least somewhat* controlled by eyewitnesses who anchored enthusiasm in real history. The words spoken by the prophets, representing the resurrected Lord, did often seem more real and important than the words once heard by others long ago on some hillside in Galilee; yet, even those who had known him continued to be active in the communities in which the Jesus traditions were transmitted. We must not be so enamored by perennial myths and editorial additions that we fail to see that additions were by editors who inherited and reshaped *traditions.* Our evangelists were certainly editors with theological and Christological tendencies, but let us not fail to perceive that editors always work on what has been handed to them. Additions reveal traditions.

The production of Mark, then Matthew, Luke, and John—and sometime before 125 C.E. the Gospel of Thomas (see ch. 4)—is unthinkable if from the beginning there was only preaching (kerygma), especially the *focused* proclamation that God had raised the crucified one or that preaching was the force that created the "Christian" communities. Teaching (didache) and tradition about whom the one crucified was help provide a background and disclose a process that explains the production of the Gospels. Hence, the Jesus traditions in the Gospels are the result of preaching, teaching, and even conflicts (polemics) with other Jews.

How were the Gospels written? On the one hand, the answer is simple: Mark, sometime around 70 C.E., sat down and composed the earliest Gospel, using a complex of traditions that reflected not only what had been happening since Jesus' crucifixion in 30 C.E. but also what was remembered about Jesus' actions and words before 30. Matthew and Luke depended upon Mark, but obviously not the modern eclectic Greek text of Mark. John possibly also knew Mark and inherited from him his literary creation, the genre "gospel." All the evangelists inherited traditions, some of which were unique to only one of them. Each evangelist wrote from a distinct sociological and theological perspective.

On the other hand, the answer is very complex. What sources were available to Mark and to the other evangelists? How authentic were they? How does one reliably distinguish between the true and the false, the reliable and the fabricated? How were the evangelists' traditions significantly shaped by the process of transmission? Did anyone during Jesus' life write down anything about what he had taught? Did he, like a rabbi or an Old Testament prophet, teach his disciples to memorize his most carefully crafted parables or other essential teachings? How reliable were the memories of his earliest followers? The impossibility of answering any of these questions with definitive answers has tended to produce a tone of pessimism in many academic institutions in which New Testament research has been practiced. Yet, among many New Testament specialists I am now observing a growing awareness that there was *some* historical interest among the members of the Palestinian Jesus Movement. This book contains my attempts to offer some evidence of why I am convinced this historical interest was more considerable than some critics now contend.

We must not inadvertently overlook the simplest of questions: How can we explain the appearance of a gospel? What preceded it? How was it possible for Mark to do what in fact he did, if all that preceded him were proclamations (kerygmata) *devoid* of any historical interest and content?

The sheer existence of the Gospels—which include the celebration of the life and teachings of the pre-Easter Jesus—proves that from the earliest decades of the movement associated with Jesus there must have been *some* historical interest in Jesus of Nazareth. The Gospels tell the story of one man's deeds and teachings. Not only Luke (Lk 1:1–4) and John (Jn 21:25), but also Mark and Matthew indicate that interest in the pre-Easter Jesus antedated them.

On the one hand, David Dungan, in *The Sayings of Jesus in the Churches of Paul,* demonstrates Paul's conservative and constrained use of the Jesus traditions and puts to rest the form critics' claim that "new sayings of the Lord were constantly being created and *surreptitiously or accidentally* included with the older authentic sayings, while the older sayings were being surreptitiously or accidentally discarded or modified to fit the needs of new developments, and so on."[2] Paul inherited traditions about Jesus, and he treated them with respect.

On the other hand, Charles Harold Dodd[3] correctly argued that Acts 10:36–43 does indicate that Mark's literary creation, the Gospel, was probably preceded by an *outline* that summarized Jesus' life and teaching. How reminiscent of the Marcan outline is this summary embedded in the proclamation (kerygma) that Luke attributes to the earliest community in Jerusalem:

You know the word which he sent to Israel, preaching good news of peace by Jesus Christ (he is Lord of all), the word which was proclaimed throughout all Judea, beginning from Galilee after the baptism which John preached: how God anointed Jesus of Nazareth with the Holy Spirit and with power; how he went about doing good and healing all that were oppressed by the devil, for God was with him. And we are witnesses to all that he did both in the country of the Jews and in Jerusalem. They put him to death by hanging him on a tree; but God raised him on the third day. . . .

(Acts 10:36–40; RSV)

Attempts to dismiss this outline as the invention of the author of Acts have failed; this summary developed out of pre-Lucan strata, even pre-Easter traditions. Jesus' public ministry began in Galilee and commenced after some association with John the Baptist, who indeed did baptize him. His ministry was characterized by miraculous healings, a fact now widely acknowledged by Jewish and Christian specialists on the Jesus of history. Jesus' life ended on a tree, the cross; but his followers claimed that God acted once again by raising Jesus from the dead.

The first major reason many scholars, myself included, feel compelled to continue the search for some solid understanding of the Jesus of history is not that we wish to present Jesus as a hero of the past to be admired. The task is forced upon us by two major observations: First, we perceive the multilayered quality of the gospel narratives. We are confronted with certain traditions that cannot have been devised out of nothing (*ex nihilo*) by Jesus' followers; rather, such data created the earliest Jesus communities. Foremost among such bedrock historical facts are the scandalous offenses: namely Jesus' crucifixion, Peter's threefold denial, Judas' betrayal, and Jesus' baptism by a possible rival, John the Baptist. Indeed, the leader of Jesus' followers, Peter, and the treasurer, Judas, are reported by the evangelists to have been failures during Jesus' passion.

As the evangelists passed on these traditions, they showed their creativity by struggling to change history by rewriting it. For example, in the earliest Gospel, Mark, Jesus is clearly baptized by John in the Jordan. Luke avoids such an embarrassing scene, which would make Jesus seem like an inferior person to John. According to Luke, before Jesus is baptized, John is thrown into prison. Later, the Evangelist John puts into the mouth of John the Baptist confessions of unworthiness and inferiority to Jesus. Finally, in the Gospel of the Nazareans, which may date from the early decades of the second century, Jesus flatly refuses to go to John and be baptized by him; to the invitation, which oddly enough is placed in the mouth of his mother, Mary, Jesus retorts: "Wherein have I sinned, that I should go and be baptized by him?"[4]

The second major factor that compels, indeed demands, a renewed study of the Jesus of history is our improved understanding of history, tradition, and meaning. The question before us may be articulated as follows: What is history, how do we have access to it, and how do we obtain meaning about and from it?

From Ernst Käsemann we have learned to perceive that history is accessible only through tradition, that is, what has been handed on to us by others who antedate us. There is no other means of obtaining entrance into that time prior to and separate from us. We must be informed of the past by others who pass on tradition by means of oral and written words. Merely to hand on tradition is not to hand on something meaningful or important. Tradition must be selected and interpreted. History is, therefore, accessible only through tradition and meaningful solely through interpretation. To point out that the New Testament documents are characterized by interpreted traditions is to observe that we have access to the way the gospel and pregospel traditions were meaningful to those who passed on those traditions.

It has been rather fashionable lately to claim that Jesus did not found the Church and that we must admit a gaping chasm between the Jesus of history and the Christ of the Church. Other scholars, albeit in a minority, have continued to perpetuate the authenticity of the Matthean tendency that has Jesus announce to Peter that he is the foundation of the Church. Both of these positions are actually false alternatives. The first one fails to observe that while Jesus did not found or even envision a church like that experienced by the Evangelists Matthew and John, he did call into being a separate group within Early Judaism. The second position simply ignores the Matthean tendency present in Matthew 16, especially the claim that Jesus created a "church" (an *ekklēsia*; only Matthew has this noun).

Jesus' call was not to individuals alone, as Harnack thought at the beginning of this century in his influential and controversial *The Essence of Christianity*. God's Kingdom is not exclusively individualistic, a society in the human heart (a *societas cordibus*). In one sense, Jesus could not establish something so completely unprecedented, because he inherited ancient Jewish traditions and spoke to Israel, a nation constituted and carried on by God's historical acts. As is well known, the principle of solidarity (an individual's meaning is derived only through social groups) antedates the concept of the individual in the thought of ancient Israel.

This idea continued to be operative even during Jesus' own time, even though, since Ezekiel's message, the responsibility for sin had shifted to the individual. It was in the *corporate assemblies* in the Temple and in the synagogue that the Jews found meaning and guidance.

Jesus probably began his ministry within John the Baptist's community (cf. Jn 3:22, 26; 4:1). Jesus chose twelve disciples.[5] This symbolic act was eschatological and prophetic. Perhaps Jesus intended to reestablish the nation composed of the twelve tribes.

Many scholars have claimed that Jesus did not choose twelve apostles. They argue that this idea derives from the Church. In Chapter 6 I shall present the reasons why I have slowly become convinced that Jesus did choose twelve special disciples. Suffice it for now to report that lately some outstanding scholars have argued for this possibility. G. Lohfink,[6] a Roman Catholic, and E. P. Sanders, an ultra-liberal Protestant, conclude that Jesus did call twelve special disciples to follow him.

Jesus' initiative stands out. He selected twelve apostles. They formed a distinct group within Early Judaism. One significant difference between this group and others in Palestinian Judaism is impressive: Jesus chose the disciples, but the students of the rabbis almost always chose a teacher.

Certainly, solid historical fact is encountered in the traditions that emphasize Jesus' concern only for Israel, enunciated in the narrative of his initial rebuff of the Syro-Phoenician woman, the charge to the disciples—"Do not go into the way of the Gentiles . . . but go rather to the lost sheep of the house of Israel" (Mt 10:5–6)—and his self-perception for being sent only "to the lost sheep of the house of Israel" (Mt 15:24). Surely these sayings found only in Matthew were offensive to and could not have been created by Matthew, because his church became increasingly more directed to the Gentiles (see Mt 5:13, 10:18, 21:43, 24:14, 28:19).

The Church ultimately derives from Jesus' conviction and proclamation that in his time and place God was calling into being a special group of people. This group constituted the small band of the faithful ones who prepared for and eagerly awaited God's final act before the end of all normal history and time. Jesus apparently never envisioned or founded a "Church" of Jews and Gentiles. Yet, his calling into being of an eschatological community under God's reign provided the inspiration and impetus from which the Church eventually shaped itself.

I must express agreement with the former Archbishop of Canterbury, Michael Ramsey, when he states in his book *Jesus and the Living Past* (Oxford, New York, 1980) the following:

> Without Jesus the Church could not be. Without the Church Jesus did exist as one who was rejected and crucified, and we know the event of his rejection and crucifixion. The lonely and rejected Jesus was there, before ever the Church was created. (p. 33)

For Archbishop Ramsey the reference to the "lonely and rejected Jesus" is not exhausted by the cross event. He intends it to denote also the precross Jesus. Here Ramsey is one with the great Danish philosopher Søren Kierkegaard, who claimed that Jesus' greatest suffering was during his preaching ministry when many, including his own closest disciples, namely Peter and James and John, the sons of Zebedee, failed to understand him and tended to caricature him. Ramsey is also far from Tillich and Bultmann, who assumed or tended to argue that all we can know categorically of the historical Jesus is the fact of the cross. In the following pages I shall attempt to show why I am convinced that Ramsey is absolutely correct.

I once stood in admiration of New Testament scholars who are cautiously reticent until they can defend virtually infallible positions. Now I have grown impatient with those who feign perfection, failing to perceive that all knowledge is conditioned by the observer, as Merleau-Ponty and Polanyi have demonstrated with pellucid clarity, and missing the point that all data, including meaningful traditions, are categorically selected and interpreted phenomena. Moreover, such scholars have severely compromised the axiom that historians do not have the luxury of certainty; they work, at best, with relative probabilities.

It is wise and prudent to be cautious; but, pushed to extremes, even a virtue can become a vice. As the rabbis stated, timidity is not a virtue in pursuing truth. The search for uninterpreted data, like Jesus' own acts (*bruta facta Jesu*) and his very own words (*ipsissima verba Jesu*), erroneously implies that the historian can approximate certainty, miscasts the complex structure of the Gospels, and betrays the fact that New Testament interpretation is an adventure. And, of course, that metaphor indicates that we must leave the safe and protected harbor and risk being wrecked on an unperceived reef.

METHODOLOGY

The New Testament scholar today must use the proper methodologies in order to ensure that the conclusion is discovered inductively and not posited deductively. Hence, the following work reflects some indebtedness to form criticism, redaction criticism, and other higher critical methods. The evangelists were not mere compilers of tradition; they were editors of tradition. Each shaped his own work according to certain easily recognized tendencies. Mark is fond of one adverb with which he habitually connects pericopes; it is "immediately" (*euthus*). This one word reveals how eschatologically and apocalyptically oriented are his theology and christology. In Chapters 4 and 13, and in verses 9:1 and 16:8, with which he may well have completed his work, Mark emphasizes the claim, clearly inherited from Jesus, that the final act in God's dynamic drama of moving toward a depraved humanity is now commencing.

Matthew strives to prove that all conceivable prophecies were fulfilled by Jesus; hence, he errs in portraying Jesus' triumphal entry into Jerusalem. Attempting to prove Zechariah 9, in which an ass is also a colt, he literally has Jesus riding on two animals, an ass and a colt: the disciples "brought the ass and the colt, and they placed their garments on them, and he sat on them." (Mt 21:7)

Luke tends to trifurcate universal history into three periods: the time of Israel, the middle of time or the time of Jesus, and the time of the Church. He also tones down Mark's tendency to emphasize the present as the end of time and history, and his urgent eschatological claim that Jesus will return triumphantly any moment. For example, Luke alters Mark 9:1, which reads, "And he said to them, 'Amen, I say to you, that there are some standing here who will not taste death until they see the kingdom of God having come in power.' " To "come in power" is an expression that has special importance for the apocalyptists, like the authors of Daniel, the Apocalypse of John, 4 Ezra, and 2 Baruch. It denotes a total alteration of time and the earth, and an end to normal history. Mark did not hold that this prophecy was fulfilled in the transfiguration, which does follow immediately upon it in his Gospel. Luke, however, does contend that it was fulfilled. He edits the prophecy as follows: "I say to you truly, some standing close by will not taste death until they see the kingdom of God." (Lk 9:27) Jesus' prophecy is altered so that it is clearly fulfilled according to Luke's narrative, since Luke alone contains this logion:

> "The kingdom of God is not coming with signs to be observed; nor will they say, 'Lo, here it is!' or 'There!' for behold, the kingdom of God is in the midst of you."

> (Lk 17:20–21)

Similarly, Luke stresses universalism. According to Matthew 5:15, the lamp that is lighted is put "on a stand," and it gives light to those "in the house," namely the house of Israel. In this verse we confront a typical Matthean emphasis upon the Jewishness of the gospel. According to Luke 8:16 and the doublet in 11:33 the lamp is placed on "a stand" so "that those who are entering may see the light." Luke extends the message to include the Gentiles, indeed any who decides to enter (cf. GosTh 33).

My own evaluation of where we are methodologically and perceptively regarding the gospel tradition and its transmission may be arranged under seven observations. First, the Gospels are from a later generation than Jesus' own; but, while the evangelists were not eyewitnesses,[7] they were informed by eyewitnesses. Oral tradition is not always unreliable; in fact, sometimes it is more reliable than the written word. In the beginning decades of the second century, the careful scholar Papias expressed the need to discover the living oral tradition.

Second, the Gospels and other New Testament documents reflect the needs of the Church; but while proclamation (kerygma) was one of the major tasks of the Church, there were also other functions. One of them was a concern to remember faithfully something about the precross Jesus; and dedication to historical tradition does not imply or demand perfection in transmission.

Third, the Gospels do contain legendary and mythical elements, such as Jesus' walking on the water; but surely the Gospels are categorically different from the well-known legends and myths. The evangelists collected, adapted, and expanded the traditions handed down in the Palestinian Jesus Movement. While the presence of nonhistorical and nonverifiable legends and myths in the Gospels should be admitted, the basic story about Jesus derives from authentic and very early traditions.

Fourth, Matthew clearly expands and often allegorizes Mark and Q, a lost source known only because Matthew and Luke inherit portions of it. But it does not follow from this insight that Matthew is essentially ahistorical and thoroughly creative.

Fifth, in the search for authentic Jesus material, we must acknowledge, with other scholars (notably H. Braun, J. M. Robinson, and E. Schillebeeckx), that inauthentic Jesus words may accurately preserve Jesus' actual intention. Our task sometimes is not so much to recover Jesus' own words (the so-called *ipsissima verba Jesu*) as to grasp—and for those who wish to follow him to inculcate in daily life—Jesus' own *purpose*.

Sixth, it is clear that Matthew and Luke, working from Mark and Q, did alter sayings of Jesus. And while Mark must have exercised the same exegetical freedom, it is obvious from comparing Mark with Q and Jesus sayings found only in Matthew with those only in Luke, that many of Jesus' sayings date long before 70. It simply is not true that Jesus' sayings were created by the earliest Christians or invented by the evangelists.

Seventh, Romans 1:3–4 and other early traditions may tend to indicate that Jesus' followers began to affirm he was "the Christ" only after the resurrection, when God called him back from death and exalted him (see Phil 2:6–11); but it does not follow from this perception that christology begins only after Easter, or that the cross and the resurrection were the only important aspects of Jesus' life. The claim that the Gospels are post-Easter confessionals is essentially true, but to contend that they are *only* post-Easter confessionals also fails to do justice to the abundance of pre-Easter data and traditions that are preserved, perhaps almost always in an edited form, in the New Testament.

Those who seek to discern authentic Jesus traditions in the New Testament are not involved in a salvage operation. Jesus Research is tied neither to a search for a reasonable foundation for faith nor to a need to portray the divine hero who is to be imitated.

Jesus is not to be reduced to a presupposition for New Testament theology. Even if intellectual honesty demands admitting much uncertainty about what can be known assuredly about Jesus, New Testament theology is essentially involved in confronting more than the mere existence of Jesus. As James P. Mackey states in *Jesus the Man and the Myth: A Contemporary Christology* (London, 1979, 1985), "the Christian faith is more closely bound to the person of its founder than any other faith living or dead . . . the actual person of Jesus of Nazareth, its historical founder, is more central to the Christian confession of faith than is the founder of any other religion to its formulated confessions" (pp. 2–3).

Critical scholars must not become content with ahistorical ideas and dreams. It is easy to retreat into theological or philosophical reflections, leaving for others not only the struggle to make sense of the phenomenally significant newly exposed archaeological data, but also the endeavors to understand what all our data may have to do with Jesus Research. It is not sophisticated to slip behind the contention that the task is too difficult and the results too uncertain.

There is a common portrait of Jesus in Matthew, Mark, and Luke. And despite the marked discrepancies between the Synoptics and John, a general portrait of Jesus emerges. This portrait marks Jesus out as distinctly recognizable in first-century Palestine. From any one of these sources, or even from a rough cumulative, albeit hazy, picture derived from all of them, an identifiable Jewish male emerges as a distinct historical personality. Although there were certainly some similarities between Jesus and Hillel, Jesus is recognizably different. And so Jesus is identifiable as a distinct personality, distinguishable from Hillel, Gamaliel, Ḥanina ben Dosa, Nicodemus, Banus, Johanan ben Zakkai, and even Paul. In fact, it is time for New Testament scholars to recognize that behind the later editorial layers of the Gospels lie earlier historical traditions that clarify the distinctiveness of Jesus. These traditions allow us to know more about Jesus than any other first-century Jew, with the possible exceptions of Philo, Paul, and Josephus.

Rigorous examination of the publications that postdate World War I reveals that specialists who tend to disavow knowing anything assuredly about Jesus' life, except the cross, invariably transport later into the dialogue much about Jesus' life and thought. At that stage, rigor is abandoned and illegitimate Jesus traditions are allowed to stand and become formative for developing positions.

The seeming disinterest in the historical Jesus among many scholars may in fact result neither from scholarly sophistication nor from objectivity. It may well be, as at times it most clearly is, a myopic apologetic for the soteriological principle that Christians are saved solely by grace through faith in Jesus Christ. And that perception tends to foster the claim that Christians must avoid any search for certainty, or knowledge. Yet, to affirm that the Christian is saved solely by faith begs a major question: in whom or what is this faith to be invested? As John A. Ziesler states in *The Jesus Question* (London, 1980), for the New Testament authors Jesus "is the centre, the fixed point around which everything revolves, the standpoint from which God, man, the self, and the world are to be understood" (p. 2).

The basic principle now before us seems somewhat bland and noncontroversial, but let me go on to state that my interest in this book is not primarily with Christian theology. It would be a false impression to assume that we who are studying the Jesus of history are intending, as did some of the liberals one hundred years ago, to justify a Christianity without dogma or doctrine. Our eyes are *opened* by the recent challenging discoveries—discussed in Chapters 2 through 5—and by the observation of the multilayered nature of the traditions and redactions of the earliest Christian compositions.

EXTREMES

We have glimpsed some of the problems and promise in the study of Jesus, but we must now acknowledge that there are extremes of opinion regarding such a task. Many devout Christians will retort that the study of the historical Jesus is not proper work for the New Testament scholar, because Jesus' authentic words and deeds are preserved inviolably in the canonical Gospels.

Dogmaticians may reply that Jesus Research is irrelevant, because creed and dogma have adequately and eternally grasped the essence of Jesus, who is the Christ. Some form critics might argue that such a task is futile, because Jesus cannot be known historically, since our sources show no interest in pure history; they are post-Easter confessionals. A theologian might add that all that is needed and sufficient is contained in the New Testament and that this canon must be taken seriously. Hence, the task of the New Testament scholar is to provide answers to all questions deriving from the New Testament.

Each of these replies founders on one or more major misconceptions. Devout Christians who claim to take the New Testament literally and uncritically are blind to three necessary insights: They fail to perceive that God's revelation is always directed to imperfect humanity and that revelation can never be more than imperfectly perceived and even more imperfectly recorded. They also fail to grasp that blind allegiance to the Bible ultimately breaks the Bible's first and second commandments. As Coleridge warned, bibliolatry is a form of idolatry. They likewise fail to observe that taking the New Testament authors seriously means to listen silently to their struggles to convey "the Gospel" to a specific audience. To ask historical questions is to honor seriously the conditions, concerns, and claims of those first-century thinkers. In summation, the devout Christian must inculcate the freeing truth that the Gospels are not to be treated categorically as if they were modern biographies.

Dogmaticians need to be reminded that, in the New Testament, fact and history are the raw ingredients of creed and dogma. Also, creeds are not so much derived from the New Testament documents as they are characteristic of the very first believers. Pre-Pauline tradition is liturgical and credal, as we know from studying Romans 1:1–4 and Philippians 2:6–11. Historical perception and methodology are the only means for separating dogma from superstition.

Some form critics may react negatively to my present claim; if so, they might be willing to listen to a different way of viewing the data. Today New Testament scholars cannot ignore form criticism, but many form critics now have slowly perceived that our sources are not so bereft of reliable Jesus tradition as some scholars thought between the two world wars. On the one hand, we now know that there was far more continuity between the pre- and the post-Easter communities than Bultmann tended to see. On the other hand, we are relatively certain that portions of the early preaching (kerygma) and teaching (didache) preserved in the New Testament do not derive only from the needs of the Church. They originated in real history and controlled and shaped the thought of the Church. It should be clear that faith is inextricably anchored in secular history, in real persons, events, and places.

The imagined theologian has a major point, but he or she has to understand the full import of the claim that the New Testament scholar must provide answers to all questions emanating from the New Testament. The first requisite is to recognize that the New Testament scholar works on *documents* or, better, *passages* in them that were brought into a closed canon only long after the New Testament period ended. The New Testament scholar does not study "the New Testament." The second requisite is to recognize that some generative force unites these documents, which are characterized by categorical claims and excitement. The third requisite is to grasp that while the root of almost all the theologies in the canon is the proclamation (kerygma) and explanation of Jesus' death and resurrection (with Goppelt), yet, behind this preaching— and antedating it—is the *remembrance* of Jesus' life, his teaching (especially his prayers, emphasis on Abba, and proclamation of God's rule), healings, and the shared experienced presence of God. All of these formed and demanded the earliest teachings in the Palestinian Jesus Movement (and the production of the didache). The earliest source of this excitement in Jesus, therefore, is the phenomena that considerably predate not only each of the New

Testament documents, but also Calvary. The fourth requisite is the understanding that portions of the Jesus phenomena represent historical facts that lie behind the New Testament authors and their compositions.

Unfortunately, many New Testament scholars sometimes pursue their craft as if *nothing* can be known assuredly about the Jesus of history. This situation is unfortunate. Not even Bultmann or Tillich espoused that utter pessimism. Their ideas are not to be confused with those of Bruno Bauer, Paul Couchoud, G. Gurev, R. Augstein, and G. A. Wells, all of whom *denied the existence of Jesus.* Bultmann and Tillich, as radical as they were, affirmed the existence of Jesus and the undeniable fact of his crucifixion in Jerusalem before 70 C.E. Moreover, the failure to grasp the historical particularity of Jesus, and all the scandals this entails, reduces a religion to a philosophy of existence, precisely as intended by Fritz Buri in his critique of Bultmann.

New Frontiers

Today there are three major expanding frontiers in New Testament research. The first is the development of sociological models to describe better the social phenomena of the events behind and contemporaneous with the New Testament documents. The second is a preoccupation with collections of writings, especially those we will discuss in the following chapters, namely the Old Testament Pseudepigrapha, the Dead Sea Scrolls, and the Nag Hammadi Codices. These ancient documents have helped initiate a new reevaluation of Christian origins. The third frontier is not nearly so obvious: it is a burgeoning recognition that we are able to construct somewhat reliably many aspects of Jesus' life and teachings (see Appendix 5).

The study of the historical Jesus has had an impact on international affairs. Some in the Middle East who hate Judaism and Christianity claim that the Gospel of Barnabas, a massive work of 222 chapters, alone contains the original gospel of Jesus. Barnabas, counted among the twelve in his gospel, receives Jesus' secret teachings, reports that Judas is the one who is crucified, and that Jesus prophesied the coming of Muhammad. David Sox, in *The Gospel of*

Barnabas (London, 1984), presents ample evidence showing that this work is a medieval forgery by an enthusiastic convert to Islam.

Today Jesus is claimed by widely differing groups. He is portrayed as a Marxist who provides the blueprints for an economic and social reform; as a Black Messiah who stood against an exploitative white nation, Rome, as a liberator who proclaimed that God's Kingdom belongs to the poor; and as the Prince of Peace who shows the way for nuclear disarmament. Other portraits are also common: we hear of the charismatic Jesus, the demythologized Jesus, and the doctrinal Jesus. Jesus is once again very popular; and he is important for more people than armchair historians.

The search for the historical Jesus is also demanded because these portraits are mutually incompatible; some reconstructions simply exclude the possibility of others. Somewhere the Jesus of history has been lost. Far too often, a Jesus is fabricated out of ideologies that are not biblically based, and then this construction is employed deceptively to articulate the platform for some revolutionary movement. Obviously, such endeavors are categorically different from Jesus Research.

Jesus Research is clearly essential, because no longer is it possible simply to pick up a canonical gospel and read it as if it were a modern biography. We are forced to ask, Who was Jesus? What was he really like? To these simple initial questions, a flood of others follow. Jesus Research begins primarily because the data in the New Testament force us to raise these questions.

OVERVIEW

The purpose of this review was limited primarily to the demonstration of one fact: a new phase in the study of the historical Jesus commenced in the eighties. I have labeled it "Jesus Research" in order to distinguish it from the former "Quest for the Historical Jesus," which was characterized by dogmatic or theological interests. Even the so-called "New Quest for the Historical Jesus," which began in the fifties, was grounded in theological concerns. While Jesus Research does certainly have theological implications and is possible only because of the utilization of theological methodologies and sensitivities,[8] it is not initiated by them. The impetus has come from new discoveries, as indicated intermittently in the preceding pages and developed in the following chapters.

The new climate surrounding Jesus Research has enabled a new sensitivity to the perennial questions. The major impediments to the task of trying to say something definite about the historical Jesus have eroded. First, the theological one has crumbled. It had been constructed out of a twofold claim: in the past some critics argued that faith alone is sufficient for the Christian; others added that Jesus the Christ is known solely existentially. Now the best minds perceive that it is better scholarship to deal with Jesus in the context of history, rather than in some sort of philosophical or existential framework.

Second, formerly we were lost in a wasteland of history, which was caused by the lack of sources from pre-70 Judaism. Now—since the 1940s—we possess hundreds of documents that are pre-70 and Jewish. Somehow, in decades of confused apologetics and well-meaning attempts to refine an infallible methodology, we forgot two essential dimensions of the search for Joseph's son. Historical research is scientific by a critical method but not necessarily by conclusion. The historian at best can provide us not with certainty, but with relative probability. Hence any talk about searching for the pure facts *(bruta facta Jesu)* or Jesus' precise words *(ipsissima verba Jesu)* is imprecise, imperceptive, and impossible. Likewise, any search for Jesus is a relative task: it must be acknowledged that within our day it has slowly become clear that Homer and Hesiod were real people, but also that Hippocrates' writings are almost all pseudonymous, and that we know practically nothing reliably about Hillel, Jesus' contemporary.[9] Like the study of the historical Homer and Hesiod, the study of the historical Jesus is possible and fruitful. It is timely, therefore, to assess where we New Testament scholars are today in our search for reliable historical knowledge of Jesus of Nazareth.

The new research on Jesus will be different from and more informed than previous attempts, primarily because of the increased documentary evidence and phenomenal archaeological discoveries; hence it is pertinent to organize an assessment according to those categories. Our discussion will proceed with an attempt to evaluate the importance for Jesus Research of the Old Testament Pseudepigrapha, the Dead Sea Scrolls, the Nag Hammadi Codices, Josephus, and archaeology. I shall conclude with an examination of Jesus' concept of God and his self-understanding.

Since the field to be covered is broad and complex, the procedure must be focused and selective. This approach demands judgments that obviously cannot be explained here. Suffice it to state that only two questions will be raised: Are the data significant in Jesus Research? If so, why and in what important ways?

The discoveries will be discussed according to the following organization: a review of the discovery; reactions by journalists or scholars; the false claims that have inhibited perceptions; an assessment of the significance of the find; a selection of representative and major examples; and a summary of the significance of the new insights for Jesus Research.

NOTES

1. The titles and bibliographical data for the publications being referred to can be obtained by reading the bibliography at the end of this book.

2. D. L. Dungan, *The Sayings of Jesus in the Churches of Paul: The Use of the Synoptic Tradition in the Regulation of Early Church Life* (Philadelphia, 1971). The quotation is from p. 142; the italics are his.

3. C. H. Dodd, *The Apostolic Preaching and Its Developments* (Chicago, New York, 1937) pp. 36–37.

4. Jerome, *AdvPelag.* 3.2

5. See the discussion on pp. 136–38.

6. G. Lohfink, *Jesus and Community: The Social Dimension of Christian Faith,* transl. J. P. Galvin (London, 1985).

7. The evangelists were not eyewitnesses to Jesus' acts and teachings. Unfortunately, many Christians still cling to this idea, which was disproved by New Testament scholars during the nineteenth century. It is not clear who the evangelists were; but it is possible that Mark had been Peter's companion, and Luke Paul's fellow traveler. Matthew and John were produced by circles or groups of highly trained Christians, some of whom were certainly Jews who had converted to Christianity.

8. Sanders fails to realize that he is using theological concerns and methodologies (see esp. *Jesus and Judaism,* pp. 150–56, 235) and certainly theological texts; yet he impugns theology. Note how he maligns "theology": "I am interested in the debate about the significance of the historical Jesus for theology in the way one is interested in something that he once found fascinating." (*Jesus and Judaism,* p. 2)

In *Jesus and the Constraints of History,* Harvey is "concerned to press his discussion towards the problem of christology, and he spends considerable effort on the question how a modern can make sense of ancient thinking. I prescind from both topics." (*Jesus and Judaism,* p. 9) Bornkamm's claim that "the essential mystery of Jesus" was to "make the reality of God present" is "more *post factum* theological evaluation than historical description." (*Jesus and Judaism,* p. 30) Kümmel's view that Jesus understood his death was demanded by his concept of the dawning of God's Kingdom, and his mission is "a retrojection of Christian theology back into the mind of Jesus." (*Jesus and Judaism,* p. 37)

9. J. Neusner concludes that the traditions about Hillel were shaped after 70 and sometimes after 140, when there "was interest in recovering usable spiritual heroes from within Pharisaism itself, in place of Bar Kokba and other messianic types." (p. 85) See Neusner, "The Figure of Hillel: A Counterpart to the Problem of the Historical Jesus," in *Judaism in the Beginning of Christianity* (Philadelphia, 1984) pp.63–88.

Chapter 2

Jesus and the Old Testament Pseudepigrapha

The apostle Paul referred to the Scriptures as the *graphē:* "Paul, a slave of Christ Jesus, called to be an apostle, set apart for the good news (gospel) of God, which he promised beforehand through his prophets in the holy scriptures (*graphais*). . . ." (Rom 1:1–2) Matthew, Mark, Luke, and John also used the term *graphē* to denote the writings collected into the Hebrew scriptures, or Old Testament. Post-first-century Christian scholars referred to other ancient documents, sometimes perceived as inspired or scriptural, as the *apocrypha* or the *pseudepigrapha.* These ancient terms are still used today to denote the Jewish religious books written roughly between 250 B.C.E. and 200 C.E., and especially before 70 C.E., when Judaism was permanently altered by the results of the great war against Rome (66–70 C.E.). Speculations that at least some of these documents are Jewish, Palestinian, and pre-70 have been dramatically confirmed. Fragments from 1 Enoch, Jubilees, and the archetypes of some of the testaments in the Testaments of the Twelve Patriarchs have been discovered in the caves just west of the Dead Sea, specifically in the same caves that sheltered the Dead Sea Scrolls. These fragments were scattered among the fragments of other scrolls.

During the time of the European Enlightenment, of the seventeenth and eighteenth centuries, interest was turned, as in the Renaissance and in our own day, to the ancient world. In the early decades of the eighteenth century Jo. Albertus Fabricius published the first edition of the Old Testament Pseudepigrapha; it was titled, naturally in Latin, *Codex Pseudepigraphus Veteris Testamenti.*

Not until the end of the Victorian Era, and just before the beginning of World War I, was there an English edition. In 1913 R. H. Charles published the first English edition of the Old Testament Pseudepigrapha. It was selective and directed to scholars. In 1983 and 1985, with an international team of specialists, I edited a new English edition of the Old Testament Pseudepigrapha. The first English edition contained seventeen pseudepigrapha; the new has fifty-two documents plus thirteen writings preserved only in ancient, sometimes lengthy quotations and added as a supplement to Volume 2 (for a list of these documents see Appendix 1). The astronomical leap from seventeen to sixty-five documents will disturb some scholars who have grown content with a personal view of Early Judaism; other scholars, alive to and excited by new challenges, will thrive on the vast new territory for exploration.

Scholars who examine the hundreds of early Jewish documents now available will find how difficult it is today to separate Jewish from Christian writings. Are the Odes of Solomon essentially Jewish, as A. Harnack, B. W. Bacon, and many others—up unto the present—have claimed, or Christian with penetratingly deep Jewish ideas and phrases, as others, including myself, have concluded?[1] Is the Testaments of the Twelve Patriarchs a Christian composition that incorporates received Jewish traditions, as M. de Jonge maintains, or a Jewish document that must have been interpolated and redacted, as H. C. Kee and most others—including myself—argue? Are the Hellenistic Synagogal Hymns actually Christian hymns that are heavily influenced by Judaism, or a Christian reworking of an otherwise lost set of Jewish hymns, perhaps a synagogal hymnbook? These questions reveal how difficult it frequently is to judge if a document is essentially Jewish or Christian. Perhaps it is also time to reexamine some old problems; for example, have we assessed accurately James, Hebrews, and Revelation by labeling them simply "Christian"?

Students will also grow to perceive what it means to state that earliest "Christianity" for at least forty years, from 30 to 70 C.E., was a group within Judaism. For four decades—from 30 to 70—the Palestinian Jesus Movement was a Jewish group that used Jewish traditions to articulate allegiance to Jesus of Nazareth, a Jew from Galilee. This movement developed into what is commonly called Christianity. In seeking to understand the Pseudepigrapha, specialists will ultimately be forced to reconsider Jesus' place within first-century Judaism.

As always with sensationally new and exciting developments, there have been misrepresentative statements. It is clear that Jesus' warning to let an answer be merely "yes, yes" or "no, no," according to Matthew, and his reference to the many shelters (or mansions) in heaven, according to John, is paralleled impressively in one pseudepigraphon from the first century. It is called 2 Enoch. C. F. Potter, in *Did Jesus Write This Book?* (New York, 1965, p. 27), became enthusiastic about these parallels. He concluded that "it may well be that" Jesus "wrote" 2 Enoch "or part of it." Fortunately, no scholar has been guilty of such claims.

In assessing the significance of the Pseudepigrapha for Jesus Research, one aspect is noncontroversial and indeed obvious. Many of the Pseudepigrapha are roughly contemporaneous with Jesus and are Palestinian. Along with the Apocrypha, the Mishnah, and the Dead Sea Scrolls, they are our major source for describing the religious phenomena in pre-70 Judaism. The Mishnah, however, was not compiled until 200 C.E., whereas all the Apocrypha and the Dead Sea Scrolls and many of the Pseudepigrapha predate 100 C.E.

The "sectarian" Dead Sea Scrolls represent the literary products of one small Jewish group that had withdrawn from Jerusalem and isolated itself in the desert. The Pseudepigrapha are a wide variety of texts; some are also products of small groups with well-defined boundaries, but they had much wider distribution than the documents produced by the isolated and closed Qumran group. The Pseudepigrapha help clarify the intellectual landscape for first-century, pre-70 Jews, such as Jesus. And that is exceedingly important, because creative geniuses like Jesus do not live in one country, one city, or one house; they live in an intellectual world. The Pseudepigrapha help us perceive Jesus' intellectual homeland.

To a certain extent, reading the early Jewish Pseudepigrapha is like reading the New York *Times.* One is forced to enter a particular world; one is obligated to share the fears and aspirations of a particular people. But there is more. The Pseudepigrapha are religious texts, and they are highly charged with emotions and claims; they must not be dismissed categorically as polemical or apologetic. They are historical creations of religious people who are suffering from a *loss* of social values, rules, and norms (*anomie*), and also from incredible oppression.

Three examples can now be brought forward to illustrate some significances of the Pseudepigrapha for Jesus Research. The three that I shall emphasize now are apocalypticism, eschatology, and the consciousness of sin and need of forgiveness.

APOCALYPTICISM

In 1960, E. Käsemann claimed that the mother of all Christian theology is "apocalyptic" thought.[2] He certainly is perspicacious, but his understanding of apocalypticism must be refined in two ways.

An attempt to define apocalypticism or apocalyptic documents must be based on a study of *all* the Jewish apocalypses and apocalyptic literature. These, except for the apocalyptic chapters in the Old and the New Testaments, Daniel and the Apocalypse of John, and the quasi-apocalyptic writings found among the Dead Sea Scrolls, are published together in the first volume of *The Old Testament Pseudepigrapha*. In some scholarly discussions the term "apocalyptic" (used incorrectly as a noun) is used synonymously and even interchangeably with "Pseudepigrapha." The documentary evidence for apocalypticism has been greatly expanded, and any understanding of this phenomenon (or these phenomena) must take cognizance of *all* pertinent writings. No scholar has yet attempted to perform this essential task; and Käsemann did not include a discussion of the Jewish apocalypses in his insightful publication.

Likewise, Käsemann's understanding of the origins of Christian theology must be refined. Today we have an improved perception of Jesus' relationship with and alteration of Jewish apocalypticism. We are more familiar now with the alterations of some Jewish apocalypses by Jesus' followers in light of their formative belief in the appearance of "the-one-who-was-to-come" and in the resurrection of Jesus by God. The discovery at Qumran of the passage in 1 Enoch quoted by Jude (see Illus.3) has helped clarify such alterations.

Käsemann reminisced that the study of apocalyptic thought was simply not a suitable topic during his years as a student and almost all of his long career as a professor. Today we can report that this vast field is a main area for research and discussion; it is central to the New Testament discipline. For example, in Princeton, New Jersey, Professor J. Christiaan Beker has astutely argued that the heart of Paul's theology is shaped by Jewish apocalyptic thought.[3]

So much progress has been made in the study of apocalyptic thought, the apocalypses, and apocalypticism that a scholar's competence is revealed immediately by his or her use of these three terms. The learned German scholar G. von Rad, in his *Old Testament Theology,* warned long ago that the term "apocalypticism" cannot be used to denote both a literary phenomenon and a theological perspective.[4]

Today the leading scholars agree that the term "apocalypse" refers to literary phenomena. I would stress that this concept does not refer to a well-defined, easily described genre, but we do recognize it, in all its manifold varieties, and attribute it to many documents, such as 1 (Ethiopic Apocalypse of) Enoch, 2 (Slavonic Apocalypse of) Enoch, the Fourth Book of Ezra, 2 (Syriac Apocalypse of) Baruch, 3 (Greek Apocalypse of) Baruch, the Apocalypse of Abraham, and the Apocalypse of Elijah. These writings are in the Old Testament Pseudepigrapha; to this list we must add Daniel and the Apocalypse of John, as well as numerous apocalyptic writings such as the Testaments of the Twelve Patriarchs and the Testament of Moses.

The apocalypses, produced by apocalypticism, portray an entire world of being, including an absorbing perspective on everything that touches human existence, from reflections on the beginnings of creation (protology) to professed revelations of what shall occur at the end of all time and history (eschatology). They range from cosmic disclosures of the remotest regions of the universe (usually defined as the highest heaven, which is sometimes portrayed as the seventh heaven) to allusions regarding the social setting (*Sitz im*

Leben) of the group or individual that is behind the production of the texts.

Apocalypticism, in contrast to apocalypse, does not refer to a text. It denotes the sociological phenomena lying behind and producing such documents as those named above. It encompasses far more than a world of *thought* behind the apocalypses.

Apocalypticism usually originates out of the collapse of meaningful social structures. It is characterized by a lament over the failure of solutions or salvations to come out of normal historical developments (God is no longer working through history—*Heilsgeschichte),* a eulogy over an exhausted, worn-out earth, and an age often called "this age of suffering" (2En 66:6). It culminates in anticipatory celebration of indwelling a new age in which, using the words of the preapocalyptic prophet Isaiah, the lamb shall lie down with the wolf, peacefully, contentedly, and eternally. (Isa 11:6) It is this ethos, this social setting, that produces the literary masterpieces called apocalypses.

Cézanne, the Impressionist painter, once said that the landscape of southern France painted itself in him. In a similar vein, apocalypticism expressed itself in the apocalyptists. Writing was an important dimension—indeed an obligatory principle—of apocalypticism. As the author of 2 Enoch recorded, Enoch was "a wise man, a great scholar" (2En [A] 1a:1), who is reputed to have written 366 books (2En [J] 23:6).

The third term, "apocalyptic," is an adjective, although regrettably it is used incorrectly as a noun. Ironically it is used as a noun in the title of Hanson's book *The Dawn of Apocalyptic.* Yet Hanson himself forcibly and correctly argued that this term must be used only as an adjective.[5]

What, then, is apocalyptic thought? Many definitions have been published; most are inaccurate or imprecise, and it would be unwise to attempt in a few words what others have devoted whole books to elucidate. Yet, some clarity is necessary before proceeding further.[6] The essence of apocalyptic thought is *transference.* The individual is moved, through vision or audition, from here to there, from a land conquered by pagans to a world—or age—full of God's glory. The transference is from here to there, or from now to then; from a helpless finality *(telos)* to a paradisiacal conclusion *(eschatos).* Such transference embodies *redefinition;* so that from the Maccabean times (second century B.C.E.) to the decade of the Apocalypse of John (the end of the first century C.E.) one could talk about "living" through "dying." By being faithful to Torah and God, one can "conquer" by being "conquered" (see Rev 2:7, 11, 17, 26; 3:5, 12, 21).

A mother reportedly said to her seven sons who were soon to be martyred: "Therefore the Creator . . . will in his mercy give life and breath back to you again, since you now forget yourselves for the sake of his laws." (2Mac 7:23; RSV) According to the author of the Apocalypse of John, "one like a son of man" (= Christ; Rev 1:13) affirms, "I died, and behold I am alive." (1:18) Then, at the end of the message to the seven churches, he promises: "He who conquers, I will grant him to sit with me on my throne, as I myself conquered and sat down with my Father on his throne." (Rev 3:21) In the Apocalypse of John, "to conquer" is to face, indeed to suffer, martyrdom; to conquer is to be conquered publicly before the earthly rulers who reverse the meaning of reality, power, and truth.

The dynamics of apocalyptic thought create new possibilities for discourse and display fresh symbolic language. It is a transference of meaning. Primarily it is a *redefining* of essential concepts, even of reality itself.

Power is redefined: now on earth is the apparently invincible power of conquering Rome and the powerlessness of the conquered. Soon to come from heaven to this earth are the only powerful ones, who shall conquer Rome and powerfully vindicate the faithful so that the conquered become conquerors.

Reality is redefined: from a world or age that is only apparently real but is actually finite and condemned, to a new world or age replete with a restoration of Adam and Eve's original joys and fellowship with each other, nature, and especially God. The harmony of Eden is not the luxury of Rome, but the luxuriance of Paradise.

The transference and redefining of meaning characterizes the apocalypses and apocalyptic literature. It also affected other literatures of Jesus' time. It left its imprint on many early hymns and even hymnbooks of the Second Temple Period, including, for example, the earliest Christian hymnbook:

But Truth was proceeding on the upright way,
And whatever I did not understand he exhibited to me:

All the drugs of error,
And pains of death which are considered sweetness.
And the corrupting of the Corrupter,
I saw when the Bride who was corrupting was adorned,
And the Bridegroom who corrupts and is corrupted.

And I asked the Truth, Who are these?
And he said to me: This is the Deceiver and the Error.

And they imitate the Beloved and His Bride,
And they cause the world to err and corrupt it.

And they invite many to the wedding feast,
And allow them to drink the wine of their intoxication;

So they cause them to vomit up their wisdom and their
     knowledge,
And make them senseless.

Then they abandon them:
And so they stumble about like mad and corrupted men.

Since there is no understanding in them,
Neither do they seek it.

But I have been made wise so as not to fall into the hands
     of the Deceivers,

And I myself rejoiced because the Truth had gone with me.

(OdesSol 38:7–16)

To obtain this transference of place (*Lebensraum*) and redefinition demands three factors: a means, an invitation, and full pictorial involvement. According to one apocalypse (2En), Enoch is awakened, led by the hand by two angels, and journeys to and through vividly experienced heavenly worlds. The author of the Apocalypse of John sees a door that has been opened in the heaven (Rev 4:1), hears the command *"Anaba hōde"*: "Come up here" (Rev 4:1), and then describes how he experienced the most phenomenally colorful celestial events. Others, like Paul (2Cor 12:1–10), remember only the event, experience, and inarticulate wisdom. They are unable to categorize the journey as either a dream or an actual bodily ascent (cf., e.g., 1En 1:2, 12:1–2, 14:2, 15:1, 17:1).

In summation, the unearthly claim of the apocalyptists is that humanity can go home again. We can return home, not back into the womb à la Freud, and not back to an esoteric world via knowledge (*gnosis*); we can return to a paradise that is to be reopened. To a certain extent, Gunkel was perceptive in seeing that the end of time is a return to the beginning, but when the authors of the Psalms, the Odes of Solomon, 4Ezra, and 2Enoch stress that paradise is preserved only for the righteous, the point is well made that paradise regained will be freed of any possibility of a fall, or failure to embody God's will. The end surpasses the beginning.

The significance of the Pseudepigrapha, and the apocalyptic literature collected among them, for understanding Jesus of Nazareth is decisive. To what extent was he influenced by apocalypticism?

Certainly, Jesus was not one of the apocalyptists. They were repeatedly exhorted to write down what they had seen and heard. Jesus wrote nothing. The apocalyptists were often scribes, influenced by Wisdom literature and preoccupied with encyclopedic, scientific knowledge. Jesus was an itinerant teacher who, rather than debate about esoterica, was obsessed with the need to proclaim to all Israel the approaching nearness and importance of God's Kingdom.

The apocalyptists tended to be vengeful, often calling upon God to destroy the Jews' enemies. Jesus was more concerned with inward dispositions and an attitude of compassion and outgoing love (but see 2En 52). He even exhorted his followers to "love your enemies" (Mt 5:43–44 = Lk 6:27; cf. Rom 12:20). This aspect of Jesus' thought is the most distinctive or unique aspect of his ethical teachings. As far as we now know, no other Jew, or Jewish group, drew that extreme inference from the relevant ethical passages in the Old Testament.

The apocalyptists denigrated the earth; they frequently speculated about, or claimed to receive revelations concerning, a purified earth, or even a totally new earth. Jesus celebrated God's creation, and uses the lilies of the field—which bloom so gloriously for so short a time—as examples of God's concern for his people (Mt 6:25–33).

The apocalyptists talked about the future age drawing closer.

Jesus—sometimes in conflicting ways, according to the evangelists —affirmed that only God really knew the time of the end (Mk 13:32),[7] but that it appeared somehow *already* to be *dawning* in his ministry (Mk 9:1), namely in the miracles and proclamations (Mk 1:14–15).

Most important, the apocalyptists tended to situate God farther and farther from the living world of humanity. Jesus stressed the nearness, indeed the presence, of a compassionate Father, who should be called, in a childlike way, *Abba* (see Chapter 6).

Yet, the apocalypses and apocalyptic literature are important for understanding Jesus. Both the apocalyptists and Jesus shared a feeling for the oppressed (cf. 1En 102–4 and 2En 63); and both uttered woes against the rich (1En 94:8–9, 96:4–8, 97:8–10; Mk 10:23–25). Both presupposed a profound dualism, especially of two categorically different ages. Both were ultimately optimistic. God's promises and the greatest of all human dreams—peace and harmony throughout the universe—would be realized by God's own actions, perhaps mediated through an intermediary. Both stressed transferring and *redefining;* for example, the author of 2 Baruch and Jesus claimed that the first shall be last (2Bar 51:13; Mk 10:31). Both sided with the poor (Mk 10:21) against the wealthy, exhorted righteous conduct (e.g., 1En 104:6; 2En 61), uttered beatitudes (viz. 2En 42, 52; Mt 5), and demanded purity of hearts (cf. 2En 45; Mk 7:14–23).

The most surprising—and to many scholars astounding—development in research on the Pseudepigrapha is a decisive shift on the evaluation of the character and date of the Parables of Enoch (1En 37–71), which is a book that describes the heavenly Son of Man, the Messiah, the Elect One, and the Righteous One. Clearly, these are four terms for the same intermediary of God.

J. T. Milik, who was responsible for publishing the Aramaic Enoch fragments found among the Dead Sea Scrolls, emphasized that the Parables of Enoch, so clearly aligned with Jesus' reputed words, was unattested among the Qumran Aramaic fragments. He judged that it was a Christian composition from around the beginning of the third century C.E.[8] Many New Testament scholars were persuaded by his judgment and refused to use 1 Enoch 37–71 to assess Jesus' life and the theology of the earliest Christians.

Today, no specialist on the Parables of Enoch agrees with Milik's judgment. During international seminars in Tübingen and a year later in Paris, experts on this book agreed that it is certainly a Jewish document.[9] All Enoch scholars, except one, M. Knibb, are convinced the work is Jewish and must predate the destruction of Jerusalem in 70 C.E. In his masterful commentary on 1 Enoch, M. Black wisely concludes with these words:

> In brief, Halévy and Charles were right in proposing a Hebrew *Urschrift* (original writing) for the Book of the Parables, which I would date to the early Roman period, probably pre-70 A.D.[10]

Hence, the term *"Son of Man,"* which looms so conspicuously in the Parables of Enoch, was already developed by Palestinian Jews long before 70 C.E.

In the New Testament, "the Son of Man" is almost always found only in collections of Jesus' words. Is it not possible that this phrase derives authentically from Jesus himself? Why do the disciples never refer to him as "the Son of Man"? Are there not some of these Son of Man sayings that may help us comprehend Jesus' self-understanding and his perception of his mission? Is it not difficult to categorize all of the Son of Man sayings as circumlocutions for the first-person-singular pronoun, or as another means of referring generically to humanity? What indeed was denoted and connoted by the words "Son of Man" during the early decades of the first century C.E.?

Now we must focus our attention not only on Daniel 7 and the Gospels, but also on the Parables of Enoch. For example, what importance—if any—does the following passage have in our search for an understanding of Jesus:

> Furthermore, in that place I saw the fountain of righteousness, which does not become depleted and is surrounded completely by numerous fountains of wisdom. All the thirsty ones drink (of the water) and become filled with wisdom. (Then) their dwelling places become with the holy, righteous, and elect ones. At that hour, *that Son of Man* was given a name, in the presence of the Lord of the Spirits, the Before-Time; even before the creation of the sun and the moon, before the creation of the stars, he was given a name in the presence of the Lord of the Spirits. He will become a staff for the righteous ones in order that they may lean on

him and not fall. He is the light of the Gentiles and he will become the hope of those who are sick in their hearts. All those who dwell upon the earth shall fall and worship before him; they shall glorify, bless, and sing the name of the Lord of the Spirits. For this purpose *he became the Chosen One*; he was concealed in the presence of (the Lord of the Spirits) prior to the creation of the world, and for eternity. And *he has revealed the wisdom* of the Lord of the Spirits to the righteous and the holy ones, for *he has preserved* the portion of *the righteous* because they have hated and despised this world of oppression (together with) all its ways of life and its habits in the name of the Lord of the Spirits; and because *they will be saved in his name* and it is his good pleasure that they have life. In those days, the kings of the earth and the mighty landowners shall be humiliated on account of the deeds of their hands. Therefore, on the day of their misery and weariness, they will not be able to save themselves. I shall deliver them into the hands of my elect ones like grass in the fire and like lead in the water, so they shall burn before the face of the holy ones and sink before their sight, and no place will be found for them. On the day of their weariness, there shall be an obstacle on the earth and they shall fall on their faces; and they shall not rise up (again), nor anyone (be found) who will take them with his hands and raise them up. For they have denied the Lord of the Spirits and *his Messiah.* Blessed be the name of the Lord of the Spirits!

(1En 48:1–10)

Are not "that Son of Man," "the Chosen (or Elect) One," "the Righteous One" (53:6), and "the Messiah" different titles or descriptions for the same person? Note, in particular, a statement in 1 Enoch 53: "After this, the Righteous and Elect One will reveal the house of his congregation." (1 En 53:6) Although the tense of a verb seldom clinches an argument, it is significant to observe that the verb is not in a plural form (they will reveal); it is singular (causative, imperfect, third-masculine, singular): "he (the righteous and elect one) will reveal (or cause to be seen)."

Yet it is also clear that the functions and descriptions of the "Son of Man" in 1 Enoch are manifestly contradictory and complex; they are not simply parallel with the traditions about the Jesus of history. For example, what is stated about the Son of Man in 1 Enoch 46—he will dethrone kings and crush the teeth of sinners—contrasts with Jesus traditions, but the description in Chapter 48—he will be a staff for the righteous, a light to Gentiles (Lk 2:32), and the hope of the sick—is consonant with them.

The impact of Jewish apocalypticism and apocalyptic thought upon Jesus is undeniable and pervasive. Although I know of no apocalypse that clearly affected him directly, I am persuaded that he knew and was influenced by Daniel and 1 Enoch 37–71, even if it was via the traditions that flowed to, or through, or from these apocalypses. It is along these lines of inquiry that I have begun to rethink, and ultimately reject, Bultmann's claim that it is impossible to know anything about Jesus' self-understanding (see Chapter 6).

As Perrin confided in me, the Son of Man sayings of Jesus are the most complex and perplexing passages in which to discern possible authentic Jesus tradition. The present book is not the place to develop a solution to this problem, but an attempt to provide some details seems demanded.

I am convinced that *all* three classes of Jesus' Son of Man sayings —those that depict the Son of Man's authority, future coming, and present suffering—were *not* invented by the *Church* (*pace* Vielhauer and Conzelmann). Beyond that certainty it is difficult to proceed further; yet, it is conceivable that under the influence of the Enoch traditions (1En 62–63, 69), perhaps indirectly through oral traditions, Jesus used the term Son of Man to stress his own charismatic authority that amazed his contemporaries (see Mk 1:22, 7:37, 11:18; Mt 7:28; Lk 4:32, 19:48; Jn 7:46). Perhaps the apocalyptic and judgmental form of his message caused him to talk about the coming powers of judgment attributed to the Son of Man—which probably did not denote another future figure—and here again he may have been influenced by the apocalyptic Enoch traditions (1En 62, 69). In light of the martyrdoms of the prophets and of his friend John the Baptist, and as an explanation of the sufferings he endured and expected, he may even have created the suffering Son of Man sayings. All these possibilities may never move beyond the realm of scholarly speculation, but it seems assured that there are reasons now to go beyond Bultmann's contention that only the eschatological Son of Man sayings derive from Jesus himself and that they refer to a future deliverer.

ESCHATOLOGY

We now turn to the second example of the importance of the Pseudepigrapha for Jesus Research. The belief, even contention, that the
present was both the end of this age and the dawn of a new age
permeated most sectors of Early Judaism. The major mine for this
perspective, called eschatology, is the Old Testament Pseudepigrapha. The end, or *eschatos,* of all linear history was set in motion "in
the beginning" (Gen 1). The history of God's creative acts in human time and on this earth has almost completed its course. The
Jew of Jesus' time talked about "the end of time" in a way that was
nearly synonymous for "in our time." Eschatology is not to be
confused with apocalyptic thought, even if the latter is almost always eschatological in perspective.

Eschatology, as J. Carmignac reminded us, is thought that is
focused on *eschatos,* the end.[11] Time is assumed to be bifurcated; the
author of 4 Ezra, for example, talks about this age (or world) and
the future age (or world). The present is the last day or days of the
first age. The apocalyptists tended to perceive the last days as a time
of tribulation; indeed the present suffering embodied the birth pangs
of the new age—an idea inherited by Paul when he talked about the
cosmos moaning and groaning in travail (Rom 8:22). The time of
judgment of sinners was about to commence. The new age would
dawn by God's decisive act from the world above and the coming
age. Jesus inherited this dual chronology and cosmology.

Both the Woes and the Beatitudes in the Gospels probably derive
from Jesus, and indicate he inherited from contemporary Judaism
both God's judgment (1Bar, 4Ezra) and his forgiveness (PrMan).
Yet, he replaced the stress on a distant, vengeful God about to
annihilate the wicked—Jews and Gentiles—with an emphasis on a
present, forgiving Father who wished repentance from all Jews. The
eschatological prophets urged the righteous to remain faithful to
Torah and its moral laws; Jesus urged *all* Israel (and perhaps the
Gentiles also) to repent and believe the good news of God's final
act. Jesus was not extremely different from the contemporary eschatological prophets or thinkers. Like them and most of the biblical

prophets, he held a balanced view of God's wrath and love; but he tended to place the emphasis on God's compassion and desire for a return to righteousness.

Jesus probably did warn about an impending war with Rome, as we know from traditions embedded in Mark 13; but that is different from proclaiming an eschatological war with Satan. Unlike some apocalyptists and eschatologists, Jesus did not yearn for God's cataclysmic punishment of the wicked. His message included them. Here the *exhortations* of the eschatologists and Jesus were different.

Despite the objections by R. Bultmann long ago and E. P. Sanders recently, Mark 1:14b–15 is an accurate summary of Jesus' message, even though the words employed to articulate this summary derive from Mark and his community. This exegesis is not novel; it has been amply demonstrated by the major commentators on Mark, including Hugh Anderson. According to Mark 1:15, Jesus' message was the following:

> The time *(ho kairos)* is fulfilled
> and the kingdom of God is at hand;
> repent and believe in the good news.

The eschatological prophets in Early Judaism (cf. 1QM, PssSol, 4Ezra, 2Bar) envisioned doom and destruction in the face of the impending end; they tended to portray a vengeful God. Jesus proclaimed the welcome nearness of God's own rule and the need to repent; he emphasized a loving Father. The eschatological prophets tended to predict woe; he stressed a call for decision.

One additional comment should be made in passing. As is well known, Jude 14–15 quotes from what was considered long ago to be —perhaps—a lost Jewish document. Now we know Jude quotes from 1 Enoch 1:9:

> In the seventh (generation) from Adam Enoch also *prophesied* these things, saying: "Behold, the Lord came with his holy myriads, to execute judgment on all, and to convict all the ungodly of all their ungodly deeds which they have committed in such an ungodly way, and of all the harsh things which ungodly sinners spoke against him."
>
> (Jude 14–15)

Unexpectedly, as already mentioned briefly, this quotation, preserved in pre-70 Aramaic, was discovered on a strip of leather found among the Dead Sea Scrolls (see Illus.3).[12] Biblical theologians and others, will now be forced to reassess our understanding of scripture, inspiration, and canon, since a book in the closed Christian canon quotes as prophecy a passage in a book rejected not only from the Jewish canon but also from the Protestant and Catholic canons, although it is in the canon of Ethiopian Jews (Falasha).

Obviously, in the first century there was considerable fluidity regarding the limits of scripture, inspiration, and canon. We must devote more time exploring the question of Jesus' concept of how God had spoken and was speaking to his creation.

THE CONSCIOUSNESS OF SIN AND THE NEED OF FORGIVENESS

The apocalypses and apocalyptic literature belong to only one of the numerous divisions in the Old Testament Pseudepigrapha. To be representative of this vast corpus, some brief reference should be made to at least one other division. It is tempting to draw attention to numerous unexplored Jewish philosophical tracts and Wisdom works and attempt to assess Jesus' wisdom sayings in light of them. Here I shall limit my comments to a section of the Old Testament Pseudepigrapha that is important primarily because of the misconceptions harbored by many Christians.

Many Christians, including some who are erudite and sophisticated, tend to assume that Jesus must have been unique and have had little relation with his contemporaries. To begin with, this improper perspective—or unexamined presupposition—ensures that any conclusion will be deficient, and certainly docetic (a denial of Jesus' humanity). Any Christian theology based upon it would be at best only partly "Christian." It fails to do justice to the concept of the incarnation and is dangerously susceptible to anti-Semitism or anti-Judaism.

Jesus is frequently falsely portrayed as one who broke with a rigid and stale—even false—piety. It is assumed that he alone proclaimed the sinfulness of all and God's loving forgiveness for repentant sinners. The sources for this misleading impression are the well-known passage that contrasts the praying styles of the sinner and the Phari-

see (Lk 18:9–14-only in Luke) and Jesus' polemic against the Pharisees who wash only the outside of the cup and leave the inward
things impure (Mt 23:25–26, Lk 11:39–40).

The historical reconstruction behind this portrayal is false and
needs to be corrected. Even though there were Jews "who trusted in
themselves that they were righteous and despised others" (Lk 18:9),
the preceding portrait is a sad caricature. Jesus did meet righteous,
God-fearing fellow Jews. The harsh portraits of the Pharisees reflect
not so much Jesus' time as the clashes between the Christians and
the Pharisees after 70 C.E.

Before shattering the portrait of Early Judaism as a legalistic and
dogmatic system, let me illustrate how deeply entrenched is this
view. Napoleon's conquest of Africa and the Near East opened up
an interest in the antiquities of the Near East including Egypt.
Eventually a Frenchman deciphered the hieroglyphics.

This story of deciphering an unknown, ancient, and holy script is
so fascinating and important for an understanding of the advances
in the early decades of the nineteenth century that it warrants repeating briefly at the present time. A Frenchman, Jean François
Champollion, almost singlehandedly opened the door to the secret
world of the ancient Egyptians. He discerned some signs in the
bewitching, enigmatic, and famous Egyptian hieroglyphs by, among
other insights, finding in hieroglyphics some symbols that had already been correctly identified as proper names in the Rosetta
Stone, which contains inscriptions in Greek, demotic, and hiero-
glyphic. He wisely identified some forms as alphabetic signs for *p, o,*
and *l.* Two names sprang to life; they are *"Ptol*emy" and "Cl*eo*pa-
tra."

The treasures in the Bibliothèque Nationale are a permanent rec-
ord of nineteenth-century conquest and exploration under the great
Napoleon. The subsequent success of the British Empire not only
brought hundreds of manuscripts to the British Museum, it also
brought home to Western consciousness the importance of Palestine. Archaeology of the Holy Land had begun.

All this growing awareness and exploration of the Near East
went not so much hand in glove, as contemporaneously, with the
search for Jesus. The hallmark of the nineteenth-century excitement
was, on the one hand, Harnack's liberal life of Jesus, with the two

1. 4QMMT. Early Hasmonean script of c. 150 B.C.E. A letter from a leader at Qumran to the Wicked Priest, the high priest of the Temple cult. This is the most recently published fragment among the Dead Sea Scrolls.

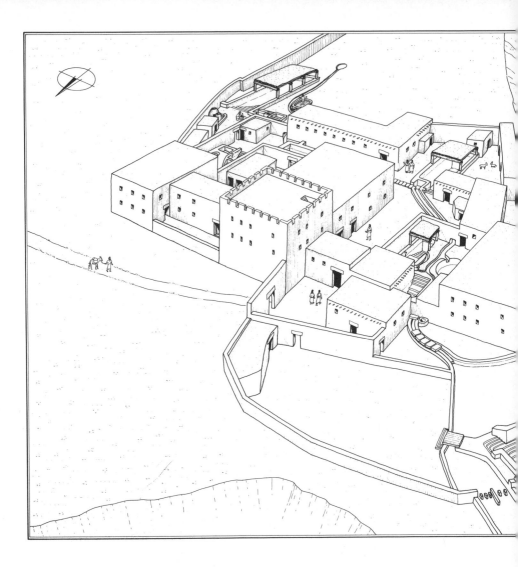

2. This artist's rendering of the Qumran monastery follows the lead of the excavators of the Qumran ruins. Note the extensive installations for the directing and storing of water, the entrance by the massive tower, and the overall size of the monastery.

Lane Ritmeyer

3. 4QEn^{c}1 i (top fragment). An Aramaic fragment of so-called 1 Enoch that contains the passage quoted by the author of Jude in verses 14 and 15. It was found among the Dead Sea Scrolls and predates the destruction of Jerusalem by less than a century.

Courtesy of the Israel Department of Antiquities and Museums

4. Qumran. The caves in the marl terrace, especially Caves V and IV, and the ruins of the monastery in which the Dead Sea Scrolls were composed or copied.

Werner Braun

5. The famous leather scroll of Isaiah (1QIs^a) found in Qumran Cave I. The Great Isaiah Scroll from Qumran is over one thousand years older than the Hebrew manuscript from which editions of Isaiah were translated prior to the discovery of the Dead Sea Scrolls. The scroll shows the wear to the leather from hands of pre-70 Jews; it is opened to Isa 40:3 in the left column, second line, beginning to the left after the space (Hebrew reads right to left). Isa 40:3 was important to the Qumran Essenes, perhaps to John the Baptist, and to the evangelists as well (Mk 1, Mt 3, Lk 3).

Courtesy of John C. Trever and the American Schools of Oriental Research foci of the Fatherhood of God and the brotherhood of humanity, and, on the other, the classical tomes of Emil Schürer. His multivolumed *Geschichte des jüdischen Volkes im Zeitalter Jesu Christi* was translated into English as *A History of the Jewish People in the Time of Jesus Christ.*

Schürer's volumes are the apex of the nineteenth century's pyramid of scholarly advancement. Unfortunately, he succumbed to the tendencies of his day, using the apologetics, even polemics, in some New Testament passages to distort his evaluation of early Jewish piety. It is shocking today to read his claim that in Jesus' time Jewish prayer "was bound in the fetters of a rigid mechanism." He even continued, and argued that the *Shema* (Deut 6:4) and the *Eighteen Benedictions,* the two great liturgical statutory prayers of the synagogue, were "degraded to an external function."[13]

Schürer's voice echoed what had been reverberating through Gothic arches for centuries. Medieval artisans, seeking to celebrate the triumph of church over synagogue, depicted a once-attractive woman with flowing garments and a crown, but she also had a blindfold over her eyes, a large and broken candle in her right hand. Sometimes a broken spear or staff was pressed against her side. The artisan has depicted the synagogue in or on the cathedrals in Paris, Strasbourg, Freiburg, and elsewhere. The sculpture is more than chiseled anti-Semitism or anti-Judaism; it is a failure of the Church to be attuned to Jesus of Nazareth. It also usually mirrors a move away from an essential Christian affirmation, that Jesus, as well as being divine, had been a truly human person who had preached in synagogues.

Centuries before the medieval craftsman, the prayers of Jews were denigrated. This degradation was characteristic not only of the lowly or uneducated; it was also typical of the most scholarly persons. Jerome, the great biblical scholar of the fifth century in Caesarea, defined Jewish prayers as *grunnitus suis, et clamor asinorum,* "the grunting of a pig and the crying of donkeys." (*In Amos* 5.23)

These pejorative evaluations of Judaism included Early Judaism. They placard the failure of the Church to grasp that *Jesus was a Jew* and that the earliest Christians were almost all Jews. The vision was distorted. It is time to acknowledge these failures. The proper beginning is to locate and study the prayers of Jews contemporaneous with Jesus. Almost all of these are now collected within Volume 2 of *The Old Testament Pseudepigrapha,* within the corpus of the Dead Sea Scrolls, and within the Mishnah. Studying these prayers will awaken in the Christian an embarrassment for placarding pious Jews with terms of reprobation. Two dimensions of these hymns, odes, and prayers are eminently significant.

There is a profound recognition of sin. A virtually unparalleled confession of unworthiness and of sinfulness is found in the Prayer of Manasseh. Two verses should be quoted:

> And now behold I am bending the knees of my heart
> before you;
> And I am beseeching your kindness.
> I have sinned, O Lord, I have sinned;
> But I certainly know my sins.

> (Vss. 11–12, from the Syr.)

The author of these verses must not be dismissed as a miserable wretch, or a Jew who has committed disgusting sins. He was conscious of his infirmities, and he confessed the weaknesses that any introspective person sees daily. The author was a devout Jew, and a near contemporary of Jesus.

How enlightening it is to observe that this Jewish prayer has often been falsely categorized as "Christian." The judgment was given by such premier scholars as Fabricius, Migne, and Nau.[14] Today the prayer is recognized by specialists as Jewish and from the century preceding the destruction in 70 C.E.

Again we must emphasize the importance of the proper methodology. It is a travesty of honesty and integrity to define "Christianity" according to some ideological schema and then attribute to it all revered thoughts and documents. Judaism is thereby robbed of all attractive features, and it becomes impossible to perceive either Jesus as a Jew, or the earliest Christians, like Peter and Paul, as faithful Jews committed to Jesus.

Moreover, the Prayer of Manasseh must not be set aside as an eloquent exception. It is very close to Psalm 51, sometimes labeled the prayer of the penitent sinner, and to Psalms 25 and 103. Somehow inexplicably many scholars who study Christian origins fail to realize the full implications that the Psalter was the hymnbook of the Second Temple (and it remains the premier "hymnbook" for Jews and Christians). These prayers were recited by Jews. Many were memorized by faithful Jews—like Jesus.

Early Jewish prayers frequently parallel the confession of sin in the Prayer of Manasseh. The hymn that concludes the Rule of the Community (1QS) and the Thanksgiving Hymns (cf. esp. 1QH 5.5–6) are replete with confessions of sin, and the need for forgiveness. Only one parallel to the Prayer of Manasseh can be considered now; it is an unrecognized parallel. Aseneth, the Egyptian who will eventually marry Joseph, laments her unworthiness, according to the author of the pseudepigraphon titled "Joseph and Aseneth," once called "The Prayer of Aseneth." She utters the following lament:

> I have sinned, Lord,
> Before you I have sinned. . . .
>
> Rescue, O Lord, me
> The desolate and solitary. . . .

(JosAsen 12:5–12)

The faithful Jew, moreover, acknowledged that *only God* can forgive the sinner. Pervasive throughout the theology of Early Judaism, despite innumerable uninformed disclaimers by modern scholars, is the recognition that all contemporary Jews have sinned[15] and therefore cannot earn righteousness before God. The author of 1 Enoch 81:5 has the angels exhort Enoch to teach his children that "no one of the flesh can be just before the Lord; for they are merely his own creation." The author of 4 Ezra, relying on older traditions, has Ezra ask, "For who among those who have come (into this world) have not sinned? Or who of those born have not transgressed your commandment?" (4Ezra 7:46, from the Syr.; cf. Ezra 9, Neh 9) During the Day of Atonement the high priest in the Temple *confessed repeatedly his own sins and the sins of God's people:*

> O God, *I have committed iniquity and transgressed and sinned* before thee, *I and my house and the children of Aaron,* thy holy people. *O God, forgive,* I pray, the iniquities and transgressions and sins which I have committed and transgressed and sinned before thee, *I* and *my house and the children of Aaron,* thy holy people. . . . (m.Yom 4:2; italics mine).[16]

Returning to the Prayer of Manasseh, we confront the confession of sin and inability to save oneself in a crystallized form:

> You, O Lord, according to your gentle grace,
>> promised forgiveness to those who repent from their sins,
>> and in your manifold mercies
>> appointed repentance for sinners as the (way to) salvation.
>
>> (PrMan 7b)

The recognition of sin, the need for forgiveness, and the perception that God alone can supply absolution is insightfully articulated in the Thanksgiving Hymns (cf. esp. 1QH 4). The author confesses that everyone is in iniquity from birth and remains in sin until death. Then comes the memorable acknowledgment that righteousness is not possible for humans and that "all the works of righteousness" belong solely to God (1QH 4.31). Humans can only sin and repent and seek forgiveness from God; God makes one righteous because of his power, mercy, and lovingkindness (1QH 4.29–33). This concept must no longer be attributed in the history of ideas to the creative genius of Paul. These prayers and psalms, and the many now preserved in the Mishnah that are roughly contemporaneous with Jesus, reveal that it is ever necessary to say, "I am sorry," and that Jesus' religious genius was partly possible because of the deep, penetrating advances in early Jewish theology.

Jesus has often been called a holy man (*hasîdh*) by many scholars, especially those who are Jews. He was clearly religious. His life was regulated by the daily order of prayer, and not, as we are, by the omniscient hour hand on our wrist or wall. He may have even occasionally spent all night in prayer, as Luke states:

> But it happened in these days (a pre-Lucan Semitic phrase, and probably tradition) he (Jesus) went on to the mountain in order to pray; and he was throughout the night in prayer (with) God.
>
>> (Lk 6:12)

He probably taught his disciples a special prayer, which is recognizable in the Lord's Prayer, said regularly by Christians today. Jesus' prayer is strikingly similar to Jewish prayers, especially the Qaddish, and his appeal to God to "forgive our debts as we also forgive our debtors" is not a "Christian" invention, but a Jewish tradition reflected, for example, in the Prayer of Manasseh.

Jesus' concept of God as Father, of the importance of the present, and the embodiment of outgoing compassionate and forgiving love —represented in that brief phrase "as we also forgive our debtors (trespassers)"—is represented in other lives who have been touched by him. Mother Teresa of Calcutta, for example, lives out her prayer:

> Let the sick and the suffering find in me a real angel
> of comfort and consolation.
> Let the little ones of the street cling to me because
> I remind them of him, the friend of all little ones.

In the Prayer of Manasseh, whose author employs the imagery of the bended knee of the heart, in Jesus' life and prayers, and in Mother Teresa's prayers, we confront prayer that is not confined by adjectives like "Jewish" or "Christian." Authentic prayer is not defined by such adjectives; it is the heart speaking directly to another heart (*cor ad cor loquitur*). And Jesus emphasized that the heart open to God is attuned always to the "little ones."

The foregoing reflections are obviously selective. The full significance of the Pseudepigrapha for Jesus Research is not yet envisioned or written. But it is becoming clear how important the Pseudepigrapha are for an understanding of pre-70 Judaism and of Jesus himself.

The preceding discussions, out of necessity, have exceeded the limits of the Pseudepigrapha by including some ideas preserved in the Mishnah and in the Dead Sea Scrolls. This inclusiveness is necessary because one corpus of Early Jewish literature must not be studied in isolation from others. We now can continue by examining the Dead Sea Scrolls more directly.

NOTES

1. For a bibliography of recent publications on the Pseudepigrapha, see Charlesworth, *The Pseudepigrapha and Modern Research with a Supplement* (SBL SCS 7S; Chico, Calif., 1981). Also consult both volumes of Charlesworth (ed.), *The Old Testament Pseudepigrapha.*

2. See the English translation: E. Käsemann, "The Beginnings of Christian Theology," in *Apocalypticism,* ed. R. W. Funk (JTC 6: New York, 1969) pp. 17–46. It is often forgotten that Käsemann was talking about Jesus, and the powerfully

influential dictum is often misquoted; hence it bears repeating: "Apocalyptic—since the preaching of Jesus cannot really be described as theology—was the mother of all Christian theology." (p. 40)

3. J. C. Beker, *Paul the Apostle: The Triumph of God in Life and Thought* (Philadelphia, 1980, repr. 1984).

4. G. von Rad, *Old Testament Theology*, 2 vols., transl. D. M. Stalker (New York, 1962, 1965) vol. 2, p. 330.

5. P. D. Hanson, *The Dawn of Apocalyptic: The Historical and Sociological Roots of Jewish Apocalyptic Eschatology* (Philadelphia, 1979 [rev. ed.]); note p. 429: "That is to say, careful attention must be paid to this work in defining the genre *apocalypse,* the perspective of *apocalyptic eschatology,* and the type of religious movement we call *apocalypticism.* While being precise in our definition and use of these three terms, we can apply the adjective *apocalyptic* when referring to the overall phenomenon in a less differentiated manner." This corrective to Hanson's nomenclature should not be misinterpreted; I admire his work and learn from his insights. We both are endeavoring "to refocus the discussion of apocalypticism upon the ancient texts themselves and upon the sociological matrices within which those texts took form." (p. xi)

6. For my further comments see *The New Testament Apocrypha and Pseudepigrapha: A Guide to Publications with Excursuses on Apocalypses* (ATLA Bibliography Series, No. 17; Metuchen, N.J., London, 1987).

7. This verse is ultimately traceable to the Jesus of history *(pace* Perrin and many other excellent New Testament scholars). The ignorance of Jesus regarding the end of time is *not* easy to attribute to a community that idolizes Jesus. The reference to "son" is now seen to be deeply Jewish, Palestinian, and pre-70, as we know from studying 4 Ezra traditions, 1En 37–71, and the rabbinic references to the Galilean miracle workers roughly contemporaneous with Jesus (See ch. 6).

8. J. T. Milik, *The Books of Enoch: Aramaic Fragments of Qumrân Cave 4,* with the collaboration of Matthew Black (Oxford, 1976). Note in particular p. 96: "In conclusion, it is around the year A.D. 270 or shortly afterwards that I would place the composition of the Book of Parables." Milik came to this solution partly because 1En 37–71 "draws its inspiration from the writings of the New Testament, the Gospels especially, beginning with the titles of the pre-existent Messiah: 'Son of Man' (Matt. 9:6; 10:23; 12:8; etc.) and 'Elect' (Luke 23:35)." (pp. 91–92) In scholarly works I expect both sides of an argument to be explored; why did this esteemed Aramaic scholar not recognize the Jewishness of 37–71 and consider the possibility that it had influenced the evangelists, and perhaps Jesus himself? The abundant and significant parallels between 1En 37–71 and the gospel traditions are pellucid. They need to be assessed and weighed from every conceivable angle.

Scholars are neither apologists nor polemicists. Attempting to be unbiased, they attend to data (texts and archaeological discoveries) and amass evidence for arguments pro and con. They are at the same time prosecuting *and* defense attorneys; the jury is the best pool of international colleagues. But the judge is always the data.

9. See Charlesworth, *The Old Testament Pseudepigrapha and the New Testament: Prolegomena for the Study of Christian Origins* (*SNTS* MS 54; Cambridge, New York, 1985) pp. 102–10.

10. M. Black, *The Book of Enoch or I Enoch: A New English Edition with Commentary and Textual Notes,* in consultation with J. C. VanderKam, and an appendix by O. Neugebauer (SVTP 7; Leiden, 1985) p. 188, parentheses mine.

11. J. Carmignac, *Le mirage de l'eschatologie* (Paris, 1979).

12. See the photograph, transcription, and philological notes in Milik, *The Books of Enoch.*

13. E. Schürer, *A History of the Jewish People in the Time of Jesus Christ,* transl. S. Taylor and P. Christie (Edinburgh, 1898) 2d division, vol. 2, p. 115.

14. See my discussion in *OTP,* vol. 2, pp. 625–33.

15. In a future publication I shall draw attention to the list of those who are sinless in the history of Israel and Early Judaism. Those named are always religious giants of the past.

16. The translation is by H. Danby, *The Mishnah* (Oxford, 1933, repr. repeatedly), p. 166.

Chapter 3

———— ·◆◆◆· ————

Jesus and the Dead Sea Scrolls

The most sensational discovery of ancient manuscripts in modern times occurred in 1947 in Palestine during the last months of the British Mandate. Three cousins, Ta'mireh Bedouin, were leading their flocks of sheep and goats on the plateau just to the west of the Dead Sea. Jum'a Muhammad Khalil found two holes in the sides of a rocky, gently sloping cliff to the west of the plateau. After throwing a rock through the smaller hole, he heard it clatter off apparently large earthen jars inside. A few days later, early in the morning while the others slept, Muhammad Ahmed el-Hamed slipped away from his cousins. He climbed the cliff, raised himself up to the cave opening, and because he was a teenager and smaller than the others slipped through the gaping hole.

According to this Bedouin, who is also called ed-Dîb ("the wolf"), he spied ten large earthen jars. None contained immediately recognizable treasures, like gold, silver, or precious gems. Only one, which was covered, contained something interesting: two cloth bundles and a leather roll. Eventually these three packages were transported to a place near Bethlehem. They hung for weeks in a bag attached to a tent pole.

These three old and foul-smelling lumps eventually, after much debate, were identified. They are the first of the Dead Sea Scrolls discovered: the Rule of the Community (1QS), the Habakkuk Pesher (Commentary, 1QpHab), and a copy of Isaiah (1QIs^a; see Illus. 5) that is over a thousand years older than the one that had been used to establish the critical text of the Hebrew Bible, the Old Testament.

These three scrolls wound up in Bethlehem in a cobbler's shop in the vicinity of Manger Square. The cobbler, Kando (Khalil Eskander Shahin), won the confidence of the Bedouin. He promised they would receive the major portion (2/3) of the profits from their sale. Before these were sold, four more scrolls were brought to Kando. They had been found also in the same cave, buried beneath nearly two thousand years of collapsed ceiling rock, desert sand, and accumulated waste. Through avenues of intrigue and danger, Kando and a Syrian Orthodox Christian (Isha'ya) attempted to have them appraised and to sell them.[1] The age and value of the scrolls were unknown. Those who had seen them could not identify the ancient handwriting, were ignorant of Hebrew, and dismissed them as medieval copies.

Eventually some scrolls were obtained by the famous scholar Eliezer L. Sukenik of the Hebrew University; others were photographed and identified in the American Schools of Oriental Research. Over the next decade more caves and more scrolls were found. The community in which they had been copied was excavated and identified. Father Roland de Vaux proved that a mass of stones belonged to other structures under the sand and that these were not remains of a Roman fort. They were the ruins of a Jewish monastery that was burned and destroyed in 68 C.E. by the Romans on their way to besiege Jerusalem.

The story continues to unfold even up until the present. The years leap into decades. It seems so long ago that I left the United States, as Thayer Fellow of the American Schools of Oriental Research, to study in the École Biblique de Jérusalem with Father Benoit and Father de Vaux. Yet I shall never forget standing with de Vaux, our backs to the east and the ruins; we were looking down on the marl terrace and the craggy opening to Cave IV (see Illus. 4), which once held well over four hundred manuscripts. These were not found by the archaeologists, who were excavating the ruins. They were found by Bedouins, after the archaeologists had commenced the excavations in 1951. The main treasures of the Qumran community were not found by scholars, because they knew "too much": they judged that the marl cliffs were too brittle to support caves.

Father de Vaux turned to me and said something like the following: We had studied geology and knew that only the rocky cliffs could support caves. We had searched up there on those massive cliffs and to the north; we found really only one cave, Cave III, that rewarded us with a full scroll. The Bedouin had less scientific knowledge and more sense. With the twinkle still in his eye and his ever-present cigarette streaming smoke, he turned and walked away.

And so the so-called Dead Sea Scrolls were first discovered in the late 1940s in caves just to the west of the Dead Sea. The first photographs and translations appeared shortly thereafter.

But there was more to come. The largest scroll yet discovered was acquired by Y. Yadin, Sukenik's son, who changed his name into a Hebrew form, a common practice for his generation. In the mid-1960s he obtained it from Kando, the erstwhile Bethlehem cobbler. It was not translated into English until 1983. A voluminous body of fragments of other writings has not yet been published.

With the publication of the Leviticus Scroll from Cave XI, all the relatively complete scrolls have been published. As of the present—not including the biblical texts—I count more than ninety published "sectarian" scrolls and portions of documents (see Appendix 4). Only thirteen of these are well known (viz., 1QS, 1QSa, 1QSb, 1QM, 1QH, 1QapGen, 1QpHab, CD, 3Q15 [= Copper Scroll], 11QTemple, 11QPsᵃ, 11QpaleoLev, 11QtgJob).

A major international project has been launched to make available reliable texts and translations of all the Qumran documents already published and in the public domain. Within a decade we will have in three volumes the photographs, texts, translations, and concordances to these numerous documents.[2]

No collection of ancient literature has excited the imagination of our contemporaries so fully as have the Dead Sea Scrolls. And among the new questions raised, none has caught the fancy of the Western world as much as this one: Was Jesus influenced by the unique ideas found in these Qumran scrolls? Now placed before our eyes are leather scrolls once written, held, and read by Jews contemporaneous with Jesus.

The Dead Sea Scrolls have evoked mutually exclusive claims for almost forty years. Some widely read—and too influential—authors have claimed that the Dead Sea "Scrolls are really 'God's Gift to

the Humanists,' for every unrolling reveals further indications that
Jesus was, as he said, 'The Son of Man,' rather than the deity 'Son
of God' his followers later claimed."[3] The authors of such statements are untrained and rely basically on secondary sources and
even journalists' articles. Their claims are not merely uninformed;
they are preposterous.

Other writers conclude with the opposite contention. U. C. Ewing claims that the Dead Sea Scrolls present sufficient evidence "to
ameliorate the position of the Christian religion," demonstrate that
Jesus' gospel is undeniably historical, and disclose Jesus to be "a
symbol of love in its highest and purest state."[4] It is easy to perceive
Christian apologetics practiced by a popularist.

During the battles that resulted from the discovery of the scrolls,
self-styled scholars who could not read the scrolls in their original,
but were dependent upon frequently inaccurate English translations, picked up the debate between scholars as if it were a fallen
mace. Some journalistic writers began to attack the citadels of
Christendom, others flayed away in defense of the faith. The Dead
Sea Scrolls do not, and cannot, support polemical claims—or
counter theological claims—because they do not refer to Jesus either explicitly or implicitly.

The books published by sensationalists are frequently referred to
by scholars as examples of crackpot literature. Yet it is precisely
such publications, one of which promises to restore the lost years of
Jesus' life, that have won the attention of so many individuals. The
public has simply not been reading the careful and erudite publications on the scrolls published by internationally established scholars
like D. N. Freedman, J. T. Milik, A. Dupont-Sommer, F. M. Cross,
J. A. Sanders, M. Black, R. de Vaux, J. Strugnell, H. Lichtenberger,
G. Vermes, J. A. Fitzmyer, K. Stendahl, S. Talmon, and J. Murphy-
O'Connor.[5]

Unfortunately, I cannot report that the excesses are committed
by only nonscholars. John Allegro, an original member of the international Dead Sea Scrolls team, continues to distort the evidence,
concluding that Christianity is a fabricated myth. His sensational
books are sad polemics against Christianity.

In the 1970s a Spanish papyrologist, José O'Callaghan, claimed
that sections of Mark and James had been identified in Greek frag-

ments from Qumran Cave 7. In a recent issue of *Biblica* (65 [1984], 538–59), C. P. Thiede argues that O'Callaghan's identification of Mark 6:52–53 is confirmed. Most text critics are not convinced. The Greek on the fragments is simply too brief for any identification.

Only two improper evaluations of the importance of the Dead Sea Scrolls for Jesus Research will be singled out for discussion now. Each is published by a fine and widely respected scholar.

William S. LaSor is well known for his contributions to the study of the Dead Sea Scrolls. In his *The Dead Sea Scrolls and the New Testament* (Grand Rapids, Mich., 1972), he confronts primarily the following question: "What have the Dead Sea Scrolls done to Jesus and the New Testament?" Basically I wish to voice agreement with LaSor: The real importance of the Scrolls is not that they reveal the sources of the New Testament authors; they clarify the complexity of Early Judaism and provide unedited documents, indeed manuscripts themselves, that without any doubt are early Jewish writings.

LaSor is primarily interested in assessing the possible relation between Jesus and the Dead Sea Scrolls. In pursuing this comparison he makes numerous claims about Jesus that are extreme and, to me, untenable. It is impossible for me to concur that the sayings of Jesus recorded in the Gospels are usually authentic or unedited.

I agree with him that the scrolls do not support the claim that Jesus was an Essene or even significantly influenced by the Essenes; yet I think he has overreacted against such claims. His concerted attempt to show that Christianity is essentially unique and that Jesus' deeds and words are unparalleled is reactionary or at least tendentious. His book concludes with sixty-two comparisons between the Dead Sea Scrolls and the New Testament. It is informative of his position and method to note that only two parallels are clearly similar.

LaSor's judgment is basically sound when he claims that both the Essenes and the Early Christians were Jewish "sectarian" movements that emphasized humanity's sinful state and inability to please God. His conclusion, however, does not seem to follow from this judgment: the Essenes and Christians were "moving in different orbits" (p. 254).

What I find missing in the discussions that lead up to this judgment is a recognition of the complexities and diversities in Early Judaism; the striking similarities—at times—between the Essenes and the Palestinian Jesus Movement; and the recognition that they *shared the same* old *traditions* (the Hebrew scriptures, especially Isaiah and the Psalms, and at least some of the Pseudepigrapha), *nation, area* (Palestine), *and time* (c. 26–70 C.E.). These shared similarities are impressive, but they are lost by the contention that the Essenes and Jesus' group were "moving in different orbits."

LaSor's attempt to evaluate the possible relation between Jesus and the Dead Sea Scrolls falters at a fundamental level. He, like some other scholars, fails to appreciate the vast difference between the *edited* documents in the New Testament and the *earlier traditions* that lie behind them. Most New Testament specialists today would concur that the failure to comprehend fully this distinction invalidates much New Testament research over the past two hundred years.

Jesus' death predates the first Gospel by about forty years. The crucial issue is not the comparison of documents, namely the Scrolls, which predate 70 C.E., and the Gospels, which postdate 70. The critical questions concern Jesus and the Essenes and the more than forty years when the Essenes and Jesus and his followers shared the same territory, nationality, and adversaries (namely, the Romans and the Sadducees, and intermittently the Pharisees and the Zealots). Can there be no relationship between the Essenes and Jesus (and his group) when both emphasized the sinfulness of all humanity and need for God's grace, the two ages and the approaching end of all time, the establishment of the new covenant according to Jeremiah 31:31–34, the presence and power of Satan (or Belial) and the demons, the similar indebtedness to apocalypticism, a cosmic dualism, and the clarion call of Isaiah 40:3? Can all these similarities—many of which are strikingly impressive—be dismissed legitimately as mere coincidences?

Certainly it has become clear that the Essenes and Jesus (and his followers) emphasized essentially the same hermeneutical principle: All scripture and prophecy pointed *only* to their own time and group. Surely, both were Jewish groups who emphasized (at least in the early decades of the Palestinian Jesus Movement) shared possessions with "brothers." Obviously, as has become palpable lately, both were products—and to a certain extent examples—of Jewish apocalypticism. Clearly, the two Jewish groups shared also an eschatological emphasis, an absolute commitment to their own ideas and beliefs, and were related to a somewhat minor phenomenon in Early Judaism: a messianic theology. Was there no relationship or cross influencing?

These reflections thrust before us one major question: what were the relationships between Jesus (and his followers) and the Essenes? They also awaken in us an appreciation for the proper methodology.

Floyd V. Filson, in an article bearing the same title as LaSor's book, rightly begins with the following judgment: "For the study of the New Testament background the discovery of the Dead Sea Scrolls is the most significant manuscript find ever made. . . ."[6] Two emphases, however, made by Filson are inaccurate and methodologically imprecise.

He claims that the New Testament writers could not have been influenced by the ideas in the Dead Sea Scrolls, because of the secret character of the essential teaching in them. He correctly stresses that the scrolls reveal that Essene wisdom was reserved for only the fully initiated members. He forgets, however, the following facts: Before the discovery of the Dead Sea Scrolls, long articles on the Essenes had appeared in major works like Schürer's *Geschichte* and The Jewish Encyclopedia. Josephus and other ancient writers described with impressive details the life and thought of the Essenes. The modern but pre-World War II publications and ancient descriptions of the Essenes explain why most scholars rightly judge the Dead Sea Scrolls to belong to the Qumran type of Essenism.

If Josephus knew so much about the Essenes, is it likely that his contemporaries, the authors of Mark, Matthew, Luke, and John, could not have known something about the theology of the Essenes? Some Essene novitiates rejected, or were rejected by, the Essenes; can we be certain they never divulged what had been learned?

Filson continues his comparison by claiming that Jesus could not have been influenced by the Essenes because they lived in the wilderness of Judea near the Dead Sea and Jesus certainly never visited their monastery. At one point he dismisses Essene influence on Jesus and his followers with a question: "Are we to believe that

John the Baptist, Jesus, the author of the Gospel of John, Paul, and the author of Hebrews had all joined the sect and later left it without that fact being recorded?" (p. 149) The implication behind this question is that only Qumran Essenes knew Essene theology and that Jesus and others had to visit the monastery to learn such esoterica.

The implication distorts first-century Palestinian Judaism. According to both Philo and Josephus, four thousand Essenes lived in Palestine. Since no more than approximately three hundred Essenes could have lived at Qumran and nearby, the vast majority, or—if you take four thousand literally—around thirty-seven hundred, dwelt elsewhere. Philo and Josephus also stressed that the Essenes lived in villages and cities, preferring to congregate on the fringes. The reference, by Josephus, to the Essene gate in the walls of Jerusalem is now apparently confirmed by recent archaeological discoveries just to the southwest of the present wall of Jerusalem, and by the Temple Scroll itself. The latter scroll even seems to prove, according to some scholars, that Essenes lived in the southwestern sector of Jerusalem.

These perspectives are significant. Jesus could have met Essenes during his itineraries; maybe he talked with one or more of them. Perhaps they discussed common values and the need for full dedication to God and his covenant. Historical research into pre-70 Palestine convinces me that to ignore these possibilities is to retreat behind some unexamined dogma.

The Essenes are not mentioned in the New Testament. This fact may be because Jesus' adversaries are the ones who tend to be prominent in the Gospels. Also, we do not know the title or name chosen for self-identification by the group we call "Essene," a term that itself is a subject of scholarly debate. What do we actually know today about the authors of the Dead Sea Scrolls?

The handwriting on the scrolls and the archaeological evidence have enabled critics of widely divergent faiths and perspectives to obtain an impressive consensus. Thanks to decades of tedious and time-consuming research by such scholars, we can now report that the Dead Sea Scrolls are Palestinian, pre-70 compositions, linked with the ruins at Qumran, and related in some way to the Essenes.

The monastery in which the scrolls were written was inhabited by

Palestinian Jews from around the middle of the second century B.C.E. until 68 C.E., when the Romans conquered and burned the monastery, leaving behind a layer of black ashes. The handwriting on the *sectarian* scrolls *composed at Qumran* is dated from the second century B.C.E., at the earliest (4QS [the earliest copy of the Rule of the Community]), to the first half of the first century C.E., at the latest (the Pesharim; viz. 4QpHos^a). The archaeologists found an abundance of coins in the ruins of the monastery; 143 of these are Jewish and were minted during the reign of Alexander Jannaeus, who ruled from 103 to 76 B.C.E. These coins were found in the second stage of occupation; hence the earliest stage must be dated at least as early as the reign of John Hyrcanus I, who ruled from 135 to 104 B.C.E. The coins indicate that some Essenes had begun to live in the Qumran monastery by *at least* the reign of John Hyrcanus I.

Roman coins from 67/68 C.E. above and Jewish coins to 68 C.E. below a layer of iron arrowheads and black ashes is palpable proof of the successful march toward Jerusalem by the Roman Tenth Legion. We learn from Josephus that in June 68 C.E. the Tenth Legion occupied Jericho, a city only a little to the north of the Qumran monastery (Illus. 2).

Thus, the handwriting of the Dead Sea Scrolls, the date of occupation of Qumran, and the striking evidence of the Roman conquest of the monastery in 68 C.E. cumulatively show that Jews lived in the monastery from the second half of the second century B.C.E. until 68 C.E. Only for a few years during this interval was the monastery abandoned; and that was from about 31 B.C.E. until about 1 B.C.E. It is necessary to emphasize that Jews were living in the monastery and even composing new writings during the youth and public ministry of Jesus of Nazareth. Unfortunately, several studies on the relationship between Jesus and the Qumran Scrolls imply that the comparison is between Jesus and Essenes of a previous century.

The Dead Sea Scrolls are linked with the ruins at Qumran. The caves in which the scrolls were found are close to the ruins, and Caves 4, 5, 6, 7, 8, 9, and 10 are extremely near, a mere few minutes' walk away (see Map I). Pottery found in the caves and that found in the ruins are virtually identical, and a pottery workshop was unearthed in the ruins. The handwriting on the scrolls is similar to the handwriting on pottery fragments found in the ruins; the differences can be explained by alterations demanded by writing on pottery rather than on leather and by the distinguishable personal habits in writing attested in the scrolls, especially in the two hands of the Thanksgiving Hymns. Finally, the caves and the ruins were occupied during precisely the same periods in history, including the exodus in the latter part of the first century B.C.E.

The scrolls are widely and wisely linked with a monastic and exiled type of Essenes, the most pious and strict group within Early Judaism. Ancient authors, notably Philo, Josephus, and Pliny the Elder, describe at some length the life and thought of the Essenes. The latter historian even places one group of them precisely where Qumran and the eleven caves that housed the scrolls are situated. The similarities between the thoughts attributed to the Essenes by these ancient authors and the ideas contained in the Dead Sea Scrolls are unmistakable and so striking that some relationship must exist between the Essenes and the scrolls. Hence, despite some recent arguments that the scrolls should not be identified with the Essenes,[7] I follow the scholarly arguments, especially those by Dupont-Sommer and Cross,[8] that the scrolls are to be identified with some type of Essenism.

There are differences, however, between the descriptions of the ancient authors and the contents of the twentieth-century discoveries. We now must acknowledge that we are confronted with numerous phenomena related to the Essenes: 1) the Proto-Essenes, probably the group that produced the early books of Enoch that date from circa 250 to 150 B.C.E., and the community behind Jubilees (perhaps the most conservative document in the Pseudepigrapha), since fragments from each of these have been found among the Dead Sea Scrolls (and some fragments of 1En antedate 200 B.C.E.); 2) the Qumran Essenes, the group of priests who left the Temple cult for the Judean desert under the leadership of the Righteous Teacher (*Môrēh haṣ-Ṣedek*) sometime around 150 B.C.E.; 3) non-Qumran Essenes, the groups of Essenes living in communities in Palestine other than at Qumran; and 4) not necessarily Essene, but related, groups of Jews who would have produced such writings as the Testaments of the Twelve Patriarchs and perhaps the later books attributed to Enoch. Our concern now is primarily with the Qumran Essenes, the monastic group of Essenes that preserved, compiled, edited, or wrote the numerous "sectarian" documents called the Dead Sea Scrolls.

With these historical, geographical, and ideological issues clarified, we can proceed with the main issue before us. What relationship, if any, was there between the Essene groups and Jesus of Nazareth?

It should now be abundantly clear that Jesus and the Essenes were contemporaries, and that there are numerous possibilities for Jesus to have heard about Essene doctrines, practices, interpretations of the Bible, and social habits. He could well have been influenced by them without having to visit the Qumran monastery; and it is likely he had observed some practices of the non-Qumran Essenes.

We are now ready to examine the evidence that Jesus may have been influenced by the Essenes. We can be relatively certain that he was influenced by them if two main criteria are met by the facts. First, we must be confident that the saying of Jesus being examined is free from the theological tendencies of the evangelists and was not created by the post-Easter believers who equated sayings of the risen Christ with the earthly Jesus. We need to limit our focus to reliable Jesus tradition.

Second, we must be relatively certain that the Essene idea under examination is peculiar to the Essenes and not an idea shared by numerous other Jews at that time. This task is extremely complicated, because we must eliminate from consideration all of Jesus' sayings and all of the Essene passages that contain ideas borrowed from the Old Testament. To do otherwise would be to ignore the fact that both Jesus and the Essenes were independently influenced from one main source, the Old Testament. We must also remove from consideration sayings and passages that could be examples of how Jesus and the Essenes were independently influenced by non-Essene contemporary Jewish documents. This task of reduction is exceedingly complex for two reasons. As we have already seen, the quantity of material from Jesus' time has increased phenomenally. For possible Essene influence upon Jesus, we must be careful to ensure that the idea under consideration is a peculiar characteristic of Essene theology.

The preceding process of reduction leaves us only with the sayings attributed to Jesus that faithfully preserve what he most probably said—not necessarily his perfectly preserved, unedited sayings *(ipsissima verba Jesu)*—and from this reservoir of reputed sayings, only those quotations that are linked with ideas, images, or symbols that were unique to the Essenes. Obviously, the flow of thought would be seriously impaired if we were forced to pause and exhaustively demonstrate why the criteria are met. Suffice it to state that the examples now to be explored are ones that have met rigorous examination.

NEGATIVE INFLUENCE

Scholars have argued habitually either for or against *only positive* influence upon Jesus by the Essenes. Jesus may have known about the Essenes and been disturbed about an aspect of their life or thought; hence, he could well have been influenced in a *negative* way by them. An example of negative influence from the Essenes upon Jesus may be one of Jesus' teachings about the Sabbath. Jesus' saying that "the Sabbath was made for man, not man for the Sabbath" (Mk 2:27) appears to go back to him.

It is difficult to attribute this saying of Jesus to the early Christian communities. They were apparently embarrassed by this teaching and the obvious potential for misinterpreting it. For example, an agraphon (a saying of Jesus not recorded in the accepted text of the canonical Gospels) records that Jesus sees a man breaking the Sabbath and tells him that he is blessed if he knows what he is doing but cursed if he does not. Here is the agraphon, which is found in place of Luke 6:5 in Codex D (a Greek manuscript of the fifth or sixth century now in Cambridge):

> On the same day, he (Jesus) saw a man performing a work on the Sabbath. Then he said unto him,
>
> > "Man, if you know what you do,
> >   you are blessed.
> > But if you do not know,
> >   you are accursed and a transgressor of the Law."

It is possible that the man thought he was following Jesus' teaching but failed to perceive that Jesus was not speaking against the observance of the Sabbath but against distortions of its original meaning.

It is significant that the saying "the Sabbath was made for man, not man for the Sabbath" is found only in Mark. Matthew and Luke refused to adopt this logion from their main source, Mark.

If the Marcan saying ultimately derives from Jesus, then he may well have been directing it against the strict Pharisaic School of Shammai (m.Shab 1.8, 3.1) or against the Essenes, who were apparently more extreme than other Jewish contemporaries of Jesus.

Devout first-century Jews took seriously the commandment to observe the Sabbath as a day of rest (Deut 5:12). The rabbis debated what was permissible on the Sabbath, with the School of Shammai almost always advocating a more severe ruling than the School of Hillel (m.Shab 1.8, 3.1). The rabbis permitted some deeds on the Sabbath, like covering up hot food with clothes (m.Shab 4.1), or tossing something from one balcony to another (m.Shab 11.2), or from one ship to another (m.Shab 11.5). And they advocated provisions to absolve guilt for unintentional (m.Shab 7.1) and intentional but perhaps necessary violations (m.Shab 7.1, 7.3). The penance was mild, merely the presentation in the Temple of a sin-offering (m.Shab 7.3, 11.6). Allowances are also provided for the deliberate profanation of the Sabbath, as when a woman who has given birth needs treatment (m.Shab 18.3), or when a son requires circumcision (m.Shab 18.3, 19.2).

The tone of these rules is serious, but it is categorically different from the tone of a document revered by the members of the Qumran community. In the Damascus Document, a large portion of two columns (10.14–11.18) concerns ordinances for the proper observance of the Sabbath. The ordinances are occasionally shockingly strict; it is forbidden on the Sabbath to lend anything to a friend or to lift a pebble or brush away dust in your home. These strictures are more rigid than those which may be traceable back to other pious Jews, like the Pharisees, who prohibited certain work on the Sabbath (m.Shab 7.2).

Matthew attributes to Jesus another statement regarding the Sabbath that it is important for us also to consider: "What man of you, if he has one sheep and it falls into a *pit on the Sabbath,* will not lay hold of it and lift it out" (Mt 12:11; italics mine)? The core of this saying in Matthew may also be traceable back to Jesus. It is quoted in different words by Luke in another passage unique to him (14:5, cf. 13:15), and it well suits Jesus' liberal attitude toward the Sabbath as revealed in his actions, which are too well known to need reporting.

In the Damascus Document, we find sufficient evidence that an Essene might have replied to Jesus' question with the words, "I would leave the sheep in the pit." The Damascus Document warns the Essene not to help a beast out of a "cistern" or *"pit" "on the Sabbath"* (CD 11.13–14; italics mine). The striking similarity between Matthew 12:11 and the Damascus Document 11: 13–14 raises an intriguing question: Was Jesus directing his words against an Essene Sabbath rule that he had observed was cruel to animals, and even broke God's injunction to Adam to have dominion over them and be responsible for them as recorded in Genesis 1:28?

Extreme caution is necessary if we are going to be relatively certain that we are working with justifiable probabilities. Jesus may not be rejecting Essene thoughts and practices. There were numerous Jews, besides the Essenes, who held extremely strict rules for the Sabbath. Many of these were Pharisees, as Mark 2:24 shows, and other groups as well may be indicated by the traditions in the Mishnah, under the tractate called Shabbath. We cannot be certain that Jesus' remarks about the Sabbath were directed against the Essenes; but this possibility must be allowed since the reference to the *sheep* (or a beast) in the *pit* on the *Sabbath* is remarkable in a saying of Jesus and in an Essene scroll and since Josephus reports that the Essenes observed the Sabbath "more rigorously than any other Jews" (*War* 2.8.147).

It is evident that there is at least one example of probable (or at least possible) negative influence upon Jesus from the Essenes. This evidence is significant, because it precludes the possibility that all possible Essene influence must come *only after* Jesus and from members of the early Christian communities who had formerly been Essenes. It is highly improbable that gentile Christians would have created an anti-Essene polemic and placed it in Jesus' mouth, or that converted Essenes would have created a saying antithetical to an Essene tradition and put it in the mouth of the one they now considered their Lord.

POSITIVE INFLUENCE

Some passages suggest that Jesus may have been influenced in a positive fashion by the Essenes. The very first beatitude in the Sermon on the Mount is "Blessed are the poor in spirit, for theirs is the kingdom of heaven." (Mt 5:3) This saying cannot have originated with Matthew and his community, because Luke records it also, and in an impressively different way: "Blessed are you poor, for yours is the kingdom of God." (6:20b) The blessing of the "poor in spirit" or "poor" is very Jewish, fits well within Jesus' own lifetime, appears to be early in the transmission of Jesus' sayings, and may very well derive ultimately from him.

It is inconceivable that Jesus wished to praise those who had poor spirits; it is also improbable that Jesus meant this blessing to be interpreted literally. He did not tell his disciples to become financially poor, or to make people poor; he exhorted them to give possessions and money to the poor.[9] The intent was to help the penniless rise out of their poverty. Certainly, Jesus and the Essenes emphasized the *reversal* of fortunes in the New Age for the faithful ones: The "poor" will be blessed fully; but this shared apocalyptic emphasis on redefinition only prompts the need for further probes to discern the possible background of Jesus' Beatitudes. If these insights are correct, then we must ask about the historical setting and metaphorical meaning of the terms "poor in spirit" and "poor."

Philo (*Apologia pro Judaeis* 11) and Josephus (*War* 2.8.122) both report that the Essenes lived frugally and rejected every form of luxury and riches. Their comments are helpful; but they do not supply us with a metaphorical meaning for "poor in spirit" or "poor."

This meaning is now supplied in the Dead Sea Scrolls. Both of these terms, "poor in spirit" and "poor," are *technical terms used only by the Essenes to describe themselves.* In 1 Enoch 97:8–10 the rich with many possessions are condemned, but the malediction does not come from "the Poor." In the Psalms of Solomon "the poor" are indeed the faithful ones, but they do not refer to themselves, as do the Qumran Essenes, as "the Poor."

In the War Scroll the Poor (*'ebhyōn*) is a self-designation by the Essenes as they foresee the glorious victory over "our enemies," who will be delivered "into the hand of the Poor (whom) you have redeemed" (1QM 11.9, cf. 11.13). A few columns later in the War Scroll the Essenes are so certain that they will win the battle that they rejoice before it begins; again they refer to themselves with a technical term, "the Poor": "But we in the lot of your truth shall rejoice because of your mighty hand. . . . Truly, your mighty hand is with the Poor" (1QM 13.12–14)!

The Essenes also conceived of themselves as "the Poor in spirit." In the War Scroll "the Poor of (or in) spirit" are identified as "the perfect of the Way" (another technical term in the Dead Sea Scrolls), and it is by this group, the Essenes, that the wicked nations shall be conquered.

Why did the Essenes use the term "the Poor" to identify themselves? The answer is found in the Thanksgiving Hymns. In these hymns we find the term "the Poor" (*'ānāw* and *'ānî*) employed seven times, and six of these are in passages that have been wisely attributed by Gert Jeremias, in his monograph on the founder of the Qumran community, to the Righteous Teacher.[10]

The Righteous Teacher suffered physical and emotional torture from the "Wicked Priest," who had exiled him from the Temple priesthood. True to his religious heritage and brilliant theological sensitivities, the Righteous Teacher, who had led his followers to the monastery in the desert before he had finished composing some hymns, looks back on his tortures with thanksgiving praises to God, who had redeemed his servant, "the life of the Poor One." How poignant is the Righteous Teacher's self-understanding of being "the Poor One":

> And you (O God) have delivered the life of the Poor One
> (*'ānî*)
> (who had been) in the den of lions,
> who had sharpened their tongue(s) like a sword.
> And you, O my God, have shut up their teeth
> lest they tear out the life of the Poor One (*'ānî*)
> and the Beggar (*wārāsh*).
> And you have forced backwards their tongue(s) like a sword
> into its sheath,
> lest the life of your Servant be slain.
>
> (1QH 5.13–15)

The author, the Righteous Teacher, continues by affirming he has been tried and tested so that God's power would be manifest to others through him, "the Poor One." (*bā'ebhyōn* 1QH 5.16; cf. 5.18, 5.21f., 2.32–34) He was "the Poor One" because of his loss of wealth, prestige, power, and most of all, his rightful place of leadership and honor in the Temple cult. Later the Qumran community referred to itself as "the Poor," at times referring to itself as "all the Poor of Grace" (*kōl 'ebhyōnēy ḥāsedh* 1QH 5.22).

It is apparent that the Essenes referred to themselves as "the Poor in spirit" and "the Poor." The terms signified that they had renounced all worldly possessions and dreams so that they might be members of God's lot, and the remnant of God's chosen elect. The Qumran community—and no other group, according to our extant sources—used "the Poor" as a technical term to refer to itself.

For our present purposes it is not necessary to discern whether Jesus uttered a blessing upon "the poor in spirit," as in Matthew, or upon "the poor," as in Luke. Studies of these passages suggest that the traditions arise ultimately from Jesus. We are confronted, thence, with an intriguing possibility: Was Jesus referring to the Essenes, "the Poor," and praising their absolute allegiance to God and desire to be purified and holy?

The first beatitude would be in harmony, then, with many of Jesus' sayings regarding the cost of discipleship; for example, Mark 10:21, "go, sell what you have, and give to the poor, and you will have treasure in heaven; and come, follow me." Like the Essene, such a follower would have become poor for the sake of God's Kingdom. It is conceivable, therefore, that Jesus could have been positively influenced by the Essenes' dedication. Perhaps the first beatitude originally meant something like the following: "Blessed are you Poor—who like the Essenes live only for God—for you already possess God's Kingdom."

The attempts to compare Jesus with the Dead Sea Scrolls—as we have seen—have foundered on numerous fallacies, misconceptions, improper methodologies, secondhand, even insufficient understanding of Jesus and the Essenes, and misguided apologetics. To be specific, the most prominent, pervasive, and significant faults are the following: the desire to prove Jesus is totally unique and the incarnate Son of God; the tendency to read red-letter New Testaments as if one has been given Jesus' unedited authentic words; the opinion that the Qumran Essenes over three centuries espoused the same theology and that those who went to Qumran in the middle of the second century B.C.E. were the ones living there in the first century C.E.; the confusion of a search for a relationship with evidence of borrowing; and the tendency to miscast the role of historian, who works only at best with probabilities, so that only what is a certainty is to be judged reliable.

NEW

What is significant and new about the Dead Sea Scrolls for research on the Jesus of history? Our reflections are organized under similarities, differences, and the milieu shared. Four similarities may be briefly sketched.

First, Jesus shared with the Essenes a theology that was thoroughly monotheistic (there is only one God) and eschatological (the present is the end of all time and history). Some sectors of Early Judaism *tended* to undermine the emphatic monotheism that derived from the Old Testament. They seem to have been preoccupied with speculations about angelology and hypostatic beings. Yet, a basic common denominator in Early Judaism is monotheism (cf. 1QS 3). This similarity between Jesus and the Essenes was shared with most other early Jews in Palestine.

It is misrepresentative to claim that the Essenes "thought of the present as the end-time, but they did not match Jesus' note of realized eschatology."[11] The best scholars, including C. H. Dodd (who erroneously coined the term "realized eschatology" in reaction to A. Schweitzer), have abandoned such descriptions of Jesus' eschatology. Like the Essenes, Jesus' theology was categorically eschatological. He preached a somewhat more imminent eschatology, but one should talk about the difference between the Essenes and Jesus in such a way that Jesus' eschatology was more realizing in terms of degree, not kind (contrast Mk 1:14–15 and 9:1 with 1QS 6). Furthermore, Jesus differed from the Essenes regarding the nature of the future, the understanding of the approaching Kingdom of God, and most significantly on how one must prepare for its coming.

Second, Jesus shared with the Essenes an utter dedication to God and Torah. Perhaps he was referring to the Essenes, the only celibate group known in Early Judaism, when he praised the men who were eunuchs for God's Kingdom. (Mt 19:10–12)

Third, Mark reports that Jesus proclaimed that divorce is forbidden. This apodictic statement was difficult to comprehend, and so Matthew relaxed it and made it casuistic. (Mt 5:31–32, 19:9) Jesus' view on divorce, according to Mark, was long considered unparalleled in the history of Jewish thought. For years, New Testament scholars were confused by Jesus' proclamation. Now a prohibition of divorce is apparently found in the longest and most recently published of the Dead Sea Scrolls, namely the Temple Scroll. According to this document, the king must remain married to only one woman: "And he (the king) must not select in addition to her another woman because she, herself alone, will remain with him all the days of her life" (11QTemple 57.17–18). What is demanded of the king is even more stringently required of others. In early Jewish and Christian sources only Jesus, according to Mark, and the author of this scroll denied the possibility of divorce. Since the Temple Scroll, according to some scholars, appears to be the quintessential Torah for the Essenes, the relationships that may have existed between Jesus and the Essenes should be reexamined.

Any comparisons between Jesus and the Essenes must ultimately be grounded in a recognition of vast differences. Unlike the Essenes, Jesus rejected a rigid observance of the Sabbath. And he involved himself with all ranks of humanity, including prostitutes and tax collectors. He and they held very different attitudes to the Jewish laws developing during his time regarding purification.

The vast difference between Jesus' liberal attitude toward purity and the Essenes' virtual paranoia about becoming unclean is now brought into sharp focus. No person was any more unclean and feared than a leper. Today, thanks to the Temple Scroll, we know there was a leper colony to the east of Jerusalem. The author (or compiler) of the Temple Scroll states that "in every city you shall allot places for those afflicted with leprosy . . . who may not enter your cities and defile them" (11QTemple 48.14–15). The lepers are to be isolated "east of the city" Jerusalem (11QTemple 46.16–17).

As Yadin states, "we learn for the first time that there were special places of isolation for lepers east of the city."[12]

As is well known, on his way to Jerusalem Jesus rested at Bethany, residing "in the home of Simon the leper" (Mk 14:3). Jesus deliberately disobeyed the Jewish laws regarding purity; he visited a leper. Bethany is a well-known village just to the east of Jerusalem. Yadin is surely correct when he concludes that "Jesus had not happened by chance to find himself in the house of a leper, but had deliberately chosen to spend the night before entering Jerusalem in this leper colony, which was anathema both to the Essenes and the Pharisees" (p. 177).

The central importance of purity in Early Judaism is clarified by the focused work of J. Strugnell and E. Qimron on fragments of a Qumran letter. In "An Unpublished Halakhic Letter from Qumran" (*The Israel Museum Journal* 4 [1985] 9–12), they announced the existence and importance of this letter.

Qimron contends that the letter was written by the Righteous Teacher around the year 150 B.C.E. It was directed against the Wicked Priest, the high priest who controlled the Temple cult. Qimron and Strugnell, on the basis of the letter, presented a significant and learned opinion (p. 10):

> During the Second Commonwealth, the observance of ritual purity was of such significance that defiling was considered a more severe transgression than bloodshed (Tosefta Yoma 1:12). Thus, the laws concerning purity, and those on the Temple cult, occupied a central place (quantitatively) in the earliest *halakha.* Indeed, most of the controversies between the Pharisees and the Sadducees concerned matters of ritual purity. Marital status was, of course, a central feature too. Any controversy on each one of these topics could create serious obstacles to communal religious life.

Let me now suggest some implications of these insights for research on the historical Jesus. His life and teachings were often in sharp contrast to the religious life of the Pharisees, Sadducees, and Essenes. E. P. Sanders, in his important *Jesus and Judaism,* underestimates the sheer magnitude of the social crises caused by Jesus' rejection of the Jewish, especially Essene, rules of purification. Jesus' examples were perhaps polemics directed against groups of

Jews who, like the Essenes, stressed separation from anything or anyone impure. Perhaps the Parable of the Good Samaritan does not in its present form derive from Jesus, but it symbolizes Jesus' exhortation: be willing to be defiled in the attempt to help or save another, even Jews of questionable beliefs and ancestry. On this principle Jesus and the Essenes stand at opposite ends of the spectrum.

Most important, Jesus emphasized the need to love others, an attitude illustrated in Luke by the Parable of the Good Samaritan and developed into a new commandment in the Johannine writings. It is conceivable that Jesus may have been thinking about and rejecting the exhortation to hate "the sons of darkness," when he stated, "You have heard that it was said, 'You shall love your neighbor and hate your enemy' " (Mt 5:43). The best, and possibly only real, parallel to the injunction to hate others is found in the Dead Sea Scrolls. In fact, according to the Rule of the Community (1QS), at the time of the yearly renewal Qumran Essenes chanted curses on all the sons of darkness, specifically those who are not Essenes, including Jews who masquerade as Essenes.

Without a doubt the most significant and uncontroversial importance of the Dead Sea Scrolls for Jesus Research is the light they shine on a previously dark period. To enter into the world of the Dead Sea Scrolls is to become immersed in Jesus' time and ideological environment. The Scrolls do more than provide the ideological landscape of Jesus' life or disclose the the spirit of the time (*Zeitgeist*) he knew. They and the *realia* of the Qumran monastery reflect dimly also the social and economic settings of pre-70 Palestinian Jews.

In addition to these brief comments, the Dead Sea Scrolls—along with the Pseudepigrapha and the Mishnah—enable us to begin to appreciate the distinctive features of Jesus' own theology. These early Jewish texts supply the framework from which to evaluate the "uniqueness" of Jesus of Nazareth. The contours of the historical Jesus begin to appear, and it is startling to discern how true it is that the genesis and genius of earliest Christianity, and the one reason it was distinguishable from Judaism, is found essentially in one life and one person.

In summation, we can report that Renan's oft-quoted dictum,

that Christianity is Essenism that succeeded, is simplistic and distorted. Christianity did not evolve out of one "sect" on the fringes of a normative Judaism. Christianity developed out of many Jewish currents; there was no one source or trajectory. The founder of Christianity is Jesus. He, of course, was not an Essene; but he may have shared with the Essenes more than the same nation, time, and place.

NOTES

1. For part of this information I am indebted to Professor John C. Trever, who was a fellow of the American Schools of Oriental Research in Jerusalem when some of the scrolls were brought to the ASOR library and hostel. See his *The Dead Sea Scrolls: A Personal Account* (Grand Rapids, Mich., 1977 [rev. ed.]).

2. The massive reference work and comprehensive edition will contain only the already published documents, which are scattered in various publications in more than one modern language. This three-volume set is edited by Charlesworth with the counsel of Professors Frank Cross, James A. Sanders, and D. Noel Freedman. It will be published by Princeton University Press. For the contents of the set, see Appendix 4.

3. C. F. Potter, *The Lost Years of Jesus Revealed* (Greenwich, Conn., 1958) p. 127.

4. U. C. Ewing, *The Prophet of the Dead Sea Scrolls* (New York, 1963) p. xii.

5. For bibliographical details to these and other publications see B. Jongeling, *A Classified Bibliography of the Finds in the Desert of Judah 1958–1969* (STDJ 7: Leiden, 1971), and J. A. Fitzmyer, S.J., *The Dead Sea Scrolls: Major Publications and Tools for Study* (SBL SBS 8; Missoula, Mont., 1977 [with an addendum]).

6. F. V. Filson, "The Dead Sea Scrolls and the New Testament." In *New Directions in Biblical Archaeology,* eds. D. N. Freedman and J. C. Greenfield (Garden City, N.Y., 1971) pp. 142–55; the quotation is on p. 142.

7. G. Ory, "À la recherche des Esséniens," *Le Cercle Ernest-Renan* (15 December 1975) 1–80; see esp. pp. 74–75.

8. A. Dupont-Sommer, *The Essene Writings from Qumran,* transl. G. Vermes (Oxford, 1961; Gloucester, Mass., 1973), and F. M. Cross, Jr., *The Ancient Library of Qumran and Modern Biblical Studies* (Garden City, N.Y., 1961; Grand Rapids, Mich., 1980).

9. See the insightful study by M. Hengel titled *Property and Riches in the Early Church: Aspects of a Social History of Early Christianity,* transl. J. Bowden (Philadelphia, 1974, rep. 1980).

10. G. Jeremias, *Der Lehrer der Gerechtigkeit* (SUNT 2; Göttingen, 1963).

11. Filson in *New Directions,* p. 151.

12. Y. Yadin, *The Temple Scroll: The Hidden Law of the Dead Sea Sect* (London, 1985) p. 177.

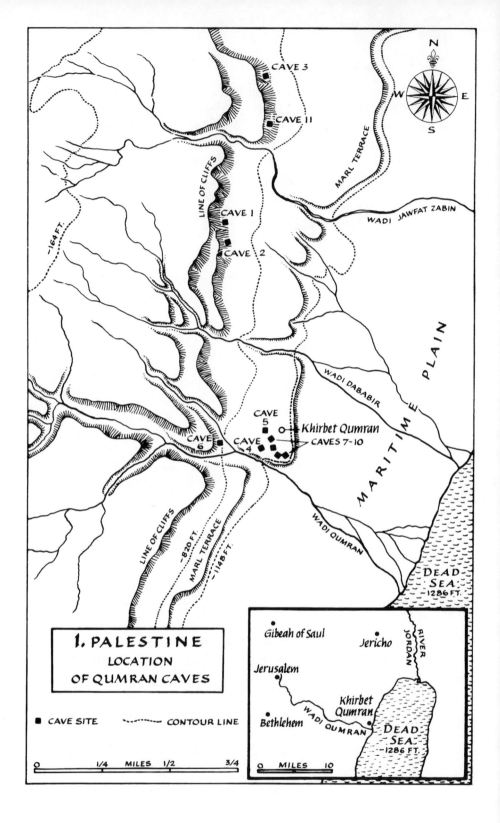

CAVE 3

CAVE 11

N

MARL TERRACE

WADI JAWFAT ZABIN

LINE OF CLIFFS

−164 FT.

CAVE 1

CAVE 2

WADI DABABIR

MARITIME PLAIN

CAVE 5

Khirbet Qumran

CAVE 6

CAVE 4

CAVES 7-10

LINE OF CLIFFS

−820 FT.

MARL TERRACE

−1148 FT.

WADI QUMRAN

DEAD SEA. −1286 FT.

1. PALESTINE
LOCATION
OF QUMRAN CAVES

■ CAVE SITE   ········· CONTOUR LINE

0   1/4   MILES   1/2   3/4

Gibeah of Saul

Jericho

RIVER JORDAN

Jerusalem

Khirbet Qumran

Bethlehem

WADI QUMRAN

DEAD SEA. −1286 FT.

0   MILES   10

Chapter 4

Jesus, the Nag Hammadi Codices, and Josephus

In December 1945, shortly before the discovery of the Dead Sea Scrolls in Jordan, two peasant brothers made a momentous discovery. Working in Upper Egypt, near Nag Hammadi, beneath a mountainous cliff pockmarked with over 150 caves, and looking for *sabakh,* a soil used for fertilizer, they found a red earthenware jar. Inside they discovered twelve Coptic papyrus codices,[1] bound in leather-covered wooden boards, that preserved fifty-three (not fifty-two as once thought) ancient writings (see the list in Appendix 3).[2]

Considerable excitement surrounded this discovery for two main reasons. Many of the documents were previously unknown, and sayings of Jesus were preserved in them.

The fifty-three documents contained in these codices may be arranged into four groups. First, most of the documents are gnostic writings, such as the Gospel of Truth. Second, several of the documents are certainly not gnostic, such as Plato's *Republic* (VI, 5). Third, some that seemed to be gnostic were probably incorrectly assessed; for example, some scholars now contend that the Gospel of Thomas was incorrectly assessed as gnostic. Fourth, a few gnostic writings are free from Christian influences, namely the Apocalypse of Adam and the Paraphrase of Shem. These two documents may evolve out of early Jewish groups that were characterized by Jewish apocalypticism. It is unwise, therefore, to brand the codices "gnostic" without checking on the character of the contents, even though the collection or library was once owned by gnostics.

Unfortunately, some scholars made rash and sensational claims about the importance of the Nag Hammadi Codices. Some brilliant scholars even judged that Bultmann's historical speculations were now receiving proof. In *The Promise of Bultmann*, Norman Perrin argued that:

> Bultmann's particular view of a pre-Christian Gnostic redeemer myth (the myth of a heavenly figure coming down to earth to secure salvation for men and opening a way for them into the heavenly realm) as an influence upon John has been strenuously resisted on the grounds that we have no evidence that such a myth is pre-Christian. But now recent discoveries in Egypt would seem to prove that Bultmann has been right all through the years on this matter.[3]

In my estimation, scholars today would agree only with Perrin's statement that "we have no evidence that such a myth is pre-Christian";[4] the remainder of it, namely Perrin's judgment, is *not* representative of recent developments.

Some critics may feel that it is unfair to cite Perrin, because his opinion may once have been valid but is obviously impossible today. Perhaps this sentiment is shared by most scholars; yet a New Testament specialist, James Robinson, has just expressed a similar evaluation. In a foreword to the recently published English translation of E. Haenchen's *A Commentary on the Gospel of John,*[5] Robinson disparages W. F. Albright's claim that the Dead Sea Scrolls and not the Nag Hammadi Codices are significant for understanding the Gospel of John. Robinson announces that "Haenchen's commentary serves in a way to mark the transition from the Qumranian orientation characteristic of much Johannine study in the first decades after World War II to the Nag Hammadi orientation that has become increasingly prominent in recent years."[6] If this statement is intended to picture a mass exodus of Johannine scholars from Qumran to Nag Hammadi, it is a mirage.

The best Johannine scholars know we are faced not with an either/or, but with a both/and: Both collections must be studied; moreover, the Semitic Dead Sea Scrolls, unlike the Coptic Nag Hammadi Codices, are clearly Jewish and anterior to the group of Jews converted to Christianity that produced the Gospel of John.

The origin of Gnosticism has been sought in Persian mythology by many scholars, especially R. Reitzenstein, R. Bousset, and R. Bultmann;[7] but in light of the vast amount of sophisticated cosmic reflections now known to be characteristic of many groups in Early Judaism, it is wise to trace the *roots* of some forms of Gnosticism in early Jewish thought, especially apocalyptic speculations on the cosmos and reflections on salvation.[8] This perspective is articulated by numerous brilliant (and independent) scholars, namely M. Friedländer, R. M. Grant, A. Böhlig, G. W. MacRae, K. Rudolph, G. Quispel, J. M. Robinson, E. Pagels, and B. A. Pearson.

Here our comments must be extremely limited; only three insights shall be shared. Each of these indicates that the *taproots* of some *gnostic* treatises are in *Early Judaism.* First, as A. Böhlig and G. W. MacRae have argued, the Apocalypse of Adam probably evolved out of Palestinian Jewish baptismal groups. For decades we have known that John the Baptist was only one well-known representative of baptizing groups who congregated especially along the Jordan.

Sibylline Oracle Four, which received its final form around 80-C.E. (because lines 130–34 refer to the eruption of Vesuvius in 79-C.E.), contains the unique Jewish emphasis that baptism is a prerequisite for salvation. This Jew exhorted "wretched mortals" to abandon licentious conduct "and wash your whole bodies in perennial rivers." (SibOr 4.165) After this baptism, God's forgiveness and acceptance are assured; the righteous ones will then be resurrected to a judgment over which God himself will preside. J. J. Collins correctly judges that this document "was presumably written in Jewish baptist circles" (*OTP* 1, p. 383). Such circles may well be the taproot of some gnostic documents.

Closely aligned with many of the ideas in Sibylline Oracle Four are the references to the salvific nature of *living water* found in early Jewish (viz. 1QH 8.7, 16; CD 19.34; Jub 24.19, 25; 1En 17:4) and Christian (Jn 4:10; 7:38; Rev 7:17; 21:6; 22:1, 17; OdesSol 6:18, 11:7; Ignatius Rom 7:2; Didache 7:1–3) documents. Certainly this tradition was inherited by Christians from Early Judaism; the technical term "living water" was eventually inherited by the gnostics, perhaps directly from Judaism, and not via Christianity, as was once thought. Note the Apocalypse of Adam (V, 5) 84 (from the translation in *OTP*):

Then a voice came to me, saying—Micheu and Michar and Mnesinous, who are over the holy baptism and the living water—"Why were you crying out against the living God with impious voices and tongues without law over them and souls full of blood and abominable deeds?"

Once it becomes clear that Early Judaism was characterized by groups, including baptist groups—and not by "four sects"—then we can begin to grasp the possible origin of some traditions in the Apocalypse of Adam. The conclusion of this gnostic apocalypse (8:16) is that "the secret knowledge of Adam . . . is the holy baptism . . ." (8:17). The conclusion helps clarify the references to "water," "holy baptism," and "living water" in the preceding verses. It is quite likely that the origin of such traditions began in Palestinian Jewish baptist circles, as Böhlig suggested.[9] These traditions were impregnated with ideas from the Adamic cycle of pseudepigrapha, namely the Life of Adam and Eve, and continued on later into the Nag Hammadi tractates titled Zostrianos and Triple Protennoia, and then on to the Bruce Codex.[10] While the Apocalypse of Adam reflects a complicated genesis, it is clearly free of palpable Christian influences; hence I concur with MacRae that we should be open to "the possibility that the work reflects a transition from some form of apocalyptic Judaism to Gnosticism" (OTP 1, p. 708).

The same situation may lie behind other Nag Hammadi tractates, notably the Paraphrase of Shem. Robinson rightly claims that both the Apocalypse of Adam and the Paraphrase of Shem evolved out of a type of Judaism "in some cases localized in the Jordan region and interacting in some way with baptismal movements."[11]

Certainly there is an anti-Jewish element, even polemic, in some gnostic writings, such as the Coptic Apocalypse of Paul (V, 2). But we have seen why early Jewish ideas and symbols lie behind at least one gnostic work. Examining the origins of the Apocalypse of Adam reveals the insight that the taproots of some gnostic treatises lie in Early Judaism. Two other insights provide even more convincing evidence of a Jewish origin for some gnostic ideas and traditions.

The second insight comes with the recognition that some of the Nag Hammadi documents may have been composed in a Semitic language. Perhaps a few tractates were written originally in a Semitic language and then translated into Greek and finally into Coptic. The Gospel of Thomas, for example, seems to emanate from Syria, where numerous documents attributed to Thomas originated, and perhaps from Semitic circles.[12] Most of the Nag Hammadi Codices were *not* composed in Coptic; hence, an Egyptian provenience for all forms of Gnosticism appears less likely today than it seemed a few decades ago. Many gnostic works were probably composed in Greek, but if some tractates were written in Syriac or another Semitic language, then a Syrian, Mesopotamian, or Palestinian origin for some aspects of Gnosticism is supported.[13] I am convinced that some documents, notably the Gospel of Thomas, derive from Syrian Christianity, which was heavily dependent upon Judaism.[14]

The third insight that the roots of some aspects of Gnosticism are in Judaism is the most important. The major emphasis in Gnosticism—namely that salvation is only through secret knowledge reserved only for the elect—is already stressed in many sectors of Jewish apocalypticism. Unfortunately this dimension of Early Judaism is not widely perceived, and it would be helpful to illustrate it.

Note the following references to secret salvific knowledge in Early Judaism: 1 Enoch concludes with the words, "Here ends the Revelation of the *secrets* of Enoch" (1En 108:15; italics mine). According to 2 Enoch the wise and great scholar Enoch (2En 1a:1) records in 366 books all knowledge of the heavens, the earth, and human creatures. God says to Enoch, "Listen, Enoch, and pay attention to these words of mine! For not even to my angels have I explained my *secrets* . . . as I am making them *known* to you today" (2En 24:3 [J]; italics mine; cf. also 3Bar, Preface). This revelation results in Enoch's being able later to tell his children the following: "And now therefore, my children, I *know* everything. . . " (2En 40:1 [J], italics mine). The import of this knowledge is moral exhortations (esp. 2En 44) because God "demands pure hearts" (2En 45:3 [J]). Enoch hands on the wisdom, and his books are to be transmitted from generation to generation (2En 48:6–7), not because of esoteric knowledge but because of moral truths. The wisdom is God's will, and obeying him brings happiness (2En 52, 61). This wisdom provides the only vehicle for the righteous to escape the Lord's judgment and pass from this age of suffering (2En 66:6

[J]) to the eternal great age (2En 65:8 [J]). The knowledge is salvific; the concepts are major ones in the search for the origins of Gnosticism.

The author of 4 Ezra emphasizes that Ezra received *secret knowledge*. Note, for example, 8:62: "I have not shown this to all men, but only to you and a few like you." The Lord instructs Ezra to write numerous books; he is to be assisted by five scribes. When Ezra has written on the tablets (4Ezra 14:24) he shall make only some of the writings public. He shall conceal many books and deliver them "in *secret* to the wise" (4Ezra 14:26, italics mine). Ezra and the five scribes—under divine inspiration—produced ninety-four books. Twenty-four were made public, but seventy were kept secret "in order to give them to the wise among your people" (4Ezra 14:46). Here we encounter many ideas later developed by the gnostics.

The Dead Sea Scrolls are also important in our search for the origins of Gnosticism. Approximately one hundred years after the Qumran Essene community was established just to the west of the Dead Sea, a follower of the Righteous Teacher claimed that the prophets had only recorded and not understood the *secrets* revealed to them by God. According to the Qumran Essenes, near the end of time all these secrets were revealed to one person, and through him to his small elect group (cf. 1QH 8). Commenting on Habakkuk 2:1–2, this Essene claimed that God (*'ēl*) made known to the Righteous Teacher (*Môrēh haṣ-Ṣedek*) "all the mysteries (*rzy*) of the words of his servants the prophets" (1QpHab 7.4–5).

About the same time, near the end of the first century B.C.E., a Qumran Essene portrayed the cosmic and terrestrial battle between "the sons of light" and "the sons of darkness." Using imagery learned from observing the movements and organization of Roman troops, which had taken control of Palestine in 63 B.C.E. under Pompey, the author confirmed the dreadful power of demonic forces and evil angels on the earth. Even with the help of God's angels "the sons of light" cannot defeat "the sons of darkness." Then after six battles conclude without any decisive victories, God himself enters and ends the war. This pessimistic view of political life on the earth and the reality ascribed to evil is a significant antecedent to the gnostics' denigration of this world. James M.

Robinson accurately states that, in this sense, "Qumran led in part to Nag Hammadi."[15]

Social, economic, and military catastrophes, however, separate the Dead Sea Scrolls from the Nag Hammadi Codices. The loss of social and traditional values and norms (*anomie*) became extreme, as represented in Josephus' account of the wealthy woman, named Mary, who during the famine in Jerusalem cooks and eats her own son (*War* 6.201–13), and in the pessimism of 4 Ezra. Loyal Jews, seeing Jerusalem burn under the hand of the pagans, would have questioned God's promises and his loving kindness. One logical reflex would be to search for another god, one who was not involved with such an evil and pain-ridden world. Was there a God above this age of suffering? The next step leads both to gnostic dualism, in which the creator is the evil god, and a transterrestrial or other-worldly metaphysic.

Some symbols, terms, thoughts, and perspectives evolved from Early Judaism into later Gnosticism. With these preliminary and necessary perspectives, we are now ready to raise the main questions: What is the significance of the Nag Hammadi Codices for Jesus Research? What document can be singled out as essential in our search for the historical Jesus? The answer to the second question is clear and readily available; but it is a document—the Gospel of Thomas, which dates from the second century C.E.—that really belongs within the New Testament Apocrypha and Pseudepigrapha. It is included in collections of the New Testament Apocrypha by such compilers as J. B. Bauer, M. Erbetta, J. A. Fabricius, M. R. James, E. Klostermann, L. Moraldi, E. Hennecke and W. Schneemelcher, A. de Santos Otero, and M. Starowieyskiego.[16] The Greek of the Gospel of Thomas is preserved only in fragments; hence the Coptic of the Nag Hammadi Codex is our major source (see Illus. 21).

The interest in this gospel by scholars is phenomenal. I have counted 397 publications on it alone.[17] Its significance for gospel research is placarded by the inclusion of translations of it in K. Aland's *Synopsis.*

The Gospel of Thomas is significant in the search for the historical Jesus because of the following factors: (1) It is a document of Jesus sayings reminiscent of the lost source (Q) apparently used independently by both Matthew and Luke.[18] (2) It contains sayings of Jesus, at least in some passages, that are independent of the so-called canonical Gospels.[19] (3) It is now becoming well recognized that it is improper to discard the Gospel of Thomas as late, derivative, and gnostic.[20]

In Chapter 6 we shall examine the Parable of the Wicked Tenant Farmers, which may be preserved with the least editorial reworking in the Gospel of Thomas. Now we turn to a perplexing saying in Thomas. This saying is intriguing and important, because it raises incisively questions regarding the transmission of Jesus sayings, the relation of the Gospel of Thomas to Luke, Luke's relation to Matthew, and all these to Mark, the lost source Q, and the lively oral tradition.

Before turning to that logion (or saying of Jesus), however, it is necessary to review another logion:

> Jesus said, "Whoever does not hate his father and his mother will not be able to be a disciple to me; and (whoever does not) hate his brothers and his sisters (and does not) take up his cross (*stauros*) in my way (ϩⲛⲧⲁϩⲉ) will not be worthy (CFI]axios) of me."

(GosTh, Logion 55)

Although reflected in Luke 14:26, and perhaps somehow related to Mark 10:29, this saying is paralleled in the canonical Gospels only in Matthew:

> He who loves father or mother more than me is not worthy (*axios*) of me; and he who loves son or daughter more than me is not worthy (*axios*) of me; and he who does not take up his cross (*stauros*) and follow after me, is not worthy (*axios*) of me.

(Mt 10:37–38)

At this stage it may seem likely that here are two *versions* of *one* saying. Note in the last phrase the Greek terms shared between Matthew, which is in Greek, and the Gospel of Thomas, which is in Coptic (which transliterates the Greek loan words).

Did Matthew, someone in his community, or some pre-Matthean person change the verb from "hate" to "love"? The more difficult reading is "hate," and it is easy to suggest that Matthew or some person prior to his Gospel altered the tradition (the reverse cannot be said of Thomas). Moreover, the priority of "hate" is confirmed by the reappearance of this (or a similar) tradition in another form, paralleled in the canonical Gospels only in Luke 14. Both Thomas and Luke preserve the verb "hate." Hence, the Jesus saying quoted above from Matthew *appears* to have been edited by someone, and maybe preserved better—at least in some details—in an uncanonical gospel, the Gospel of Thomas.

One obstacle impedes this attractive solution. Matthew 10:37–38 may not be related to the tradition in Thomas 55. There are two distinct and probably separate sayings of Jesus, as indicated by the appearance in both Thomas and Luke of *two* similar but separate sayings of Jesus that are related to the concept of "hating" or "loving" relatives. In other words, Matthew may well be an edited version of the tradition found not in Thomas 55 (cf. Lk 9:23–24) but the one in Thomas 101 (see Lk 14:26 and Mark 10:29 [cf. Mt 19:29]). In fact, the relation between Thomas 55 and Thomas 101 is unknown.

We now turn to Logion 101, which is a saying of Jesus that is perplexing and interesting.

> (Jesus said), "Whoever does not hate his fath[er] and his mother in my way (*ꙟntahe*) will not be able to be a d[isciple] to me. And whoever does [not] love h[is father] and his mother in my way (*ꙟntahe*) will not be able to be a d[isciple t]o me. . . ."[21]

A significantly different, but better known, version of this saying is found only in Luke:

> If anyone comes to me and does not hate (*misei*) his own father and mother and wife and children and brothers and sisters, and even his own soul (*psyche*), he is not able to be my disciple.

> (Lk 14:26)

Luke's version is harsh and offensive. It is easy to understand why many scholars contend that Thomas edited it, making it more attractive to Christians.

The major issue concerns the appearance of "in my way" (*ꙟntahe*) twice in Thomas and not once in Luke. This phrase may also be translated "in my manner" or "as [I] do"; but this translation is unlikely if the expression derives ultimately from Greek or a

Semitic language. It is difficult to dismiss this phrase as merely an explanatory gloss in Thomas. As is well and widely recognized, Thomas tends to be brief and esoteric, but Luke is usually full and clear. The Jesus saying now under investigation, however, stands out as being impressively contrary to these two tendencies. It is remarkable how succinct is the saying in Luke. It does not have the simple repetition—to hate father or mother in my way . . . to love father and mother in my way—and such parallelism is typical of numerous of Jesus' sayings which have been seen to be authentic.

An attempt to show that Thomas, like Matthew, strives to interpret Luke's tradition would emphasize that the saying hardest to comprehend is in the canon, and that the most difficult reading is usually earlier. For years, numerous scholars, however, have voiced uneasiness with Bengel's principle that priority in purity of transmission is to be given to the difficult reading (*proclivi scriptioni praestat ardua*). The difficult reading can be caused by omission, manuscript corruption, misunderstanding, or simple scribal error. I have seldom read a book or article that did not contain grammatical and spelling errors. Originals must not be assumed to be perfect; hence, the more difficult reading can be later. Hence, applying Bengel's principle does not solve our problem.

A critic supporting the superiority of Luke's reading might continue by claiming that the author of Thomas supplied an exegesis of the saying by adding "in my way." The author of Luke, however, is also the author of Acts, and the emphasis on Jesus' way, or "the Way," is characteristic of Acts (9:2; 19:9, 23; 22:4; 24:14, 22). Moreover, one group in Early Judaism, the Qumran Essenes, called their movement "the Way." Hence, if "in my way" was in the version of the Jesus saying available to Luke, he probably would have included it, because of his emphasis that Jesus' earliest followers in Palestine were members of Jesus' way, or "the Way."

A recurrent weakness in textual criticism's methodology is the failure to consider the tendencies of the gospel writers and the historical setting of traditions. Hence, there are difficulties in the desire here to prove a canonical tradition superior.

The strongest argument for the superiority of the Lucan reading would be the contention that it is more likely that "in my way" would have been added twice—as a clarifying exegesis—than that it was inadvertently omitted twice. It probably would not have been omitted accidentally twice. However, it would be as easy intentionally to add it twice as to delete it twice.

Any attempt to defend a claim that Luke has edited the saying in 14:26 runs aground on the recognition that it contrasts markedly with his tendencies. It cannot originate with him, and must be a pre-Lucan tradition. A comparison with the partial parallel in Matthew 10:37–38 shows that the tradition clearly predates both Luke and Matthew. The differences between them, however, raise doubts that Matthew and Luke are working here from the common Q source, as suggested perhaps by Aland's *Synopsis*. Moreover, the doublet in the Gospel of Thomas—the redundancy of sayings 55 and 101—is difficult to explain, indicates a source prior to Thomas, and may render impossible any attempt to prove a single, original version.

In this logion the major contrast between Luke and Matthew is clearly that Matthew mentions "love" and Luke has "hate." *Most important* for our purposes is the striking difference between this saying and *Luke's universalism and ethic of loving compassion.* More than Matthew or Mark, Luke emphasizes the love ethic; here he is unlike them and similar to John. Moreover, the saying is offensive, and Luke tends to omit or recast offensive Jesus sayings and systematically present his tradition, as we know from comparing his redaction of the Gospel of Mark (compare Mk 13:32 with Lk 21:33, and Mk 9:1 with Lk 9:27).

Turning back to Thomas we must ask, Why is a relatively clear statement found in a document that has a tendency toward obscurity? As S. L. Davies states in *The Gospel of Thomas and Christian Wisdom,* the logion in Thomas "is, if anything, less 'encratite' than the version in Luke" (p. 22). The renunciation of family ties is often attributed to Thomas, but this sociological phenomenon was also typical of Jesus and his earliest followers. The cumulative thrust of the preceding insights leads to the conclusion that the saying must antedate Thomas.

If the logion antedates both Luke and Thomas, and if there is insufficient reason for affirming literary dependence between them —as most scholars tend now to recognize—then we are left with two issues: The two recensions go back to a common source (oral or

written) that must ultimately predate 85 C.E., when Luke was written. Hence, we come to these questions: Does the hypothetical
source contain authentic Jesus traditions? If so, is it represented in
Luke or Thomas?

It is possible that Luke's version could derive ultimately from
Jesus. The rhetoric of shock may be the motive. The injunction to
hate others, however, is in clear contrast with the reliable tradition
that Jesus taught an ethic of love, as we saw earlier. Likewise, the
charge to hate one's own soul clashes unattractively with the Jesus
tradition to love others as the healthy person loves himself or herself. Jesus affirmed the widely influential exhortation in Leviticus
19:18 (see Mt 5:43, 19:19, 22:39; Mk 12:31; Lk 10:27; Rom 13:9;
Gal 5:14; Jas 2:8): "You shall love your neighbor as yourself" (Mk
12:31).

The parallelism of Thomas' statement, with a dual exhortation
centered first on hate and then on love, is typical of Jesus' sayings.
Many of them, especially when retroverted back into Aramaic, are
couched in pleasing Semitic poetic parallelism (*parallelismus mem-
brorum*). Thomas' version of the logion under examination, moreover, is easily distinguishable from the expansive tendency in
Thomas noted by Jeremias in his *Unknown Sayings of Jesus.*[22]

Can the saying be traced ultimately to the earliest Aramaic-
speaking communities or even to Jesus himself, who would have
uttered it in Aramaic? We can now turn to the Thomas tradition
and the Coptic phrase ϩntahe, "in my way." As in Coptic, so in
Aramaic "in my way" has a simple form: *bdrky*; hence we should
not be concerned about the loss of three words, which is the case in
Greek and English, not in Coptic or Aramaic. In Aramaic it would
not be necessary to repeat *bᵉdarkî*; once specified, it would have
been assumed in a following parallel phrase. Such style is good
Semitic syntax. The earliest communities would have known the
ruling thought was "Jesus' way."

An examination of a saying in the Gospel of Thomas thus forces
upon us probing thoughts and unresolved complexities; it brings us
close to Jesus' time and the beginnings of the transmission of his
sayings. Among the most significant questions encountered in the
preceding probe are these: Do Thomas 55, Matthew 10:37–38, and
Luke 14:26–27 derive ultimately from a lost shared source and is

this wisely called "Q"? Or does each of these passages develop independently out of a fluid oral tradition that took shape over the decades from 30 to 100 C.E.? What do the doublets in Thomas (55 and 101) and Luke (14:26–27, 9:23–24) indicate about the transmission of these Jesus sayings? How are Mark 10:29 and Matthew 19:29 related to Thomas 101, and even 55? Is "in my way" related someway to "the Way," a name for the Palestinian Jesus Movement? Are all these Jesus sayings just mentioned not indicative of one problem for the earliest followers of Jesus: the facts that his family rejected him (Mk 3:21, 31–34) and the members of his home village hated him (Mk 6:3–6, Mt 13:56–58, and Lk 4:25–30)? Despite the intriguing differences in the sayings of Jesus here, is there not a common core: alienation clearly derives from Jesus' own life? Is not Thomas essential in bringing into focus all these issues, and raising afresh the questions related to the history of the transmission of the Jesus tradition and the intractable nature of some of the problems?

In summary, we are left with one piercing question: Does Thomas 101 derive from an early pre-70 Palestinian reflection on Jesus' way, or is it a reliable statement from Jesus, perhaps somewhat altered, that is in line with his wisdom sayings? In any case, it is obvious how significant the Gospel of Thomas is in our search for the sayings of the historical Jesus. We shall return to the importance of Thomas in the study of the Parable of the Wicked Tenant Farmers in Chapter 6.

Here we have paused briefly to look at one saying of Jesus and its transmission and redaction in the first one hundred years after his death. Before continuing, it is necessary to at least stress that many other sections of Thomas deserve much more careful study than customarily given to them by New Testament scholars. For example, the whole process of transmitting the parables is frustrated by a myopic focus on only Matthew or Luke. The Parable of the Great Feast is so thoroughly altered by Matthew and his school that we are left wondering about reverence for tradition and reliable transmission (see Mt 22:1–14; Lk 14:15–24). The parable reappears in Thomas (Logion 64) and is not nearly so edited as in Matthew. Most important, Luke's and Thomas' parable about a supper or dinner is changed by Matthew and his school into an allegory about a king's wedding feast for his son. The Gospel of Thomas, and, therefore, Coptic, are sources and tools for all future New Testament research, especially that aspect of it labeled "Jesus Research."

JOSEPHUS

Josephus' writings are well known and have been important for historians studying the origins of Christianity for over fifteen hundred years. Some early Christian scholars (notably Eusebius and Sozomen) before Chalcedon (451 C.E.), where Jesus of Nazareth was declared doctrinally to be fully (or better, perfect) God and fully (or better, perfect) human,[23] refer to him as a historian worthy of trust (e.g., Eusebius, *HE* 3.9).

I have inherited four private theological libraries from scholars and preachers who have passed away. Whiston's *The Works of Flavius Josephus* was one of the very few works in each library. Our grandfathers knew the history of the first century. The discovery of the Dead Sea Scrolls awakened in our fathers a sensitivity that had been lost.

Jesus and Josephus (38–100 C.E.) were Palestinian Jews intimately linked with Galilee. Although Josephus lived later in the first century than Jesus, his early career was characterized by the struggle against and eventually the war with Rome. As is well known, Jesus was crucified by the Romans, on charges that he was a political insurrectionist; he and his followers were certainly seen as a threat to the precarious peace that existed around 30 in Palestine. Not only was Palestine, on the eastern fringes of the Roman Empire, about to explode into a multifaceted revolt, but Rome's enemy farther to the East, Parthia, was evasive, too powerful, and too near.

Jesus and Josephus are manifestly different Jews, despite the similarities of "religion," place, and time. It is impossible to contend that Jesus became pro-Roman, as did Josephus. It is also improper *(pace* Brandon) to argue that Jesus, like Josephus initially, was involved in hostilities against Rome. It is inaccurate to suggest that Jesus, like Josephus, was won over to Greek paradigms and linguistic models. There are many other differences between these first-century Palestinian Jews; in essence—and this discovery may shock many—Jesus was far more Jewish than Josephus. In no way can Jesus be categorized with Josephus as an opportunist with pro-Roman tendencies, and as an apologist who sometimes chose to write in Greek using Greek terminologies and concepts.

The significance of Josephus for Jesus Research does *not* reside in the man Josephus; it lies in his literature. He is the historian of Early Judaism. He describes the turbulent times in which Jesus lived. And, most significant, he probably referred to Jesus.

In *Antiquities* 18.63–64 Josephus, according to the received Greek text, refers to Jesus. Here is the translation by L. H. Feldman (LCL):

> About this time there lived Jesus, a wise man, if indeed one ought to call him a man. For he was one who wrought surprising feats and was a teacher of such people as accept the truth gladly. He won over many Jews and many of the Greeks. He was the Messiah. When Pilate, upon hearing him accused by men of the highest standing amongst us, had condemned him to be crucified, those who had in the first place come to love him did not give up their affection for him. On the third day he appeared to them restored to life, for the prophets of God had prophesied these and countless other marvellous things about him. And the tribe of the Christians, so called after him, has still to this day not disappeared.

Josephus' reference to Jesus, the *Testimonium Flavianum,* may also be translated from the Greek as follows (clearly Christian [interpolated] words are in italics):

> About this time there was Jesus, a wise man, *if indeed one ought to call him a man.* For he was one who performed surprising[24] works, (and) a teacher of people who with pleasure received the unusual.[25] He stirred up[26] both many Jews and also many of the Greeks. *He was the Christ.*[27] And[28] when Pilate condemned him to the cross, since he was accused by the first-rate men among us, those who had been loving (him from) the first did not cease (to cause trouble),[29] *for he appeared to them on the third day, having life again, as the prophets of God had foretold these and countless other marvelous[30] things about him.* And until now the tribe of Christians, so named from him, is not (yet?) extinct.

> *(Ant* 18.63–64)

My translation attempts to bring out the meaning most likely intended by the first-century Jew Josephus. At the outset it seems clear that either a Christian scribe added this passage *in toto* or one or more Christian copyists edited and expanded a reference to Jesus by Josephus. In order to discern whether Josephus made any reference to Jesus in *Antiquities* 18.63–64, false presuppositions and methodologies must be corrected.

Three major inaccurate presuppositions need to be exposed and discarded. First, some critics (viz. Burkitt) have argued that Josephus wrote the text essentially as it is now extant in Greek. This option is virtually impossible; Josephus is made to profess belief both in Jesus and in his resurrection from the dead. Josephus, the Jew living in Rome, could not have written the passage as it is now preserved in Greek, because of such clearly Christian passages as he "was the Christ."

Second, some critics (viz. Bauer) have supposed that Josephus (and other first-century Jews) could not have admired and said anything laudatory about Jesus without at the same time becoming Christians. Scholars generally have evidenced a biased view of the first century. They tend to portray the people on the two sides of the controversy between "Christians" and "Jews" in black and white (as in an ancient Jewish pseudepigraphon, ApAb 29), rather than use the proper shades of gray to describe the many possible positions. Scholars also have tended to fail to put a proper emphasis on the fact that almost all the earliest "Christians" were Jews. Such portraits fail to be informed of the complex issues relating to the categorization of such individuals as the anonymous rich young ruler, Nicodemus, and Joseph of Arimathea. Some Jews followed Jesus, while others admired him (perhaps only from a distance) for his honesty, charisma, integrity, and teachings.

Third, some scholars acting like formal logicians have approached the text of Josephus with an either/or mentality: either all of the text derives faithfully from Josephus or none of it does. Schürer, for example, opted for "utter spuriousness" (*History,* 1.2, p. 149). This tendency is ill-informed about the redactional nature of many pseudepigrapha and of all the Gospels. Because of the nature of the clearly Christian words, it must be acknowledged that we are once again confronted with tradition and addition: Josephus probably referred to Jesus, but Christian copyists added editorial comments.

The major methodological error committed in approaching *Antiquities* 18 is the confusion over what is meant by an alteration of text. I have become convinced that we have in this passage both interpolation and redaction. These two phenomena need to be distinguished and defined.

Interpolation is the insertion of a word or group of words into a text. Little evidence can be supplied to discern whether something has been deleted, yet we must allow for this strong possibility.[31]

Redaction denotes the reworking of a text, adding words, deleting words, altering words, and substituting words for what had been written. The presupposition is that something quite different was probably intended but is now rewritten.

Redactions are impossible to circumscribe, and can be clear only when the original text is available to be compared with the received text. This technique is possible if indeed Luke rewrote Mark, as many scholars have concluded; it may now be possible with Josephus' text, as we shall see.

Three main observations indicate that Josephus referred to Jesus in *Antiquities* 18.63–64. First, Josephus must have made a reference to Jesus, because the passage, divested of the obvious Christian words, is not Christian and is composed in such a way that it is very difficult to attribute it to a Christian. What Christian would refer to Jesus' miracles in such a way that a reader could understand them as merely "surprising works"? Would a Christian have written that "first-rate men" or "men of the highest standing" accused Jesus before Pilate, leaving the impression that he deserved a guilty verdict? Would a Christian scribe have ended a reference to Jesus by referring to "the tribe of Christians" who "are not extinct," as if they should soon become extinct?

Second, we can be confident that there was a minimal reference to Jesus in *Antiquities* 18.63–64 because once the clearly Christian sections are removed, the rest makes good grammatical and historical sense. The peculiarly Christian words are parenthetically connected to the narrative; hence they are grammatically free and could easily have been inserted by a Christian. These sections also are disruptive, and when they are removed the flow of thought is improved and smoother. For example, once the reference to the resurrection is deleted, the thought moves from Christians continuing active after the crucifixion to the nonextinct nature of the tribe.

Some of the insertions are confessional and kerygmatic; they are dissimilar from the rest of the prose. The first clearly Christian section—*"if indeed one ought to call him a man"*—looks interpolated, and it seems to reflect the doctrinal disputes of the fourth and fifth centuries C.E.

Third, some words in *Antiquities* 18 seem authentic to Josephus, because in *Antiquities* 20 he refers to a man named James as the brother of Jesus. This individual is brought to Ananus, the Sadducean high priest, who convened the judges of the Sanhedrin and was responsible for their condemnation of James and his subsequent stoning. The action was offensive and unjust to many Jews in Jerusalem. These appealed to King Agrippa, who because of complaints about the behavior of Ananus removed him from the high priesthood. Who was this "James"? Josephus identifies him clearly: Ananus "convened the judges of the Sanhedrin and brought before them a man named James, the brother of Jesus said to be Christ (*ton adelphon Iēsou tou legomenou Christou, Iakōbos onoma autō, Ant.* 20.200 [LCL]). Josephus has identified one person in terms of another; it is logical to expect the latter to have been mentioned already by him. Hence, it looms probable that Josephus had already described with some memorable details this brother of James. Indeed, he probably did so precisely where we now find the "Testimony of Flavius" Josephus (*Testimonium Flavianum*).

A study of the *Testimonium Flavianum* in its Greek form[32] leads to speculations that ultimately fall short of convincing proof. It appears likely that Josephus referred to Jesus, but certainly not in the form preserved in the Greek manuscripts.[33] Hence, many critics refuse to take a stand on the issue of reliable Josephus words in this section of the *Antiquities*. In essence, the consensus, if there is one, among New Testament scholars, is that one should not concentrate on Josephus' reference to Jesus, because it has clearly been altered by Christian scribes. The passage is frequently now ignored in research on the Jesus of history.

For years scholars dreamed of the day that a text of Josephus' *Antiquities* would be recovered in which there are significant variants in the *Testimonium Flavianum*. Then perhaps we could support scholarly speculations with textual evidence. In fact, precisely this dream has come true, and that is our good fortune.

An Arabic version of the *Testimonium Flavianum* has been discovered in Agapius' *Book of the Title* (*Kitāb al-'Unwān*), which is a history of the world from its beginning until 941/42 C.E. Agapius (or Agapios) was a tenth-century Christian Arab and Melkite bishop of Hierapolis, in Phrygia, in Asia Minor. The translation of Agapius' excerpt from Josephus by S. Pines, a professor in the Hebrew University (Jerusalem), who drew attention to it, is as follows:[34]

> Similarly Josephus (*Yūsīfūs*), the Hebrew. For he says in the treatises that he has written on the governance (?) of the Jews: "At this time there was a wise man who was called Jesus. His conduct was good, and (he) was known to be virtuous. And many people from among the Jews and the other nations became his disciples. Pilate condemned him to be crucified and to die. But those who had become his disciples did not abandon his discipleship. They reported that he had appeared to them three days after his crucifixion, and that he was alive; accordingly he was perhaps the Messiah, concerning whom the prophets have recounted wonders."[35]

What is immediately obvious—when one compares the Arabic and the Greek recensions—is that the blatantly Christian passages are *conspicuously absent* in the Arabic version. The first two Christian passages in the Greek (*"if indeed one ought to call him a man"* and *"He was the Christ"*) are missing. The third, and final, one is introduced by the words "They reported that . . ."

The final statement is contorted; how could a Jew claim that anyone "was *perhaps* the Messiah"? Or, how could Josephus state that Jesus' followers "reported that . . . he was perhaps the Messiah"? Would not the following reference to the prophets be confusing in light of the preceding "perhaps"? The possibility that anyone, including Jesus, was the Messiah, was not a proposition that could be taken lightly by any Jew, especially one with the experiences and credentials of Josephus. But it is even more apparent that no Christian could have originated such words as "he was perhaps the Messiah. . . ." It is best to assume that what Josephus wrote is not accurately preserved in any extant recension (Greek, Slavic, or Arabic); it has been at least slightly altered by Christian scribes.

It seems obvious that some Christian alterations are found in the Arabic recension, even if they are more subtle in the Arabic version than in the Greek. Agapius' quotation in Arabic was translated from Syriac, and the Syriac had been translated from a Greek version that seems to have received some deliberate alterations by Christian copyists, and the Greek itself, minus the redactions, derives ultimately from Josephus, who composed the *Antiquities* in 93 or 94 C.E. Translation from Greek into Syriac and then from Syriac into Arabic is demanded for the tradition in Agapius' work; that means the pejorative connotations at least would have been dropped by each translator, and surely the translators were Christians.

We can now be as certain as historical research will presently allow that Josephus did refer to Jesus in *Antiquities* 18.63–64.[36] To be discarded as a dated negative conclusion is A. Harnack's following judgment:

> Josephus, the Jewish writer at the close of the first century, completely ignores the Christian movement; for his so-called testimony to Jesus is a Christian interpolation.[37]

Behind the Christian interpolations or redactions is a tradition that derives from Josephus. The Jewish historian did apparently refer to Jesus of Nazareth.

Yet there may be one remaining obscurity impeding this perception. The Arabic excerpted recension is clearly more favorable to Jesus than the Greek full recension. The Greek text is also framed within and colored in the *Antiquities* by accounts of riots and "other" afflictions.

Could Josephus have written a favorable account of Jesus? Probably the Arabic tradition has been reshaped by Christian copyists as it was transmitted. Perhaps the historian Agapius, himself a Christian bishop, emphasized a positive view of Jesus. Immediately after quoting the *Testimonium Flavianum* he writes the following: "That is what is said by Josephus and his companions of our Lord the Messiah, may he be glorified." A Christian could have easily translated a quasi-polemical account so that it was more favorable. If so, then Agapius' excerpt from Josephus is still significant; it is a Christian alteration of what Josephus himself had written about Jesus.

Another possibility needs exploring. Could not Josephus have written that Jesus was "a wise man" and that his "conduct was good"? He goes on to report not that his conduct was virtuous, but that he "was known to be virtuous." Josephus could very well have written some appreciative words about Jesus. Jesus had been unjustly condemned; non-Christian Jews could have stressed that fact. Jesus argued against the zealous revolutionaries and was not an apocalyptic fanatic; Josephus would have admired this argument and position. Jesus uttered many wise and philosophical maxims and Josephus was fond of Jewish wisdom and of Greek philosophy. As the Jewish scholar Winter perceived, Josephus may well have held a "relatively friendly attitude . . . towards Jesus. . . ."[38]

The significance of the Arabic recension lies partly in the corroboration of the gospel account. Jesus was wise and righteous, attracted Jewish and Gentile followers, and was crucified by Pilate's orders; moreover, the Palestinian Jesus Movement continued after his death.

More important is the discovery that the new evidence through Agapius helps us to be more assured that a non-Christian before 100 C.E. referred to the life and teachings of Jesus of Nazareth. Indeed, this discovery is most important. Jesus' existence cannot be proved to skeptics using the New Testament accounts, because these are obviously biased in favor of Jesus. Josephus is not so biased in favor of Jesus. Certainly, he is not pro-Jesus in the Arabic version of *Antiquities* 18, which as the Jewish scholar Pines rightly judges, despite its more favorable portrait, has essentially a "non-committal attitude" to Jesus.[39]

Now we have an antidote for a poison affecting our Western culture. Last century, only one significant scholarly voice was raised against the possibility that Jesus existed. The spokesman was the German Bruno Bauer. Prior to the Second World War, only one influential critic claimed that Jesus' life was completely fabricated out of prophecies and myths; he was the Frenchman P. L. Couchoud. One would have thought that after M. Goguel's eloquent refutation of Couchoud's thesis no one would again venture to claim that Jesus never existed. Yet today in Russia G. Gurev[40] has been advancing the argument that neither Jesus nor Judas ever existed. In Germany R. Augstein, the former editor of *Stern,* published an influential book in which he claims that Jesus is merely the projected dreams and dogmas of superstitious people. In England G. A. Wells issued a book that simply claims that Jesus never existed. Many solid arguments can be presented against such distortions and polemics. Few, however, is more decisive than the *Testimonium Flavianum,* especially in the Arabic recension.

Finally, the two recensions of the *Testimonium Flavianum* should be studied by students, clergy, the laity, rabbis, and professors. The Greek recension, minus the Christian interpolations, reveals how a first-century Jew probably categorized Jesus: He was a rebellious person and disturber of the elusive peace; but he was also a wise person who performed "surprising," perhaps even wonderful, works, and was followed by many Jews and Gentiles. The Arabic version provides textual justification for excising the Christian passages and demonstrating that Josephus probably discussed Jesus in *Antiquities* 18, but certainly not in such favorable terms.

The focus of both recensions then helps shift the spotlight back on the Jesus of history, and that fact is of phenomenal importance. Our gaze is pulled away from preoccupations with ideas to confrontations with a first-century Galilean. Christians are momentarily protected from the perennial threat of docetic dogmas (the claim that Jesus was only quasi-human) and freed to reflect on the particularity of one person, Jesus. Neat paradigms are scrambled by an unnerving confrontation with *realia.* Historic dreams become anchored in historical drama.

NOTES

1. Eight leaves from another codex, the thirteenth, were pressed (around the fourth or fifth centuries) inside the front cover of the sixth codex.

2. For an engaging account of the discovery of the Nag Hammadi Codices, see E. Pagels, *The Gnostic Gospels* (New York, 1979).

3. N. Perrin, *The Promise of Bultmann* (Philadelphia, 1969, repr. 1979) p. 110.

4. See, for example, G. Quispel, "Gnosis," *Vox Theologica* 39 (1969) 27–35.

5. E. Haenchen, *A Commentary on the Gospel of John,* 2 vols., translated by R. W. Funk (Hermeneia; Philadelphia, 1984).

6. Ibid., vol. 1, p. x.

7. See the insightful discussion by G. Widengren titled "Les origines du gnosticisme et l'histoire des religions," in *Le Origini dello Gnosticismo: Colloquio di Messina 13–18 Aprile 1966,* ed. U. Bianchi (SHR 12; Leiden, 1970) pp. 28–60.

8. Persian influence is evident in Jewish apocalypticism, even in the Dead Sea Scrolls. See my comments in *John and Qumran,* ed. Charlesworth (London, 1972) pp. 87–89. Also see the important studies on the origins of apocalypticism by numerous outstanding scholars, notably S. S. Hartman, G. Widengren, H. Ringgren, and A. Hultgård, in *Apocalypticism in the Mediterranean World and the Near East: Proceedings of the International Colloquium on Apocalypticism. Uppsala, August 12–17, 1979,* ed. D. Hellholm (Tübingen, 1983).

9. A. Böhlig, "Jüdisches und iranisches in der Adamapokalypse des Codex V von Nag Hammadi," in *Mysterion und Wahrheit: Gesammelte Beiträge zur spätantiken Religionsgeschichte* (AGAJU 6; Leiden, 1968) pp. 149–61, see esp. p. 149.

10. For a discussion of the Adam cycle, see two dissertations (which I had the pleasure to direct): S. E. Robinson, *The Testament of Adam: An Examination of the Syriac and Greek Traditions* (SBLDS 52; Chico, Calif., 1982) and J. R. Levison, *"Adam" in Major Authors of Early Judaism* (to be published in the *Journal for the Study of the Old Testament,* Supplement Series; The University of Sheffield, Sheffield, England).

11. J. M. Robinson and H. Koester, *Trajectories Through Early Christianity* (Philadelphia, 1971) p. 264.

12. T. Baarda has become convinced that the Gospel of Thomas "is descended . . . from . . . a Syriac text" (p. 49). See his *Early Transmission of Words of Jesus: Thomas, Tatian and the Text of the New Testament,* ed. J. Helderman and S. J. Noorda (Amsterdam, 1983). H. Koester argues that the Coptic of the Gospel of Thomas was translated from Greek, but the Greek itself may derive from "Syriac or Aramaic." See his introduction to the Gospel of Thomas in *The Nag Hammadi Library in English,* ed. J. M. Robinson (New York, 1977) p. 117.

13. See, e.g., G. Lüdemann, *Untersuchungen zur simonianischen Gnosis* (GTA 1; Göttingen, 1975) pp. 100–3.

14. See the following works: A. F. J. Klijn, *Edessa, Die Stadt des Apostels Thomas: Das älteste Christentum in Syrien,* transl. M. Hornschuh (NS 4: Giessen, 1965); J. B. Segal, *Edessa: "The Blessed City"* (Oxford, 1970); R. Murray, *Symbols of Church and Kingdom: A Study in Early Syriac Tradition* (Cambridge, 1975).

15. Robinson, *The Nag Hammadi Codices: A General Introduction to the Nature and Significance of the Coptic Gnostic Library from Nag Hammadi* (Claremont, Calif., 1977 [2d rev. ed.]) p. iii.

16. See Charlesworth, *The New Testament Apocrypha and Pseudepigrapha,* for bibliographical details and discussion.

17. See Charlesworth, "Thomas, Gospel of," in *The New Testament Apocrypha and Pseudepigrapha,* pp. 374–402.

18. I agree with Koester's arguments on this point; see his comments in *Trajectories,* pp. 114–57.

19. This insight is now widely and repeatedly acknowledged. See, for examples, the arguments published by J. Dominic Crossan in *In Fragments: The Aphorisms of Jesus,* p. x; and B. Chilton, "The Gospel According to Thomas as a Source of Jesus' Teaching," in *The Jesus Tradition Outside the Gospels* (Gospel Perspectives 5; Sheffield, 1985) 155–75.

20. Gnosticism must not be confused with Encratism (an ascetic Syrian emphasis that is antisexual) or Docetism (the denial of Jesus' humanity). Quispel has persuaded some specialists that the Gospel of Thomas is not gnostic but encratitic. S. L. Davies, in *The Gospel of Thomas and Christian Wisdom* (New York, 1983), even though he overstates the case, clarifies why the Gospel of Thomas must *not* be branded and discarded as gnostic. Hence, potentially misleading is the following comment by Koester: "The influence of Gnostic theology is clearly present in the *Gospel of Thomas*. . . ." (*The Nag Hammadi Library in English,* p. 117) Also not representative of the lively debate on this issue is H. W. Attridge's claim that the *"Gospel of Thomas* clearly reflects Gnostic theology." See his "Gospel of Thomas," in Harper's Bible Dictionary, ed. P. J. Achtemeier (New York, London, 1985) pp. 355–56. It is not yet "clear" to scholars if the Gospel of Thomas is gnostic in its present form; it is relatively certain that this gospel preserves early, pre-gnostic traditions. It probably has received considerable editing.

21. The translation in *The Nag Hammadi Library* (p. 128) is possible, but seems too free. J. A. Fitzmyer assumes this translation, and misses the key which I am convinced opens the possibility that the Gospel of Thomas is independent of the synoptic tradition. See Fitzmyer, *The Gospel According to Luke X–XXIV* (AB 28A; Garden City, N.Y., 1985) p. 1061.

22. J. Jeremias, *Unknown Sayings of Jesus,* transl. R. G. Fuller (London, 1964 [2d. rev. ed.]) pp. 35–36.

23. An authoritative and interesting account of Chalcedon is found in H. Chadwick's *The Early Church* (Grand Rapids, Mich., 1968) pp. 203–5.

24. Gk. *paradoxos,* "strange, surprising, wonderful." Josephus would have meant "surprising"; an early Christian would have assumed he meant "wonderful."

25. Following a widely accepted emendation, which was apparently first advanced by N. Forster in 1749 (see Winter, n. 31, which follows). See H. St. J. Thackeray in *Josephus the Man and the Historian* (New York, 1929) pp. 144–45. Christian scribes could easily have changed *taēthē,* "unusual, strange" (the emendation) to *talēthē,* "truth" (the text). The possible change can also result from the unfamiliar *taēthē* or the similar appearance of the words.

26. The Greek verb *epagō* has a pejorative innuendo; however, as a strong aorist middle, it could have been interpreted by a Christian to denote "win over" (to himself).

27. As some scholars have speculated, something like "according to their opinion" preceded, and was deleted from, the confession, which obviously, in its extant form in Greek, cannot be attributed to Josephus. Another suggestion is that the Greek *legomenos,* "said to be," may have been before *christos* (and possibly taken

by some Christians to denote "proclaimed Christ" as in Mt 1:16), but was omitted intentionally to avoid any ambiguity (cf. G. C. Richards and R. J. H. Shutt, "Critical Notes on Josephus' *'Antiquities,'*" *Classical Quarterly* 31 [1937] 176). This possibility is particularly appealing because of the reference in Josephus to "James, the brother of Jesus, said to be Christ." See the following discussion.

28. An adversative *kai* is possible, denoting "but."

29. Not "did not forsake him." One perhaps should add something to explain what Jesus' followers did not cease to do; cf. F. F. Bruce, "The Evidence of Josephus," in *Jesus and Christian Origins Outside the New Testament* (Grand Rapids, Mich., 1974, 1984) esp. pp. 39–40. Immediately prior to this passage, Josephus discusses a riot (*hē stasis*); immediately after it he discusses *"another* affliction" (*heteron ti deinon*). One must see the framework for the *Testimonium Flavianum.*

30. Gk. *thaumasios,* "wonderful, admirable"; hence possibly not an assessment of Jesus by Josephus.

31. Paul Winter, who correctly traces the reference to Jesus in *Ant* 20 and 18 (minus the Christian alterations) back to Josephus, is amazed at the brevity of Josephus' reference to Jesus in *Ant* 18. He is "led to the conclusion that Josephus wrote more than has survived" (pp. 437–38). He speculates that "the passage about Jesus . . . was concerned with a riot in Jerusalem" (p. 439). Winter's article is based on careful thought and research; he also lists the scholars who argue for the authenticity, inauthenticity, or Christian interpolation of *Ant* 18.63–64. See his "Josephus on Jesus and James," in E. Schürer, *The History of the Jewish People in the Age of Jesus Christ,* rev. and ed. G. Vermes, F. Millar, P. Vermes, and M. Black (Edinburgh, 1973) vol. 1, pp. 428–41.

32. The Slavic form is even more altered by Christian scribes. See W. Bienert, *Der älteste nichtchristliche Jesusbericht Josephus über Jesus: Unter besonderer Berücksichtigung des altrussischen 'Josephus'* (Halle, 1936).

33. Also see the important observations by E. Bammel in "Zum Testimonium Flavianum (Jos *Ant* 18, 63–64)," in *Josephus—Studien: Untersuchungen zu Josephus, dem antiken Judentum und dem Neuen Testament (Otto Michel zum 70. Geburtstag gewidmet),* ed. O. Betz, K. Haacker, and M. Hengel (Göttingen, 1974) pp. 9–44.

34. S. Pines, *An Arabic Version of the Testimonium Flavianum and Its Implications* (Jerusalem, 1971).

35. The last sentence could also be translated as follows: "He was thought to be the Messiah, concerning whom the prophets have recorded wonders" (Pines, *An Arabic Version,* p. 71).

36. As G. Cornfeld states, "The discussion of Agapius' source is not at an end; but his version substantiates an earlier text of Josephus regarding Jesus, which was Agapius' source. In any case, there is evident proof of interpolation by the hands of a Christian who, by philological sleight-of-hand, transformed Josephus' historical Jewish text into an orthodox Christian text" (p. 510). See Cornfeld's *Josephus: The Jewish War: Newly Translated with Extensive Commentary and Archaeological*

Background Illustrations, ed. G. Cornfeld with B. Mazar and P. L. Maier (Grand Rapids, Mich., 1982).

37. A. Harnack, *The Mission and Expansion of Christianity in the First Three Centuries,* transl. J. Moffatt (New York, 1908) vol. 2, p. 1.

38. Winter in Schürer, *The History* (rev.), vol. 1, p. 441.

39. Pines, *An Arabic Version,* p. 67.

40. G. Gurev, "The Legend of the Man Who Sold Out Jesus," *Voiovnichii Ateist* (1964) (in Russian).

Chapter 5

The Jesus of History and the Archaeology of Palestine

The quest for the historical Jesus, for over a century, has been predominantly a German-centered European concern: from Reimarus to Strauss, from Strauss to Schweitzer, from Schweitzer to Bultmann, and from Bultmann to Käsemann and Bornkamm. This entire area of research has focused upon the New Testament writings, a study of the meaning of myth, the literary sources inherited by the evangelists, and the pregospel origin of the Jesus tradition. Except in the publications by Deissmann, Jeremias and Hengel, singularly absent in German publications has been an awareness of the importance of archaeology for a perception of Jesus' time and the early Palestinian Jesus Movement.

To a great extent, the failure to understand the importance of archaeology for biblical research has been typical of German biblical studies from the late-eighteenth century until 1953, when Käsemann "opened" the "New Quest" for the historical Jesus. American biblical scholarship has been profoundly shaped by the influence of the archaeologist W. F. Albright and his school (notably Glueck, Wright, Bright, Cross, Brown, Fitzmyer, and Freedman). British biblical scholarship was alerted to the profound significance of archaeology by many archaeologists, especially Sir Flinders Petrie and K. Kenyon. French research on the Bible has been informed by the pioneering work of numerous archaeologists, especially Vincent, Lagrange, de Vaux, and Benoit. The major advances in archaeological methodology and the phenomenal discoveries by these scholars and others has permanently altered our approach to biblical research. The successes of the American Schools of Oriental Research, the British School of Archaeology, and the École Biblique et Archéologique Française de Jérusalem are phenomenal. The role played by Israeli archaeologists is now becoming of great importance in Jesus Research (Illus. 16).

The archaeological discoveries are not known outside sophisticated circles; yet, few areas of scholarly research prick the imagination and stir the excitement of scholars and students so much as new archaeological discoveries. In the past three decades, spectacular discoveries are proving significant for research on the historical Jesus. I shall draw attention to only those that are significantly momentous for Jesus Research.

By focusing upon the recent discoveries that are significant for a better understanding of Jesus within first-century Palestine, we have been stressing from the beginning the importance of archaeology. The three main collections of writings mentioned above—namely the Old Testament Pseudepigrapha, the Dead Sea Scrolls, and the Nag Hammadi Codices—are the result of archaeological discoveries, although they were not discovered by archaeologists. Archaeological excavations have recently revealed how cosmopolitan was first-century Jerusalem.

Jerusalem was not isolated from the rest of the world. This false impression is given by a careless reading of the beginning of Mishnah *Aboth:*

> Moses received the Law from Sinai and committed it to Joshua, and Joshua to the elders, and the elders to the Prophets; and the Prophets committed it to the men of the Great Synagogue. They said three things: Be deliberate in judgement, raise up many disciples, *and make a fence around the Law.*
>
> (m.Ab 1:1)[1]

Jerusalem was a major city in a cosmopolitan culture. It contained not only the Temple, but also a large arena for chariot and horse races (a hippodrome; see *Ant* 17.255, cf. *War* 2.44), a stadium for athletic contests (a gymnasium; see 1Mac 1:14; 2Mac 4:7–20; *Ant* 12.241),[2] and massive theaters.

Herod was an athlete, built gymnasiums, and even once attended the Olympic Games. The massive arenas for athletic contests in Jerusalem and similar structures discovered in Galilee (at Magdala and Tiberias) indicate that Jews (at least some of them) were very fond of hellenistic sports.[3]

It is possible that remains of the palaces of the rulers of Adiabene, the Parthian Kingdom far to the east of Jerusalem, have been unearthed. These converts to Judaism would have brought with them to Jerusalem much of the art and culture of Parthia, a nation almost always portrayed in primary and secondary sources as foreign and hostile to Judaism.

Inscriptions have been uncovered in and around Jerusalem in many languages, especially Greek, Aramaic, Latin, and Hebrew; and these help us better comprehend the linguistic phenomenon described in Acts 2. One inscription from Caesarea Maritima contains the name of Pilate (see Illus. 10); and another inscription preserves the name of Quirinius, presumably the Syrian governor mentioned in Luke's birth narrative. Hellenistic influence is obvious in the seals on the Samaritan papyri that Frank Cross is now editing.

Yet archaeology is also revealing at least some homogeneity in Palestinian Judaism. After all, inscriptions in Aramaic and Hebrew have been discovered, and these reveal some indigenous linguistic phenomena (Illus. 20). Not only is it now clear that Galilee is culturally and archaeologically divided into upper and lower Galilee, but lower Galilee—the scene of Jesus' public ministry—is in close relationship with Judea.

The discoveries of more hymns of David, namely Psalms 151 through 155, the Qumran Hymnbook (1QH), the Psalms of Solomon, and other hymnic compositions of Early Judaism reveal the deep religiosity within Early Judaism.[4] Early Judaism was vibrant and lively; there were hosts of faithful Jews led by intelligent, pious, and articulate leaders such as Hillel, Shammai, and Johanan ben Zakkai among the rabbis, Ḥoni ha-Meaggel and Ḥanina ben Dosa among the pious, and Philo and many others among the intellectuals.

First-century Jews probably did enjoy the Greek games, as I have just suggested. But no shrine for the mystery cults has been found outside Caesarea, and the Mithraeum found there dates from centuries after 70 C.E.

The *Shema* and the *Eighteen Benedictions* protected Judaism from becoming chaotic. Indeed, the burning of the Temple and the end of the nation are certainly related to the repeated willingness of first-century Palestinian Jews to die for their faith. They repeatedly repudiated idolatrous and cruel actions by the Romans, including those by Pontius Pilate and the rogue Gessius Florus (cf. *Ant* 20. 252–57 and *War* 2.277–79). Faithfulness to Toah on the part of many Jews helps explain the war of 66 to 70 C.E.

The Roman destruction of the Temple and Jerusalem by fire in the mid-first century is a horrifying episode in Jewish history. It has certainly shaped the narratives in Luke 19:41–44 and 21:20–24 and the entire book of 4 Ezra. The one fact most clearly unearthed and palpably present in Old Jerusalem today (see Map II) is the massive destruction of, even conflagration in, Jerusalem in 70 C.E.

In 1970 Nahman Avigad and a team of trained archaeologists discovered the remains of a house—the "Burnt House"—that had been destroyed by a great fire dating from the Revolt of 66–70 C.E. Pottery, Jewish coins, and an inscription found *in situ* indicated that the Burnt House was a high priest's house torched by the Romans in 70 (see Illus. 11). Strikingly springing to life are Josephus' words:

> The Romans . . . surmounted the last wall without bloodshed, and, seeing none to oppose them, were truly perplexed. Pouring into the alleys, sword in hand, they massacred indiscriminately all whom they met, and burnt the houses with all who had taken refuge within.
> *(War* 6.403–04; transl. H. St. J. Thackeray [LCL])

In the Burnt House was found an iron spear (see Illus. 12), ashes, soot, charred wood, plastered walls now blackened, and cracked stone vessels (see Illus. 13).

Significant for the study of Jewish laws for purification is the recovery of stone vessels. Avigad states, "we were astonished by the rich and attractive variety of the stone vessels" (p. 176)[5]. Why would Jews choose to use such expensive and heavy stone wares? The answer is surely found in the Jewish laws of ritual purity. The Mishnah records the judgment that *stone* objects are impervious to ("afford protection from") impurity (m.Kel 10.1; cf. m.Par 3.2). These stone vessels, necessary for purification, are significant for Jesus Research: They remind us of the "six stone jars" prepared

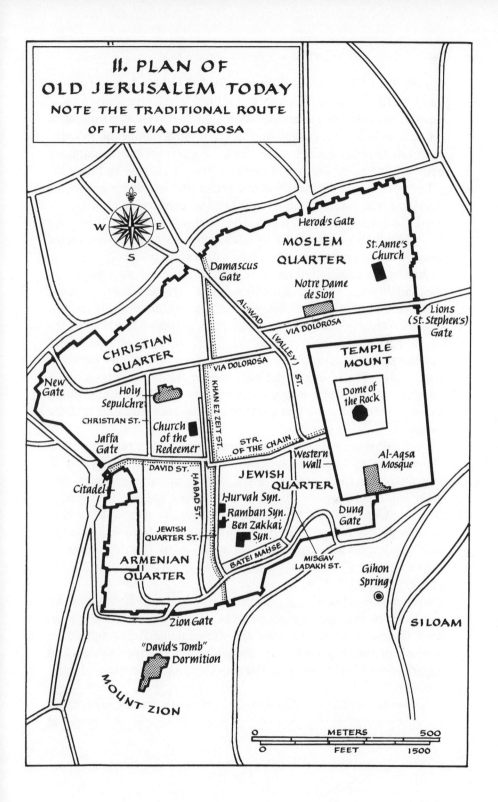

II. PLAN OF OLD JERUSALEM TODAY

NOTE THE TRADITIONAL ROUTE OF THE VIA DOLOROSA

Herod's Gate

MOSLEM QUARTER

St. Anne's Church

Damascus Gate

Notre Dame de Sion

AL-WAD

VIA DOLOROSA

Lions (St. Stephen's) Gate

CHRISTIAN QUARTER

VIA DOLOROSA

TEMPLE MOUNT

New Gate

Holy Sepulchre

CHRISTIAN ST.

Church of the Redeemer

KHAN EZ ZEIT ST.

Dome of the Rock

Jaffa Gate

STR. OF THE CHAIN

Western Wall

Al-Aqsa Mosque

David St.

Citadel

HABAD ST.

JEWISH QUARTER

Hurvah Syn.

Ramban Syn.

Ben Zakkai Syn.

Dung Gate

JEWISH QUARTER ST.

BATEI MAHSE

MISGAV LADAKH ST.

Gihon Spring

ARMENIAN QUARTER

Zion Gate

SILOAM

"David's Tomb" Dormition

MOUNT ZION

METERS 500

FEET 1500

"for the Jewish rites of purification" (Jn 2:6), which Jesus reputedly found at the wedding at Cana in Galilee. They raise questions of Jesus' relation to the contemporary heightened laws of purification.

I now wish to focus solely on the seven most significant archaeological discoveries for Jesus Research. The *seventh*-most significant discovery is the excavation of first-century synagogues in Palestine.

Ten years ago I frequently asked archaeologists digging in Israel if a synagogue clearly dating from the first century had been excavated. The reply was always no. The answer was disturbing, and it was difficult to understand why archaeologists had not discovered remains of synagogues that existed in Palestine before 70 C.E.

Origins are usually unknown. The origin of the synagogue is understandably lost in the "dark ages" that preceded Early Judaism (c. 250 B.C.E. to 200 C.E.). Yet, while it may ultimately antedate the time of Nehemiah and Ezra, when Jews gathered together in the forecourt of the Temple to hear the Torah read,[6] the "synagogue" was clearly an institution in Palestine before 70 C.E., as we know from reading Josephus and the New Testament documents. As A. J. Saldarini states, "The origin of the synagogue is obscure, but it certainly existed by the first century A.D. in both Palestine and the Diaspora."[7]

Why had no pre-70 synagogues been unearthed in the Holy Land when references to the synagogue—or at least a house of prayer[8]— date from the third century B.C.E. in Egyptian inscriptions and when some synagogues in Babylon are very old and the one in Delos, in Greece, dates from the second century B.C.E.? Why have no clear proofs of pre-70 Palestinian synagogues been found, when later synagogues are so obvious, for example, at Ḥammat-Tiberias, just southwest of the Sea of Galilee, and at Ostia Antica, the ancient seaport of Rome?[9]

Archaeological work on the synagogues in Israel had turned attention from first-century phenomena. Focus was centered on the Jews' migration to Galilee after the wars against Rome and to the building of the impressive synagogues now seen, for examples, at Capernaum, Khirbet Shema, Baram, Ḥammat-Tiberias, and Beth She῾arim.

Today the situation is different. Specialists on ancient synagogues in Palestine concur that now we have archaeological evidence of at least *three pre-70 synagogues* in Judea and Galilee, namely at Masada, the Herodium, and Gamla (see Map III).[10] The first-century Theodotus inscription, discovered in 1913–14, proves the existence of a synagogue in Jerusalem; it is palpable evidence of a Jerusalem synagogue roughly contemporaneous with Jesus.[11]

The "synagogal" ruins at Masada, the Herodium, and Gamla are distinguishable from the formalized architecture known from the third and later centuries C.E. The synagogue is indistinguishable from, and sometimes identical with, a house of prayer (in Hebrew, *beth tefilah*) and a house of study (in Hebrew, *beth midrash*). "Synagogue" is, of course, a Greek term that means "gathering-place"; the equivalent expression in Hebrew is *beth knesset.*

There were numerous "synagogues" in Jerusalem, but there were certainly not so many as Josephus and the Palestinian Talmud (*Megillah* 3.73d) reported. In the first century most synagogues were *large rooms in private homes,* which then became public rooms. When thinking about a "synagogue" of Jesus' day, it is wise to include reflections on a large room in any house, and not assume some stereotypic architectural edifice, like the three later styles: the basilica, the broadhouse, and the apsidal.[12]

The first-century house recently excavated at Capernaum beneath the octagonal church of St. Peter may well be the house Peter owned (Mk 1:29; Mt 8:14–16; see Illus. 6) and the house-church in which the earliest followers of Jesus gathered for worship and study. This possibility is so remarkable that it elicits from an audience the charge of slipping from the rigors of scholarship into sensationalism. Yet it is not the claim, but the discovery, which may well be sensational.

Seven stages in research lead to the conclusion that Peter's house may have been discovered. First, early pilgrims, like Egeria, who visited Capernaum between 381 and 384 C.E., identify the site as the place of Peter's house and of early Christian worship. Second, the house contains etched crosses, a boat, and over one hundred Greek, Aramaic, Syriac, Latin, and Hebrew graffiti from second- and third-century Christians who venerated the place. Third, the house is situated under a fifth-century *octagonal* church, a type of architecture that was used especially to venerate earlier sacred sites (an octagonal church was built by the order of Constantine over the site

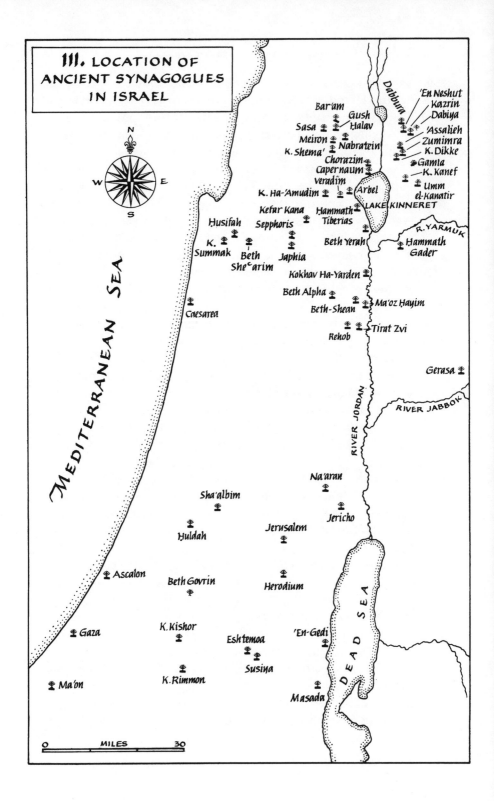

III. LOCATION OF ANCIENT SYNAGOGUES IN ISRAEL

Bar'am
Gush Halav
Sasa
Meiron
K. Shema'
Nabratein
Chorazim
Capernaum
veradim
Dabbura
'En Neshut
Kazrin
Dabiya
'Assalieh
Zumimra
K. Dikke
Gamla
K. Kanef
Umm el-Kanatir
K. Ha-'Amudim
Arbel
LAKE KINNERET
Kefar Kana
Hammath Tiberias
Sepphoris
Husifah
K. Summak
Beth She'arim
Japhia
Beth Yerah
R. YARMUK
Hammath Gader
Kokhav Ha-Yarden
Beth Alpha
Ma'oz Hayim
Beth-Shean
Tirat Zvi
Rehob
Gerasa
RIVER JORDAN
RIVER JABBOK
Caesarea
MEDITERRANEAN SEA
N
W   E
S
Na'aran
Sha'albim
Jericho
Huldah
Jerusalem
Ascalon
Beth Govrin
Herodium
Gaza
K. Kishor
Eshtemoa
'En-Gedi
DEAD SEA
Ma'on
K. Rimmon
Susiya
Masada

0   MILES   30

6. Capernaum. The commercial and fishing town to which Jesus moved from Nazareth. The Sea of Galilee or Lake Kinneret is in the south (bottom) part of the photograph. The octagonal structure is situated above a pre-70 house. It is conceivable that it is the house of Peter. The later synagogue can be seen in the ruins with columns to the right.

Werner Braun

7. Herodium. The mountain constructed by Herod in the Judean desert south of Bethlehem. He was reputedly buried in it, but his tomb has not yet been found.

Werner Braun

8. Jerusalem. The family tomb of King Herod the Great. Note the large rounded stone that can be rolled in front of the entrance, exactly as with Jesus' tomb described in the Gospels. *David Harris*

9. Deep in the Judean desert, on a mountain, can be found the remains of Herod's lavish palace at Masada. This artist's rendering helps us understand why historians consider Herod the Great to be one of the greatest builders of antiquity. *Lane Ritmeyer*

© L. RITMEYER

10. The famous Latin inscription in which the name of Pontius Pilate appears. Note the name "Pilatus" on the second line. This limestone Roman inscription was found in Caesarea. *Courtesy of the Israel Department of Antiquities and Museums*

11. Jerusalem. The "Burnt House." This house was burned by the Romans in 70 C.E. The evidence of ash and charred wood is poignantly visible. The house belonged to a priestly family, Bar Kathros, and is situated within the walls of first-century Jerusalem, in the Upper City. *Zev Radovan*

12. Jerusalem. The iron spear found in the "Burnt House." The spear was found abandoned and leaning here in the corner of a room. It may have belonged to one of the priests or a member of the family and was left unused because of the catastrophe and conflagration that overtook them. Note the evidence of burning and intense heat on the wall to the right of the spear. *Zev Radovan*

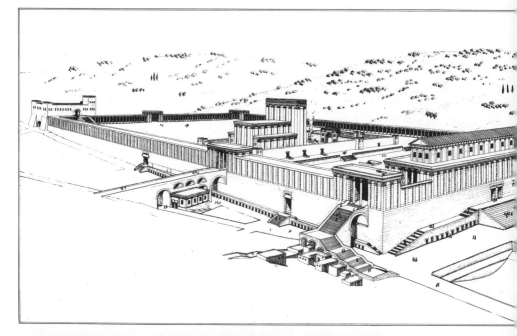

13. Jerusalem. Stone table and vessels from the "Burnt House" in Jerusalem. Stone vessels like these are characteristic of pre-70 Jerusalem. Probably these stone vessels and table were made in Jerusalem. The widespread use of cumbersome and costly stone vessels derives from the Jewish laws of ritual purity. Stone was not susceptible to ritual contamination, and therefore preserved its purity. Pottery vessels became ritually unclean through contact with an unclean substance or object.

Courtesy of the Israel Department of Antiquities and Museums

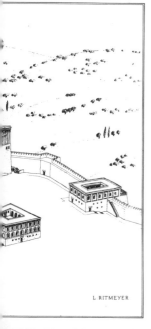

L. RITMEYER

14. One of the wonders of the ancient world was the Jerusalem Temple, especially with Herod's majestic expansion of the Temple Mount. From the western, upper city in Jerusalem, Jesus and his disciples would have seen something similar to this artist's rendering. *Lane Ritmeyer*

15. Jerusalem. Notice the massive stones; the southern and western lower courses are Herodian. The monumental stairway of the first century can be seen in the excavated area south of and adjacent to the walls. *Werner Braun*

16. Jerusalem. Notice the sharp fall of the Kedron Valley, the rise to the left on which David had built his city, and the massive Temple area to the north.   *Zev Radovan*

commemorated as Jesus' birthplace in Bethlehem). Fourth, the house can be traced back to the first century B.C.E. (it probably was constructed originally sometime between 100 and 60 B.C.E.), because of the stratigraphic conditions and the recovery of early Herodian lamps and coins. Fifth, fishhooks have been found under the pavement of what is identified to be a house-church; hence it is conceivable that a fisherman lived here. Sixth, early paving is evident, notably the early Roman Pavement B, but what is remarkable is the discovery that the floor and walls of the house were plastered no less than three times, beginning about the middle of the first century C.E. The large room was apparently altered for some public use around the middle of the first century C.E. Seventh, the large room, after it was plastered, was probably converted into a "house-church" (no other houses in Capernaum have been discovered with plaster). In this large room only large storage jars and oil lamps have been unearthed; *no ordinary household* pottery has been recovered.

Since there are no rival options for Peter's house, and since it was clearly where the house has been discovered or somewhere extremely close to it, it seems valid to conclude that Peter's house may have been excavated and identified. The discovery is virtually unbelievable and sensational.

Despite the sensational nature of the find, learned archaeologists and historians have slowly come to the same conclusion. The insights of V. Corbo, the Franciscan excavator who discovered "the house of Peter" and announced them in his *The House of St. Peter at Capharnaum,*[13] have been critically reviewed by Jews and basically supported. In *The Historical Jesus,* discussed in the review of Jesus Research in the eighties in Chapter 1, the Jewish popularist Cornfeld states boldly that "Jesus instructed the people and worked miracles in this house" (p. 78). Christian scholars have also voiced agreement; for example, the learned Dominican Father Jerome Murphy-O'Connor, who teaches at the École Biblique de Jérusalem, offers this sane advice:

> Certitude as to the original ownership of this room is, of course, impossible, but the evidence of consistent veneration in the pre-Constantinian period demands an explanation. It was of central importance to Chris-

tians. The most reasonable assumption is the one attested by the Byzantine pilgrims, namely, that it was the house of Peter in which Jesus may have lodged (Matt. 8:20).[14]

Publications coauthored by Jewish and Christian scholars have also reached this conclusion. James F. Strange and Hershel Shanks contend that "all signs point to the likelihood that the house of St. Peter where Jesus stayed, near Capernaum's famous synagogue, is an authentic relic." They conclude that the Franciscans "discovered what was probably St. Peter's house where Jesus stayed when he lived in Capernaum."[15]

Meyers and Strange conclude that "the excavator's conclusion (that this is indeed Peter's house and was venerated continuously until the fourth century [this parenthetical clarification is theirs]), . . . is really a working hypothesis to be tested with further excavation. . . . In the meantime we have, provisionally speaking, the oldest Christian sanctuary unearthed anywhere."[16] In the face of the evidence for a momentous discovery, I tend to hesitate to claim certainty or even overwhelming probability; but the data are impressive: Peter's house in which Jesus lived when he moved to Capernaum from Nazareth has probably been discovered.

The first-century walls of the house are too weak to support a tiled roof, as in Rome or Pompeii. The roof would have been constructed of tree branches covered with palm leaves and caked mud. Scholars have rightly reflected on the following episode:

> When he returned to Capernaum, some time later word went round that he was in the house; and so many people collected that there was no room left, even in front of the door. He was preaching the word to them when some people came bringing him a paralytic carried by four men, but as they could not get the man to him through the crowd, they stripped the roof over the place where Jesus was; and when they had made an opening, they lowered the stretcher on which the paralytic lay. Seeing their faith, Jesus said to the paralytic, "My child, your sins are forgiven."
>
> (Mk 2:1–5; NJB)

Thinking on such possibilities, or even probabilities, draws the individual interested in Jesus away from ideas, no matter how noble, to reality and history. Christians, and perhaps others, are prompted to

IV. Outline of Jerusalem in various periods

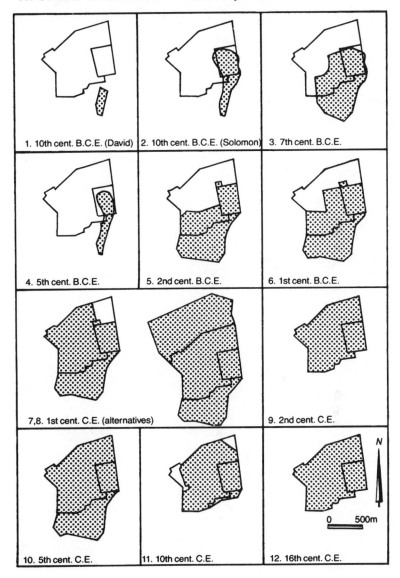

1. 10th cent. B.C.E. (David)
2. 10th cent. B.C.E. (Solomon)
3. 7th cent. B.C.E.
4. 5th cent. B.C.E.
5. 2nd cent. B.C.E.
6. 1st cent. B.C.E.
7,8. 1st cent. C.E. (alternatives)
9. 2nd cent. C.E.
10. 5th cent. C.E.
11. 10th cent. C.E.
12. 16th cent. C.E.

N

0   500m

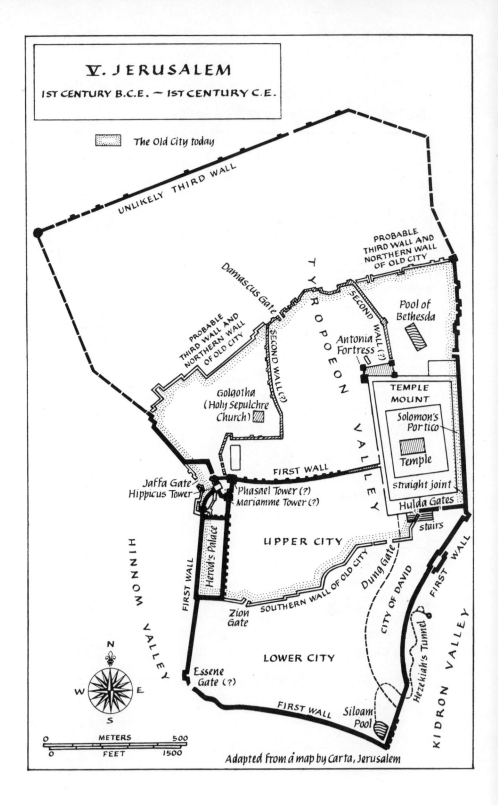

V. JERUSALEM

1ST CENTURY B.C.E. — 1ST CENTURY C.E.

The Old City today

UNLIKELY THIRD WALL

PROBABLE THIRD WALL AND NORTHERN WALL OF OLD CITY

PROBABLE THIRD WALL AND NORTHERN WALL OF OLD CITY

Damascus Gate

SECOND WALL

TYROPOEON VALLEY

SECOND WALL (?)

Pool of Bethesda

Antonia Fortress

Golgotha (Holy Sepulchre Church)

TEMPLE MOUNT

Solomon's Portico

Temple

FIRST WALL

straight joint

Jaffa Gate
Hippicus Tower

Phasael Tower (?)
Mariamme Tower (?)

Hulda Gates

stairs

Herod's Palace

UPPER CITY

FIRST WALL

HINNOM VALLEY

Dung Gate

CITY OF DAVID

FIRST WALL

Zion Gate

SOUTHERN WALL OF OLD CITY

Hezekiah's Tunnel

KIDRON VALLEY

N
W   E
S

LOWER CITY

Essene Gate (?)

FIRST WALL

Siloam Pool

METERS   500
0
FEET   1500
0

Adapted from a map by Carta, Jerusalem

think about what it must have been like back then, over there, and with Jesus. Was it here in this house that Jesus performed miracles, including the healing of Peter's mother-in-law (Mk 1:29–31)?

It is along such lines of reflection that we shall probably approximate more closely the social setting of the earliest traditions and of Jesus' own life. We must put aside the Hollywood distortion that depicts thousands attending Jesus' sermons. We should imagine a small, select group of about thirty crowded together in a private home to hear a challenging teacher.

The impact of these discoveries for Jesus Research, however, is not yet examined. In my opinion we shall again be confronted with the nonpriestly house church "synagogal" character of earliest Christianity, the multiplicity of responses to God's recorded will (Torah), the unifying force of a charismatic Jewish miracle worker who spoke enthusiastically, dynamically, categorically, and captivatingly, and his followers' penchant for the freedom of reflection and expression.

Archaeological research on the synagogues and house churches suggests that some allegiance to Jerusalem and its Temple is also demanded by the frequent architectural orientation to the holy city. The first-century synagogue at Gamla (see Map III), which is northeast of the Sea of Galilee or Lake Kinneret, has an entrance that faces south toward the Jerusalem Temple. The later "Galilean" synagogue usually had three entrances that faced south toward Jerusalem. The synagogue at Susiya, south of Jerusalem, was entered from the east, and the worshiper turned right toward the north wall, the wall of orientation, and toward Jerusalem. In such settings we are brought closer to the tradition of Jesus' first sermon in the synagogue (Lk 4:16–30) and the raising of the daughter of a synagogue ruler named Jairus (Lk 8:41–56). We need to think historically and sociologically, as well as theologically, about the meaning of Luke's summary, that Jesus "was preaching in the synagogues of Judea" (Lk 4:44).

The *sixth* most significant archaeological discovery pertains to the walls and gates of Jerusalem (see Map V). In 1968 K. Kenyon told me the large stone just north of the École Biblique was from the defensive dike built by the Roman army. Now, some Israeli archaeologists contend that this stone signals the place of Josephus' famous third wall. The northern wall of Jerusalem would then be over 450 meters north of the present Turkish wall. This distance is considerable, when one walks northward from the present walls of Jerusalem down Nablus Road or Salah-ed-Din Street (see Map V).

The physical size of Jerusalem, therefore, would be significantly increased. Nevertheless, Josephus' estimate that more than 2.5 million were entrapped in the city by the Romans is an exaggeration (see *War* 6.425; in *War* 6.420 he states that 1.1 million Jews died in Jerusalem during the war; see m.Pes 5.5–7).

I do not agree with the conclusion that the third wall has been definitively identified by excavations that disclose the foundations of massive towers; these may well be much later than the first century. We must also remember that the area enclosed by the third wall is *not* the Jerusalem Jesus knew. The third wall was begun by Herod Agrippa I (37–44 C.E.) shortly after 41 C.E. (*War* 5.152), or eleven years after the crucifixion. The fact is confirmed by the Herodian ashlars and sherds discovered near the Damascus Gate where they were placed or fell in the first century, as well as Josephus' description of Agrippa's third wall (*War* 2.218, 5.148, 152–60). Hence, I doubt the recent contention regarding the place of the third wall, and continue to support the claim that the northern wall of Jerusalem that was begun by Herod Agrippa lies beneath the present Turkish walls.

During Jesus' life the figure of 20,000 inhabitants and 180,000 celebrants at Passover surmised by J. Jeremias in his *Jerusalem in the Time of Jesus*[17]—if a little low—may not be far off the mark. Yet, by 30 C.E. there also would have been many people living in houses just to the north of Jerusalem's walls.

Far south of the northern third wall, archaeologists have discovered a small gate in the southwest corner of the second wall. Some excitement has been aroused regarding the possibility that the small gate is indeed the Essene gate mentioned only by Josephus (*War* 5.145). The recently published Temple Scroll describes a latrine just northwest (11QTemple 46.14) of Jerusalem's walls: "And you shall make for them a latrine outside of the city to which they shall go out thither. . ." (11QTemple 46.13). This latrine is undoubtedly the "Betsoa," or house of excrement, mentioned by Josephus as just northwest of the Essene gate in the western wall.

If archaeologists have discovered the Essene gate, then Essenes probably lived in the southwest section of Herodian Jerusalem.[18] The discovery and its implications are significant for a study of Christian origins, because precisely in that area Jesus most likely held his last supper, and it was here that tradition (cf. Epiphanius, Eusebius) seems to have placed the home of Jesus' family, especially his brother James and his mother, Mary. Are we confronted here with unhistorical legends, or faced with an intriguing possibility that Essenes and Christians inhabited the same section of Jerusalem? If so, then the possibility that the Essenes influenced the early Christians is raised to a new level for research. Yet, proximity does not necessarily mean similarity, and clear evidence of Essene influence on Jesus' followers is not to be confused with Essene influence on Jesus.

The *fifth* major archaeological discovery pertains to the Temple Mount in Jesus' time. We now have unexpected discoveries that help us better comprehend Jesus' righteous indignation in the Temple. Formerly, we thought that Jesus may have "cleansed" the Temple, but that the mention of "oxen" and "sheep" by the author of John (Jn 2:14) was simply another clue that the Fourth Evangelist was ignorant of Jerusalem.

This impression and evaluation may now be disproved. The double and triple Hulda Gates, in the southern wall of the Temple, have been discovered, as well as portions of the massive pre-70 stone stairway, plazas, and walks (see Illus. 15). The money changers could have been just inside these massive gates; and a passageway from this area, indeed from the Double Gates, to the so-called Solomonic Stables has now apparently been discovered. Formerly, we knew that the latter held stalls for large animals in Herodian times, but no connection with the Temple could be found. It is now clear that large animals could easily have been led from these stalls (which still reveal niches in which large animals were tethered) to the halls of money changers.[19]

From the straw bedding or tethers accompanying such large animals, Jesus could easily have fashioned a whip, as the evangelist John states: "And making a (kind of) whip from cords, he drove them all, with the sheep and oxen, out of the Temple. . ." (Jn 2:15). The verisimilitude seems impressive. It is easy to imagine this occurring. The major entrances to the Temple were the Hulda Gates, in the south, only a few yards south of this scene depicted in John. The skirmish caused by Jesus' justified wrath may well have occurred in the lower level of the three-storied Royal Portico, Herod's meat market, *Hanûth* (cf. *Ant* 15.393, 411–17), which Josephus claimed was an "edifice more noteworthy than any under the sun" (*Ant* 15.412). As archaeological work and related discussions continue, it should become clearer whether we can move from imaginative storytelling to possible historical reconstruction.

It seems much clearer today than it did a few years ago that at least in some ways Jesus' arrest resulted from his anger in the Temple. I agree, therefore, with the arguments by many scholars (viz., Bernard, Hoskyns, Dodd, Barrett, Lightfoot, Brown, and Sanders) that Jesus was probably arrested because of his actions in the Temple against the wealthy priestly aristocracy. The case for the authenticity of some details in the Johannine account of Jesus' last days is stronger than the case for the superiority of the Johannine sequence of events, which has Jesus "cleanse" the Temple at the beginning of his ministry. The Synoptics' account, which has Jesus cause a disturbance in the Temple just before his execution, seems to be more likely.

The details in the Gospel of John are significant: the large animals—sheep and oxen—and the whip fashioned by Jesus are mentioned only in the Gospel of John. It is unwise to continue to brand the Gospel of John as only a theological work devoid of historical facts. John may well preserve reliable historical information on Jesus' actions in the Temple. He is obviously using traditions independently of the Synoptics, as Dodd, Schnackenburg, Brown, D. M. Smith, and others have argued.[20]

Even more archaeological discoveries related to Herod's Temple are significant for Jesus Research. The size of the stones used to build the Temple are described by Josephus as astronomically massive (*Ant* 5.224; 15.392). Scholars have tended to reject Josephus' figures as inflated and exaggerated.[21] Archaeological discoveries, however, at the Herodium (see Illus. 7), Masada (see Illus. 9), and especially Jerusalem have proved that Herod the Great was one of the most ambitious and successful builders in antiquity. The distinguished Israeli archaeologist who has been excavating the Jewish

Quarter of the Old City of Jerusalem, Nahman Avigad, reviews what is now known about Herod's accomplishments and offers the opinion that he was "undoubtedly the greatest builder Palestine had ever known."[22]

The stone that connected Robinson's Arch to the western retaining wall of the Temple Mount is massive; it probably weighs over twenty tons. As Jesus and his disciples walked to the Temple, they could easily have seen it above their heads. The massiveness of this stone—which has been exposed for approximately two thousand years—becomes clear when one realizes that the heaviest stone in the Pyramids is probably less than fifteen tons, and the most gigantic stone at Stonehenge weighs about forty tons.

Yet, an even more massive stone has just been discovered. It is part of the foundation of the western retaining wall. Its weight has been estimated to be an amazing 415 tons.[23] The size and majesty of Herod's Temple Mount has surprisingly loomed large before us (see Illus. 14).

The recent excavations reveal that Herod's Temple was one of the marvels of the ancient world. The Babylonian Talmud (*Succah* 51b) records a reliable tradition; it emphasizes that Jerusalem was the perfect example of a splendid city. Pliny the Elder caught the magnificence of Jerusalem when he saluted it as the most celebrated metropolis in the East (*Natural History* 5.15.70). Professor B. Mazar, the archaeologist who has directed the excavation of the area south and west of the Temple walls, utters these remarkable words:

> The most striking conclusion of the excavations is that they revealed a city every bit as splendid as the ancient writers described, confirming in almost uncanny detail many of the specific descriptions of the city we find in Josephus.[24]

We come much closer today in feeling the Galilean disciples' awe when, according to Mark, one of them exclaimed, "Look, Teacher, what magnificent stones, and what magnificent buildings!" (Mk 13:1).

The *fourth* most significant archaeological discovery for Jesus Research is the realization that inside the Sheep Gate, or Lions Gate, are two pools, having a total of five porticoes. Archaeologists have unearthed massive and extensive Roman ruins, numerous columns from an original reservoir that had porticoes on each side, including the center area that divided the twin pools. The Eleventh Column of the Copper Scroll, found in Qumran Cave 3, mentions a pool in Jerusalem. The text is uncertain; but the name of the pool seems to be *Beth Eshdathayin* (cf. DJD 3, p. 297; Plate LXVIII), the dual ending for the well-known "Bethesda" (following the superior reading of Codex Alexandrinus, Codex Ephraemi Rescriptus, and others in Jn 5:2).

Prior to these discoveries, John's reference to the Pool of Bethesda near the Sheep Gate (Jn 5:2–9) was dismissed as allegorical theology. No such *five*-porticoed pool was known to exist; it is not noted in the ancient descriptions of Jerusalem. The theologian John must have been simply caricaturing the inefficacy of the Pentateuch, the *five* books of Moses, and even the pool of water as symbolizing the Torah (Dodd). The sick man could not be healed by the old covenant; the new—embodied in Jesus—brought an immediate cure.

The Gospel of John is certainly a very theologically oriented work, but, as Bultmann showed, the five porticoes do not allegorically denote the Pentateuch, because John does not portray Jesus as one who liberates Jews from the Torah. John cannot be dismissed as a document devoid of historical information. The author, and editors, of John clearly altered traditions; but the Gospel preserves some impressive facts about Jerusalem, as Albright, Goodenough, and Torrey claimed as long ago as 1924.

It is unwise to force into John 5:1–9 any contrast between the Torah and "the life-giving word of Christ," as did C. H. Dodd.[25] Archaeological research reveals how dated and inaccurate were early commentators, such as J. H. Bernard, who contended that the Pool of Bethesda (or Bethzatha) was the Virgin's Well *(Gihon)* "south of the Temple, in the Valley of Kidron."[26]

Archaeology tends to confirm some of John's description. The Copper Scroll's name for Bethesda means "the Place (geographical sense of *byt*) of the Twin Pools" (literally "poured-out water").

The final three most significant discoveries help us better understand the Passion narrative, the earliest written traditions behind the Gospels. The *third* pertains to Jesus' trial in the Praetorium, a term for the official residence of the *praetor,* "leader" or governor.

Today Christian pilgrims to Jerusalem are told the trial took place in the Antonia Fortress, and they follow the *Via Dolorosa,* the celebrated pathway Jesus supposedly walked to his execution. The *Via Dolorosa,* however, has little to do with the Jerusalem Jesus knew; it is a later routing. What was the route taken by Jesus? It was probably from Herod the Great's palace in the western Upper City to Golgotha (see Maps II and V). Pilate and other authorities responsible for maintaining peace in the city did not have to move from the palace to the fortress to monitor activities in the Temple. As Père Benoit showed me in the late 1960s, one can look from the citadel on the western hill down upon the Temple to the east. Pilate and the governing authorities could relax in the sumptuous palace and still be able to view any activity in or near the Temple Mount.

Archaeologists have been able to show that the traditional "Praetorium" was the headquarters or barracks of a Roman garrison. The "King's Game," on the so-called *Lithostrōtos,* in what is now the monastery of the Sisters of Zion, dates from Hadrian's rebuilding in the second century C.E. Benoit, who has studied the archaeological remains of Jerusalem for over forty years, showed me a Herodian column that was absorbed by and hence antedates the massive floor stones in the aforementioned monastery. It and the Ecce Homo Arch belong to Hadrian's Aelia Capitolina of the second century C.E.

In his *Jesus and the Gospel,* Benoit has shown that the *praetorium* denotes the *residence* of the prefect (not procurator, as stated in contemporary popular works) in Jerusalem.[27] Likewise, *en tō praitōriō tou Hērōdou* (Acts 23:35) indicates the abode of the Roman prefect in Herod's former palace in Caesarea. The Greek term *lithostrōton* specifies the large stoned public square in front of Herod the Great's palace, or the praetorium. The Aramaic term *Gabbatha,* associated with *lithostrōton,* means "height," or "high" place. It would be an apt description for Herod the Great's palace in the Upper City, or western elevated section of Jerusalem. Josephus indeed calls the area of Herod's Palace "the Upper City": *hē anō polis* (*War* 1.402; *Ant* 15.318).

It is easier now to imagine the magnificent stones, perhaps even mosaics, of the *lithostrōton,* because of the recent excavation of a patrician, perhaps Sadducean, home in the Upper City. The dwelling features a bathroom with a *mosaic floor*. Research helps clarify what occurred according to John 19:13: "Hearing these words, Pilate led Jesus outside; and he sat down on the judicial bench (*Bema*) in a place called *lithostrōton,* which in Aramaic[28] (is called) *Gabbatha.*"

The *second* most significant archaeological discovery for Jesus Research is the recovery of the bones of a man, named Jehoḥanan, who had been crucified.[29] Jehoḥanan's ankles remain attached to the wood portions of a cross, because the spike driven through them bent when it hit a knot. The man was crucified in his thirties, in Jerusalem, and near the time of Jesus' own crucifixion. Previous to this archaeological find, we had no remains of one who had been crucified.

The significance of this discovery for Jesus Research is obvious, even though we cannot conclude that Jesus was crucified in an identical manner. Three insights are important. First, we have a grim reminder of the horrors of crucifixion. There is wide agreement today that death would have resulted from a slow, excruciating process of asphyxiation. In order to breathe, the victim would have to push up with the legs in order to free the lungs from the weight on the chest from the upper torso. Jehoḥanan's body on the cross was probably not upright; it had apparently been pushed up and twisted. If so, then the resulting muscle spasms would have caused unbearable pain. Second, if Jehoḥanan's legs had been broken to prevent him from raising up to breathe, then death would have come swiftly to him and not after prolonged daily torture as was the case with Spartacus' followers and Josephus' friends.

If Jesus' torso had also been twisted on the cross, then we can understand why he seems to have died so rapidly. It is now somewhat easier to understand why Jesus died so quickly; he was crucified just outside the walls of the Holy City, and just before the greatest festival of the year and the beginning of the Sabbath. It is now easier to comprehend the tradition that Pilate was astounded by the report that Jesus was already dead (Mk 15:44). The passage, unfortunately, is sometimes mistranslated; note now the excellent rendering in The New Jerusalem Bible:

Pilate, astonished that he should have died so soon, summoned the centurion and enquired if he had been dead for some time.

(Mk. 15:44)

Third, the old hypothesis that Jesus' corpse *must* have been dumped into a pit set aside for the corpses of criminals and insurrectionists and not buried is disproved. Jehoḥanan's bones had received a proper Jewish burial.

Finally, the *most* significant archaeological discovery for Jesus Research is the growing proof of the site for the crucifixion. Jesus was crucified around 30 C.E. just outside Jerusalem's walls, as the author of Hebrews states (Heb 13:12).

Today pilgrims are shown the Garden Tomb, near Gordon's Calvary; both are just north of the present Turkish walls of the Old City. Most lay Christians choose this serene spot, clearly outside the present walls, as the location of Jesus' own burial. They are absolutely right in one particular: Jesus was crucified outside Jerusalem's walls.

The traditional site for Calvary is sometimes not attractive. It can be a noisy menagerie of competing ecclesiastical authorities within the Church of the Holy Sepulchre and within the present walls of the Old City (see Illus. 18, 19; Map II, V).

In the late sixties, Kenyon discovered proof that the wall now encompassing the traditional site for Calvary in places lies on a foundation that was constructed in or shortly after 41 C.E. by Herod Agrippa. Hence, in 30 C.E. the traditional site would have been outside the city. Also, in the late 1960s Père Charles Coüasnon showed me in the Church of the Holy Sepulchre columns still in use from the fourth-century church of Constantine.[30] Hence, the traditional place can be traced architecturally to the early centuries of Christianity. And moreover, there are no competing places for Calvary or Golgotha prior to the last century.

In the late 1970s, excavators working at the site of Golgotha exposed part of the foundations of Hadrian's Roman Forum, in which the Temple of Aphrodite was constructed around 135 C.E. The Romans had probably intentionally built this temple to cover Golgotha, and perhaps Jesus' tomb. Now, two major discoveries confirm, in my opinion, that the Church of the Holy Sepulchre houses the rock on which Jesus was crucified (see Illus. 19).

M. Broshi, in 1976, discovered remains of a Herodian wall in the northeast section of the church itself. Consequently, in 30 C.E. Golgotha was just outside the western wall. More important, it is now clear, thanks to the excavations in the late 1970s by D. Katsimibinis, that the rock of Calvary still rises approximately thirteen meters above bedrock. The exposed rock bears the marks of ancient quarrying; it is a rejected portion of an ancient preexilic Israelite white stone, *malaki,* quarry.[31] By the first century B.C.E., this site had evolved from a seventh- or eighth-century rock quarry to a refuse dump, and finally to a burial site, since Jewish tombs predating 70 C.E. are visible. It is possible, as the Evangelist John reports, that the final evolutionary phase in the first century before 70 was a garden: "In the place where he was crucified there was a garden, and in the garden a new tomb, in which no one had been placed" (Jn 19:41).

On this exposed rejected rock it is probable that Jesus had been crucified. It had been outside the walls and near a public road in 30 C.E. The site fits all the Jewish (see Lev 24:14; m.Sanh 6.1) and Roman requirements of a spot for executions.[32]

Perhaps the early Christians living in Jerusalem knew what archaeologists only recently have discovered, namely, that Golgotha is a rejected quarry stone. It is possible that they commemorated Jesus' crucifixion by reciting Psalm 118:22:

> The stone which the builders rejected;
> this has become the head of the corner.
> (1Pet 2:7)

In fact this tradition, recorded in 1 Peter, is also attributed by Luke to Peter when he spoke to the high priest in Jerusalem: "This is the stone which was rejected by you builders, but which has become the head of the corner" (Acts 4:11). The pronoun "this" may well have a double meaning, denoting both Calvary and Jesus. Perhaps the proclamations in the early Palestinian Jesus Movement influenced the retelling of Jesus' parable of the vineyard so that it was expanded by a new conclusion:

The stone which the builders rejected;
this has become the head of the corner.
(Ps 118:22, Mk 12:10, par.)

Père Coüasnon was convinced that the site of the crucifixion had been found. He had no doubt that Jesus' tomb had been conclusively identified. He argued that the biblical

> story of the burial of Jesus can reasonably be accepted as being historically true and one must conclude that "the first Church of Jerusalem had an exact, and well-attested, knowledge of the location of the tomb of Jesus." Moreover, it is evident that many details of the Gospels are more easily explainable if, at the moment the texts were written, there still existed a living knowledge of the tomb.
>
> To summarize: the new tomb (Matthew, John) was hewn in the rock (Matthew, Mark, Luke) in a garden (John) near to the city (John), the owner of which was known (Matthew), being Joseph of Arimathea (Matthew, Mark, Luke, John), a well-known counsellor (Mark, Luke); in the tomb, a mortuary couch is situated on the right-hand side (Mark), while the low door obliges one to stoop to look inside (John).[33]

The new discoveries encourage us to speculate on the possible liturgical customs of Jesus' followers in Jerusalem before 70. Did the followers of Jesus ever stand before a tomb (perhaps Jesus' tomb) and recite Psalm 118?

Separating tradition from redaction in Mark 16 has given me the impression that Jesus' earliest followers revered his tomb. Some of them probably added to the need to make an annual pilgrimage to the Holy City and Temple a desire to venerate the traditions associated with Jesus' death (Illus. 8) and resurrection. This action would have seemed quite natural; pilgrimage to the tombs of Jewish sages was an old custom in pre-70 Palestinian Judaism.

Jesus' earliest followers could have attributed to all of Psalm 118 a meaning appropriate for this setting. Recall especially verse 23: "From the Lord is this (deed);/ it is marvelous in our eyes." The refrain *kî lĕcôlām ḥasdō*, "forever (is) his covenant love," is repeated four times. It is an appropriate celebration for Jesus' followers; but we certainly must admit that we have no evidence Jesus' followers ever recited it standing before Calvary or the nearby tomb in reverence of the last episodes in the life of their Lord.

Twenty years ago, Old Testament colleagues tended to dismiss the importance of archaeology for New Testament studies. They told me on more than one occasion that the New Testament covered only one hundred years and represented primarily non-Palestinian settings. The celebration was for "Albright's great plan and expectation to set the Bible (namely, the Old Testament narratives) firmly on the foundation of archaeology buttressed by verifiable data. . . ."[34]

On October 21, 1984, at a gathering of Albright's students, now distinguished professors, for the "Homage to Albright," David Noel Freedman, one of the acknowledged geniuses in biblical studies, admitted publicly that "Albright's great plan . . . seems to have foundered or at least floundered." In his words, "the Albrightian synthesis has become unglued. And we are further from a solution than we ever were."[35]

What had not been expected is proving significant. Archaeological discoveries are responsible, at least in part, for the new collections of documents significant for the study of Christian origins, namely, the Old Testament Pseudepigrapha, the Dead Sea Scrolls, the Nag Hammadi Codices, and the vast amount of Aramaic material from Jesus' time and country. We are better able to comprehend Galilee (especially Capernaum and a first-century house church) and Jerusalem (especially the Temple and Golgotha) before the denouement of the great revolt against Rome.

Helen Keller, in *Three Days to See*, reflects on what she would look at if she were given three days of sight. If given the opportunity to see an aspect of first-century Palestine as Jesus and Josephus knew it, many Jews and Christians would choose Jerusalem. Now, thanks to sensational discoveries, this erstwhile romantic wish is partly yet palpably realizable.

The foregoing discussions reveal that a purely theological and literary approach to the New Testament or Christian origins is improper and misleading. Examining documents roughly contemporaneous with Jesus and studying archaeology, however, never should be seen as an attempt to prove or support any faith or theology. Authentic faith certainly needs no such shoring up. Philologists, historians, and archaeologists cannot give Christians a risen Lord;

but they can help them better understand Jesus' life, thought, and death.

There are often tensions between scripture and science. I would tend, however, to join Bernard W. Anderson, who confessed:

> In the face of the tension between the Biblical account and the archaeological evidence, my position would not be that ascribed to Tertullian, "I believe because it is absurd," but rather that of Augustine, "I believe in order that I may understand."[36]

As incredible as it once may have sounded, archaeologists are not throwing up debris in the way of Christian faith. In terms of New Testament history they are exposing the arena and bedrock on which faith is founded. Jesus Research is influenced by archaeological research. The Jesus of history is now less incomprehensible thanks to the archaeology of Palestine.

NOTES

1. Italics mine. The translation is by H. Danby, *The Mishnah* (Oxford, 1933, repr. frequently) p. 446.

2. An authoritative discussion is found in J. A. Goldstein, *I Maccabees* (Anchor Bible 41; Garden City, N.Y., 1976) pp. 117, 200–1; and in Goldstein, *II Maccabees* (Anchor Bible 41A; Garden City, N.Y., 1983) pp. 228–30.

3. H. A. Harris corrects the one-sided interpretation by such influential authors as Zev Vilnay who contend that Jews boycotted the athletic contests. Harris correctly concludes as follows: "There is no evidence that orthodox Jews stayed away from the Games in Palestine, any more than those very orthodox Jews, Philo and Paul, stayed away from the similar games in Alexandria and Tarsus" (p. 96). A significant corrective to our understanding of this dimension in Early Judaism is provided by H. A. Harris' *Greek Athletics and the Jews,* ed. I. M. Barton and A. J. Brothers (Trivium, Special Publications 3; Cardiff, 1976).

4. References to each of these and translations of many are found in *OTP* 2.

5. N. Avigad, *Discovering Jerusalem* (Jerusalem, Nashville, 1983). For a vivid discussion of the excavation of the "Burnt House" and color photographs, see pp. 120–36.

6. Hence, I concur with the position of S. Safrai, who concluded that "the institution did not begin in the Diaspora but in the very precincts of the Temple and in Jerusalem itself. This is not to affirm that Ezra founded the synagogue, but merely that the elements on which it was based and from which it developed may be traced back to certain activities of Ezra" (p. 913). Safrai, "The Synagogue," in *The Jewish People in the First Century: Historical Geography, Political History,*

Social, Cultural and Religious Life and Institutions, vol. 2, ed. S. Safrai and M. Stern, with D. Flusser and W. C. van Unnik (Compendia Rerum Iudaicarum ad Novum Testamentum I.2; Amsterdam, 1976) pp. 908–44.

7. A. J. Saldarini, "synagogue," in *Harper's Bible Dictionary,* p. 1007.

8. For the Greek texts and English translations see G. H. R. Horsley, *New Documents Illustrating Early Christianity,* vol. 3 (Sydney, 1983) pp. 121–22. Saldarini correctly points out that "it is not certain that these (inscriptions) refer to a synagogue." See his discussion in *Harper's Bible Dictionary,* p. 1007. Safrai contends that the inscriptions do refer to a "synagogue." See his comments in *The Jewish People in the First Century,* pp. 911–13. The problems involve not only nomenclature—"house of prayer" and "synagogue"—but also the movement from a generic structure to an architecturally identifiable "synagogue," and the establishment of an institution called either a "house of prayer" or a "synagogue." Obviously, the synagogue was sometimes referred to as a "house of prayer," but houses of prayer certainly predate the establishment of the institution of the synagogue. For example, what does the author of 3 Maccabees mean by these words: "They consecrated them with an inscription on a pillar, and having dedicated a place of prayer on the site of the banquet, they went away. . . ." (3Mac 7:20)?

9. Long after completing this chapter, I read about the discovery of a synagogue in Bova Marina, Italy. It dates from the fourth century C.E.; but beneath it is a much older structure, perhaps an earlier synagogue. See R. Suro, "Italian Synagogue May Be Oldest in Europe," New York *Times* (Mar. 4, 1986) p. 22.

10. The definitive work is by F. Hüttenmeister and G. Reeg, *Die antiken Synagogen in Israel. Teil 1: Die jüdischen Synagogen, Lehrhaüser and Gerichtshöfe; Teil 2: Die samaritanischen Synagogen* (Beihefte zum Tübinger Atlas des Vorderen Orients, Reihe B, Nr. 12/1 and 12/2; Wiesbaden, 1983). Popular English works on the discovery of pre-70 Palestinian synagogues are the following: E. M. Meyers and J. F. Strange, *Archaeology, the Rabbis, and Early Christianity: The Social and Historical Setting of Palestinian Judaism and Christianity* (Nashville, 1981). L. I. Levine, ed., *Ancient Synagogues Revealed* (Jerusalem, Detroit, 1981). J. Gutmann (ed.), *Ancient Synagogues: The State of Research* (BJS 22; Chico, Calif., 1981).

11. It was discovered by R. Weill; see his *La cité de David,* 2 vols. (Paris, 1947). For a photograph of the inscription and an English translation, see H. Shanks' *The City of David: A Guide to Biblical Jerusalem* (Washington, 1973, 1975) pp. 103–4, and Levine (ed.), *Ancient Synagogues Revealed,* p. 11.

12. The synagogues at Bar'am and Meiron are examples of a basilica. The ones at Khirbet Shema, Khirbet Susiya, and Eshtemoa are broadhouses. The Beth Alpha synagogue is apsidal. For excellent photographs and discussion of these types of architecture, see E. M. Meyers, "From Temple to Synagogue," in *Judaism, 200 B.C.–A.D. 200,* ed. J. H. Charlesworth (Evanston, Ill., 1983). This slide lecture is distributed by the Religion and Ethics Institute, Inc., P. O. Box 664, Evanston, Ill. 60204, U.S.A.

13. V. Corbo, *The House of St. Peter at Capharnaum,* translated by S. Saller (Publications of the Studium Biblicum Franciscanum, Collectio minor 5; Jerusa-

lem, 1969). The monograph contains numerous important photographs of "the house of Peter." Noteworthy are Corbo's following observations: "Owing to these soundings below the pavement of the house church of the Jewish Christians the chronology of the origin of the veneration of the house of St. Peter, with the consequent creation of a place of cult or a primitive house church, must definitely be fixed already in the first century A.D." (p. 44).

14. J. Murphy-O'Connor, *The Holy Land: An Archaeological Guide from Earliest Times to 1700* (Oxford, New York, 1986) p. 191.

15. J. F. Strange and H. Shanks, "Has the House Where Jesus Stayed in Capernaum Been Found?" *BAR* 8 (1982) 26–37. The quotations are respectively from pp. 26 and 30.

16. Meyers and Strange, *Archaeology*, p. 130; see also p. 26.

17. J. Jeremias, *Jerusalem in the Time of Jesus: An Investigation into Economic and Social Conditions During the New Testament Period*, transl. F. H. and C. H. Cave (Philadelphia, 1969) p. 84.

18. Y. Yadin correctly contended that Essenes lived in Jerusalem and that they resided in the quarter near the Essene gate. See Yadin's popular work on the Temple Scroll *The Temple Scroll: The Hidden Law of the Dead Sea Sect* (London, 1985) pp. 181–82.

19. For photographs of the underground gate and the galleries that connect it to the so-called Solomon Stables, see Cornfeld, *The Historical Jesus*, pp. 144–53.

20. D. M. Smith rightly concludes as follows: "In any event, the life, interests, and controversies of the Johannine community provided the primary material and inspiration for the author of the Fourth Gospel. The influence of the synoptics was at best secondary and perhaps in some cases even second-hand" (pp. 170–71). See Smith's *Johannine Christianity: Essays on Its Setting, Sources, and Theology* (Columbia, S.C., 1984).

21. See R. Marcus and A. Wikgren, *Josephus* (LCL; Cambridge, Mass., London, 1969) vol. 8, p. 191.

22. N. Avigad, *Discovering Jerusalem*, p. 82.

23. See the photograph and discussion in M. Stein, "How Herod Moved Gigantic Blocks to Construct Temple Mount," *BAR* 7 (1981) 42–46.

24. B. Mazar, "Excavations Near Temple Mount Reveal Splendors of Herodian Jerusalem," *BAR* 6 (1980) 44–59; the quotation is from p. 47.

25. C. H. Dodd, *The Interpretation of the Fourth Gospel* (Cambridge, 1960) p. 319

26. J. H. Bernard, *The Gospel According to St. John*, vol. 1 (ICC; Edinburgh, 1928, repr. frequently) p. 227.

27. P. Benoit, *Jesus and the Gospel*, vol. 1, translated by B. Weatherhead (New York, 1973); see Chapters 7, 8, and 9.

28. Jn 19:13 has *"hebraisti,* which literally means "in Hebrew"; *Gabbatha* is Aramaic. The Evangelist John, like many first-century Jews and Christians, did not sharply distinguish between Hebrew and Aramaic, which are closely related languages.

29. See my article in *ExpT* 84 (1973) 147–50. My research was based on the medical examinations conducted by Dr. Nico Haas, who directed a medical team from the Hadassah Medical School in Jerusalem. The remains of the crucified man have been reexamined by Joseph Zias and Eliezer Sekeles, who claim that Dr. Haas and his team committed numerous errors. See their article "The Crucified Man from Giv'at ha-Mivtar: A Reappraisal," *IEJ* 35 (1985) 22–27. Also see Shanks, "New Analysis of the Crucified Man," *BAR* 11 (1985) 20–21.

30. See now C. Coüasnon, *The Church of the Holy Sepulchre in Jerusalem,* transl. J.-P. B. Ross and C. Ross (London, 1974) p. 29 and Plates XVI, XVIII, XIX.

31. See the photographs in Cornfeld, *The Historical Jesus,* pp. 202, 212.

32. See M. Hengel, *Crucifixion: In the Ancient World and the Folly of the Message of the Cross,* transl. J. Bowden (London, Philadelphia, 1977). Also see J. A. Fitzmyer, "Crucifixion in Ancient Palestine, Qumran Literature, and the New Testament," in *To Advance the Gospel: New Testament Studies* (New York, 1981) pp. 125–46.

33. Coüasnon, *The Church of the Holy Sepulchre in Jerusalem,* p. 7.

34. I quote the recent words of D. N. Freedman; see *BAR* 11 (1985) 6; insertion mine.

35. Ibid.

36. B. W. Anderson in *BAR* 10 (1984) 74.

Chapter 6

———— • ••••• • ————

Jesus' Concept of God
and His Self-Understanding.

During my inaugural lecture at Princeton Theological Seminary I more than once referred to Jesus' "self-consciousness." Later, during the faculty seminar, I was encouraged by a revered colleague to avoid that terminology, because it might be misunderstood as reminiscent of nineteenth-century romanticism and the pursuit of a biography on Jesus. The published version of the inaugural does not contain references to Jesus' "self-consciousness."

I have preferred to focus now on this subject and try to explain why to a certain extent we can talk about *Jesus' purpose* or intent *and* his concomitant *self-understanding*. The appropriate terminology should reflect an awareness of—not a struggle to find or posit—Jesus' own self-understanding. For over fifteen years, I have been lecturing on Jesus and the two-hundred-year search for the Jesus of history. During that period, I tended not to refer to Jesus' self-consciousness or his intentionality. Yet, there are at least three major passages in the New Testament that now convince me we are thrust into a confrontation with Jesus' self-understanding. The texts themselves have forced me to change my mind. Now I am convinced that an exegete interested in Jesus Research is obligated to reflect on Jesus' self-understanding.

Bultmann's influence on the biblical academies not only in Germany, but throughout the world, has preempted a careful study of "Jesus' self-consciousness." On the one hand, I thoroughly agree with Bultmann that it is not justifiable to present Jesus "as a historical phenomenon psychologically explicable."[1] On the other hand, for years I used to quote with approval what I can now no longer endorse. I am referring to the following quotation in Bultmann's *Jesus and the Word:*

> I do indeed think that we can now know almost nothing concerning the life and personality of Jesus, since the early Christian sources show no interest in either, are moreover fragmentary and often legendary; and other sources about Jesus do not exist (p. 14).

I certainly agree with Bultmann that the nineteenth-century lives of Jesus, which attempted to present his personality and the development of his "inner life," are "fantastic and romantic" (p. 14). Bultmann's understanding of the Christian sources, namely the tradition embedded beneath the redaction in the Gospels, is quite different from my own. I differ from Bultmann not only in conclusion, but also in methodology. In particular, what separates my work from his is a deeper involvement in the study of Early Judaism, and a decidedly different understanding of the origins of the gospel tradition within Early Judaism.[2]

A search for Jesus' self-understanding probably should begin with his concept of God. Here, I am pleased to report, there is an international consensus. Jesus conceived of God as a heavenly, loving, and intimate father, who was very near and not isolated in some distant heaven. From the distinguished publications by J. Jeremias, it is clear that Jesus chose one particular Aramaic noun to articulate his conception of God.[3] Jesus refers to God by the word "Abba," which is a determinative Aramaic noun, "the Father." It is employed frequently as a vocative form, meaning "O Father," and, since the pronominal suffix is often omitted in colloquial speech, it also means "my Father." Occasionally in Jerusalem I hear children call their fathers with the sounds "Abba, Abba," which is, of course, Hebrew for "Daddy."

There can be little doubt that Jesus used this formula when addressing God. It is represented in all five independent layers of the gospel tradition. It is in Mark, Q (a hypothetical sayings source that is lost and known only because Matthew and Luke independently quoted from it), Special Matthew (words preserved only in Mt), Special Luke (words found only in Lk), and John.

"Father" is the opening word in the prayer that Jesus taught his disciples (Mt 6:7–15 [*pater hēmōn*], Lk 11:1–4 [*pater*]): "Father, may your name be held holy" (Lk 11:2). The Evangelist Matthew, or someone in his community, probably altered Jesus' "*Abba*"— represented in Luke as, "*pater*," "Father," which is unusual—to a common Jewish address: *ʾābînû* (Heb.), *pater hēmōn* (Gk.), "our Father."

In the Greek of the Gospels, the Aramaic form sometimes is first transliterated and then translated into Greek. For example, Mark 14:36 records that Jesus, when he was deep in prayer on the Mount of Olives the night he was arrested, prayed, "*Abba ho patēr*" (Gk.), "Abba, Father. . . ." The Aramaic formula, which clearly goes back to Jesus, even influenced the liturgy of the early Church. It is embedded in Romans 8:15, which states that the Christian cries out saying, "Abba, Father." Paul, in Galatians 4:6, states that because Christians are God's sons the "Spirit of his Son" has been sent into their hearts crying, "Abba, Father."

Far too often, on the basis of Jesus' preference for Abba, New Testament scholars have argued for Jesus' *uniqueness*. The arguments often devolve into asides about the impoverished theology of Early Judaism, and Jesus' unique perception of God as a loving Father. Such arguments have developed without the requisite caution, and without any intensive study that is both sensitive and thorough, of the prayers preserved from Early Judaism.

Jesus' unique use of *ʾabbāʾ* (Aram.) for God builds upon the Jewish custom to call God " *ʾābînû* (Heb.)," "our Father." God is invoked as "Our Father" in a version of the second benediction before the Shema in the morning synagogal service, namely the Ahabah Rabbah. This prayer can be dated with some probability in form and content, but not exact wording, to pre-70 Palestinian Jewish liturgical settings. Even today it is recited in Hebrew in the morning synagogal service, and before the Shema. Note the following excerpt (both forms of "father" are from *ab*):

> Our Father (*ʾābînû*), merciful Father, thou who art ever compassionate, have pity on us and inspire us to understand and discern, to perceive, learn and teach, to observe, do, and fulfill gladly all the teachings of thy Torah.[4]

Jesus' concept of God as "merciful Father" is paralleled in a syna-gogal prayer. The term "Father" for God is found in other Jewish sources.[5] Notably, shortly after 100 C.E. Rabbi Akiba emphasized that Israel is made clean only because of the merciful actions of "your Father in heaven" (m.Yom 8.9). In these excerpts the term is "'ābînû,'" which means "our Father" (=Mt 6:9, *pater hēmōn*) or *ªbîchem*, which means "your Father."

Jesus' term is very similar, but not identical. It is Abba, "Father," which can also connote the familiar "Daddy." In Eleazar's prayer in 3 Maccabees 6:3 and 6:8 (in the *OTP* 2) we do find "Father" used in the absolute form: *pater* (LXX). We certainly do not have all the prayers used in Early Judaism; hence it is precarious to build upon the above data a unique theology for Jesus. There is not a world of difference between "our Father" and "Father"; both expressions evoked a loving and intimate God!

Yet, Jesus chose to use *'abbā'* not *'ābînû* when addressing God, and he put a unique emphasis on this word Abba. It was his habit-ual way of referring to and calling God. Is it not conceivable that he called God "Abba" because he had a conception of God that was in some ways different from that of *most* of his contemporaries? Many early Jews *tended* to conceive of God as distant, visiting humanity only through intermediaries such as angels, as we know from study-ing the Pseudepigrapha and the Dead Sea Scrolls. Jesus perceived that God himself was very near, and that he was directly concerned about each person, even (perhaps especially) sinners.

Obviously this perception must have been balanced in some way by some introspections. Jesus must have had some kind of self-understanding. At all levels of reflection, however, we must be criti-cal of our sources and methods; and we must be careful to avoid confusing what our sources may denote with what a twentieth-cen-tury Christian may wish to confess. It is not easy to be as honest as the distinguished Roman Catholic theologian Edward Schille-beeckx, who in studying "Jesus' Original ABBA Experience," wisely chose these words:

> Jesus' uniqueness in his relationship to God undoubtedly lies in its unaf-fected simplicity; and the marks of that in late Judaism, though not absent, were really rare. But we cannot build on it an awareness on

Jesus' part of some "transcendent" sonship and still less a Trinitarian doctrine, as has often happened in the exegetical and theological writings deriving therefrom. For that, more is needed. If we can find it, then in Jesus' unaffected intercourse with God as *Abba* we may justifiably perceive the natural consequences of it; not, however, the other way round.[6]

Before pursuing the search for Jesus' concept of himself, it is wise to clarify and define the major terms. Contemporary research has tended to be imprecise, and I think we must distinguish between intentionality, self-understanding, and self-consciousness.

It is clear that some purpose, some intentionality, shaped Jesus' deeds and words. What intent lies behind his authentic deeds and words? What did Jesus intend to accomplish through his life? To examine the passages that seem to contain reliable Jesus tradition eventually raises this question: What did Jesus intend by his remarkable words and actions? This question is distinct from, yet very close to, issues related to his self-understanding.

It is hard to sustain the claim that Jesus had no understanding of himself. He must have had some self-understanding. He must have reflected on his own relationship to his major proclamation: the dawning of God's Kingdom in his presence and through his words and miracles. Certainly a study of the parables and the miracles that accompanied his ministry supports this firm conclusion. He was displeased by the reputation he earned from these miraculous deeds, and he must have reflected upon who he was. He must have wrestled with the implications of his words and actions for his self-understanding.

We are therefore confronted with a major question: how did Jesus understand his role? What was his evaluation of his own personal relationship to the healings and to the proclamations of the dawning of God's reign? An attempt to understand Jesus' self-understanding must be kept distinct from, although it is somewhat analogous to, an attempt to comprehend Jesus' self-consciousness.

To search for Jesus' "self-consciousness" is to open Pandora's box. It is a dangerous term. We are liable to slip into thinking that Jesus proclaimed himself. Yet, New Testament scholars have shown that according to the synoptic Gospels Jesus did not proclaim himself. He announced the present dawning of God's rule. The term is dangerous for three other reasons: By using "self-consciousness" we may inadvertently be guilty of approaching the traditions in light of what we know from psychoanalysis. We are also liable to slip backward inadvertently into the romantic quest of the nineteenth century. Finally, a search for Jesus' self-consciousness may indeed reflect the failure to be sensitive to the limits of our biblical traditions.

Jesus was indeed conscious of a mission; but that does not clarify or indicate his consciousness of who he was, or anything to be identified *prima facie* as a self-consciousness. We must be critically honest as historians. We should not be afraid to contemplate that Jesus may well have been uncertain about who he really was—he may have left that clarification totally up to God. As I have tried to show elsewhere, according to some early Jewish sources God alone knows the identity of the Messiah. He alone will reveal who is the Messiah (see especially PssSol 17:23, 42).[7]

RETHINKING THREE MAJOR ASPECTS OF THE JESUS TRADITION

As I intimated at the outset of this chapter, there are three distinct sections in the Gospels that have forced me to rethink, and finally reject, the position, which I espoused for over a decade, that we can know practically nothing about who Jesus thought he was, that is, Jesus' self-understanding.

The first passage concerns the traditions about Jesus' choosing twelve disciples. For years I was convinced that this account was created *totally* by the Church. The early Christians affirmed that Jesus proclaimed he was the Messiah and intended to create a new Israel, consisting of twelve tribes, each ruled by one of the twelve disciples.

In favor of this argument, defended by many New Testament experts throughout the world, is the fact that, in the lists of the twelve, Peter is always first and Judas always last. Surely, I reasoned, these lists were created by the Church, and reflect the elevation of Peter and the demotion of Judas. Supporting this exegesis is the observation that the names of the twelve disciples are different in each account, specifically in Mark 3:13–19a, Matthew 10:1–4, Luke 6:12–16, Acts 1:13 (cf. Jn 1:42). The relegation of the twelve to the thoughts and needs of the Church also seems to be demanded by other apparently authentic traditions. Did Jesus choose not twelve disciples but a troika of disciples, namely Peter, James, and John? Was his following limited to twelve or did it encompass a large number of men and women?

Now I am convinced that while the lists were *shaped by* and reflect the needs of the Church, they also preserve some pre-Easter traditions. The major issue concerns Judas. If the Church created the institution of the twelve, then why was Judas placed within that institution? What is Judas doing in this elect group? Since the name "Judas" appears very early in the tradition—in Mark and pre-Marcan traditions—it cannot be argued that "Judas" derives from the anti-Semitic or anti-Jewish characteristics of the post-70 Church, even if Judas may evolve from "Judah": the Jew. "Judas" did not appear from ideology as the perfect scapegoat. Likewise, if the Church concocted "the twelve," then how can we explain the tradition that it felt compelled to replace Judas with Matthias?[8]

If "the twelve" derives only from the followers of Jesus, then it must follow that they wanted Judas to be one of the twelve. That conclusion is preposterous.

It clashes with the great embarrassment they had experienced because of Judas, and the traditions relating to him. It would have been fairly easy for the early followers of Jesus to compile a list of twelve with the name of Matthias or one of the other names in the lists of twelve. They did not have to create a list of twelve which included Judas, and then devise a means for replacing him with another.

Of course, there is the possible objection that the compilers of the lists wanted to create a Judas in light of their interpretation of scripture that it was necessary for someone to betray Jesus. But an exegesis of scripture does not accompany the lists of the twelve, not even in Matthew, which usually explains events in terms of the fulfillment of scripture. There is no evidence that "a Judas" has been created and then inserted into a fabricated twelve. Historians and exegetes are not very helpful if they merely focus upon possibilities. What we are after is probability.

I think, therefore, that it is quite probable that *Jesus appointed twelve disciples.*[9] If he did choose twelve, then it seems to follow that there must have been some intent and some understanding behind this action. A critic might reply that in this example we are faced with more clarity in trying to discern Jesus' intent, but we are far from discerning Jesus' self-understanding.

Obviously, however, "twelve" is not an insignificant number. It symbolizes Israel; it is the number of the twelve sons of Jacob, from whom the twelve tribes of Israel evolved. It is the number celebrated in the early Jewish document called the Testaments of the Twelve Patriarchs. Hence, we must raise these questions: Is there some self-understanding behind Jesus' apparent desire to have twelve special men follow him? Is he by this act not symbolically representing a belief that the end of time is now becoming a present reality? Since he is the one who chose the twelve, is he not exhibiting some perception of playing a part in the eschatological restoration of Israel? It is unwise, indeed uninformed, to follow the lead of some New Testament scholars who denounce any possibility of recovering Jesus' self-understanding; and it may no longer be wise to reject the possibility that he had some "messianic" self-understanding.

The second passage that has forced me to reconsider the conclusion that we can know practically nothing about Jesus' self-understanding is the triumphal entry into Jerusalem. If this account is in any way authentic, and if Jesus did indeed ride into Jerusalem upon an animal at the time of Passover, it certainly follows that there was some intent and perhaps understanding behind this symbolic act. If Jesus came in from the east and entered into Jerusalem through a gate riding upon an animal, and was saluted by the crowds at the time of Passover with some kind of Davidic recognition, then who did Jesus think he was? I am convinced that *some* kernel of history lies behind this account; if so, then we are obviously in some way confronted with Jesus' self-understanding.

Long ago, one of the developers of the method used by New Testament scholars throughout the world, namely Martin Dibelius, published this conclusion: "Jesus knew himself to be the Messiah chosen by God, especially when he made his entrance into Jerusalem and appeared in the Temple as Lord."[10] That conclusion may indeed be possible; but the data appear to me to be far too ambiguous to sustain such certainty.

While Jesus may not have thought himself to be the Messiah, it does not necessarily follow that he held *no* messianic self-understanding.[11] For example, Jesus may have thought that he was, or would be declared by God to be, the Son of Man; if so, then it is conceivable that the messianic overtones of this title, as for example found in 1 Enoch 37–71, would shape his growing awareness of his mission. The traditions, however, certainly do not support the conclusion that Jesus proclaimed himself to be the Messiah.

Some of the disciples could well have remembered after Easter that they had had a premonition that he was (to be?) the Messiah. Goppelt may have caught some of the disciples' pre-Easter understanding when he argued that

> the statement of Peter is conceivable not only as a vague expectation, but as a confession in the earthly days. Of course, it was such only as a confession under immediate circumstances that was overtaken by both advancing recognition and vexing doubts. And of course, it was a confession that was yet far removed, in terms of substance, from that of the first community after Easter.[12]

The third example that has shaken my confidence in knowing nothing assuredly about Jesus' self-understanding concerns a parable that has been difficult to understand. It is the Parable of the Wicked Tenant Farmers. This parable is found in Mark 12:1–12, Matthew 21:33–46,[13] Luke 20:9–19,[14] *and* the Gospel of Thomas 65. There are two primary witnesses to this parable, namely Mark 12 and the Gospel of Thomas 65. Mark 12:1–9 may be translated as follows:

> And he began to speak to them in parables. "A man planted a vineyard, and set a fence around it, and dug a trough (for the wine press), and built a tower, and leased it to tenants; then he went away.[15] When the time came (for the harvest), he sent a servant to the tenants, to collect from them (his portion) of the fruits of the vineyard. But they took him, beat (him), and sent (him) away empty-handed. Again, he sent to them another servant, him they wounded in the head, and treated shamefully. And he sent another, him they killed; then many others, some they beat but some they killed. He had still one other: a beloved son *(huion*

agapēton). He sent him to them last (of all, *eschaton*) saying, 'They will respect my son.' But those tenants said to one another, 'This is the heir; come, let us kill him, and the inheritance will be ours.' And seizing (him), they killed him, and cast him out of the vineyard. What will the owner (*ho kyrios*) of the vineyard do? He will come and destroy the tenants, and give the vineyard to others."

After this verse, Mark specifies the meaning of the parable by linking it with Jesus' death. He accomplishes this intended exegesis by referring to the prophecy in Psalm 118:22–23, which mentions the stone rejected by the builders (discussed in the preceding chapter).[16] He clarifies that "they knew" (Mk 12:12) that he had addressed the parable to them, namely the chief priests, scribes, and elders in Jerusalem (Mk 11:27). The connection between the Parable of the Wicked Tenant Farmers and the rejected-stone motif from Psalm 118 is early. It immediately follows an independent saying of Jesus in the Gospel of Thomas (logion 66); but it is Mark the Evangelist who frames the parable and clarifies the interpretation.

Jülicher was certainly correct that the parables must not be allegorized as St. Augustine and many other theologians and biblical exegetes have done.[17] Yet, New Testament scholars who still assume that Jesus never used an allegory should rethink this assumption.[18] We are confronted in Mark 12 with a parable that is probably ultimately traceable back to Jesus, and that is certainly in some ways a *partial* allegory.[19] As Anderson explains the parable, "it is an allegory in which the *vineyard* stands for Israel, the *tenants* for the Jewish authorities, the *servants* for the OT prophets, and the *son* and *heir* for Jesus."[20] All these identifications seem sound; but we must *not* go on to interpret every aspect of the parable as if it were a full-blown allegory. The landlord is not to be identified historically with a hated ruler, and then this figure interpreted to represent God.

The parable is allegorical in all the canonical Gospels. It is, however, noticeably different from the allegories produced by the followers of Jesus (recall the Parable of the Great Feast and how Matthew allegorizes a parable of Jesus), because some of the details are considerably ambiguous and underdeveloped. It is based on Isaiah 5, which is itself an allegory.[21]

A first reading gives the impression that in no way can this parable be taken back to the Jesus of history. Certainly the reference to
"a beloved son" reflects Mark's tendencies, centrally and significantly featured in his accounts of the baptism and transfiguration.
The reference to giving the vineyard to another mirrors the crisis of
66–70 C.E. and the conquest of the nation Israel by Rome in 70 C.E.
It is obvious why Jülicher, followed by Bultmann and Kümmel,
attributed the parable to post-Easter, even post-70, theological reflection.[22]

Yet, a careful rereading raises problems with the conclusion that
this parable was created totally by the post-Easter followers of
Jesus. If it refers to the death of Jesus, then we have a major difficulty: Jesus was *not* killed *within* the city, Jerusalem. His body was
not cast out of the city; recall verse 8: "And seizing (him=Jesus),
they killed him, and cast him out of the vineyard (Jerusalem)."[23] We
are, therefore, confronted with a problem: How can the *whole* parable be composed in the post-Easter communities in order to prove
that Jesus was the beloved son (Mk 12:6 and Mt 21:37) who was
killed in Jerusalem, when Jesus was *not* killed *within* the city, and
his body was *not thrown outside of it*?

It is obvious that Golgotha was outside the walls of Jerusalem, as
the author of Hebrews states (Heb 13:12–13) and as recent archaeological excavations have confirmed (as indicated in the preceding
chapter).[24] Matthew and Luke obviously felt compelled to correct
this problem, and solved the difficulty by rewriting Mark 12:8. Matthew rewrote Mark as follows: "And seizing him, they cast him *out*
(exō) of the vineyard; then they killed (him)" (Mt 21:39). Luke also
redacted Mark: "And casting him *out (exō)* of the vineyard, they
killed (him)" (Lk 20:15). Both Matthew and Luke have the son first
cast out of the vineyard (=Jerusalem)[25] and then killed. The parable, after this editorial reworking, aptly reflects the death of Jesus.
Mark's account is obviously earlier than Matthew's and Luke's versions. It is not so heavily edited, and it contains traditions that clash
with the manner in which Jesus met his death.

Another observation raises grave difficulties with the conclusion
that this parable arose for the first time within the needs of the
Church. The story prompts us to think about the wicked tenants
killing the son in the vineyard and then hurling the corpse over

something like a stone fence. The casting out of the body from the vineyard says nothing about burying the corpse. The son receives the ultimate disgrace: the corpse does not even receive a decent burial, a horrifying act in ancient, especially Jewish, societies (cf. *War* 12.517–19).

No tradition in early Christianity is so well established as the one that Jesus' corpse was placed in a tomb and a stone was rolled in front of it (cf. King Herod's family tomb in Illus. 8). In the parable, the implication is given that the corpse lies mutilated outside the vineyard. How are we to reconcile these clashing traditions? The most logical means is to trace the parable *in its earliest forms* back through the preaching in the Palestinian Jewish Movement, back before Jesus' execution, and to the Jesus of history. Therefore, I agree with Dodd,[26] J. Jeremias (who first saw the extreme importance of including in our study of this parable the version preserved in the Gospel of Thomas),[27] Anderson,[28] Dunn,[29] and Flusser,[30] that *at least portions* of the parable *must go back to the Jesus of history.* The parable does *not* reflect the way Jesus was known to have suffered and died.

Appreciably different observations also indicate that behind Mark 12:1–9 lies an authentic Jesus tradition. First, like almost all reliable Jesus traditions, this parable is clearly eschatological: the owner of the vineyard last (of all, *eschaton*) sent his son. This recognition only clarifies that the parable is harmonious with sayings of Jesus already proved to be authentic.

Second, Jesus' followers looked for his return (Acts 1:11, 1Cor 16:22, Rev *passim*). He, however, often proclaimed the coming of God and his kingdom. The core of the parable ends with these words: "What will the owner (*ho kyrios*) of the vineyard do? He will come. . . ." The rest of the parable looks edited, and it is possible Jesus' followers changed the conclusion Jesus had given to the parable. The emphasis in the parable leads up to the coming of the owner of the vineyard, God himself. This concept fits well with Jesus' message of the imminent coming of God into this world. The perception is also distinguishable from Jesus' followers' expectation that Jesus would return (come again soon) into this world. A term supports this interpretation: the term for the owner is *ho kyrios,* which is the Greek noun that usually translates the Jewish name for

17. Sinai. St. Catherine's Monastery, situated at the foot of Mount Sinai, on which Moses received the Ten Commandments, according to ancient traditions. The monastery is famous for the many manuscripts it has treasured over the centuries, notably Codex Sinaiticus, now in the British Museum, and Syrus Sinaiticus, which is a palimpsest whose underwriting preserves the oldest and best copy of the Old Syriac Gospels.

Werner Braun

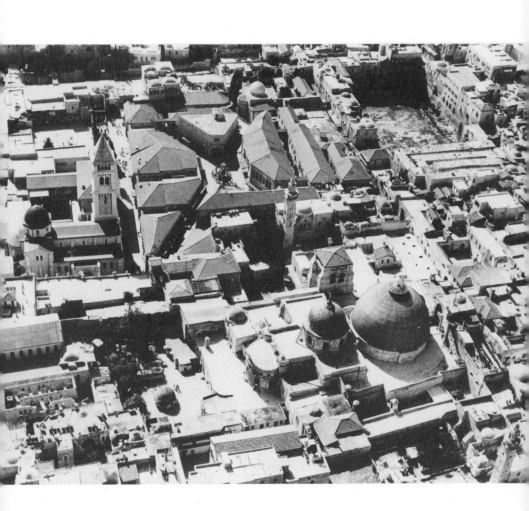

18. Jerusalem. Church of the Holy Sepulchre with its two distinguishable domes.

Zev Radovan

19. Jerusalem. Church of the Holy Sepulchre, façade. The stone of Golgotha, on which, probably, Jesus was crucified, is situated just inside the door and to the right. *Zev Radovan*

20. The name "Jesus" as written in Hebrew on an ossuary.

21. The closing page of the Coptic Gospel of Thomas.
Courtesy of Institute for Antiquity and Christianity

God, the ineffable name: Yahweh, the owner of the vineyard. In this parable Jesus cannot be both "son" and "owner" (or Lord, *kyrios*).

Third, the authentic words of Jesus are God-oriented. His followers became increasingly more Christ-oriented, indeed eventually Christian. Accordingly, the core of this parable fits with what is widely acknowledged to be authentic Jesus tradition; and it is distinguishable from the thoughts of his followers.

While there are numerous interesting questions aroused by reading the Parable of the Wicked Tenant Farmers, the one that now occupies our central focus concerns the search for *Jesus' self-understanding.* Does the section of the parable that refers to the sending of a son derive ultimately from Jesus? And if so, to what extent are we confronted here with Jesus' self-understanding?

In order to pursue this central question, we must proceed consecutively with two basic questions: the first concerns Jesus' perception of his own death, the second concerns the use of "son" in Early Judaism.

Among the edited fragments of what Jesus reputedly said and did, is there any reliable evidence that he articulated some thought that he was about to face a martyr's death? The disciples apparently contended that Jesus did say something about facing martyrdom. They repeatedly are portrayed as warning him not to go up to Jerusalem and confront the chief priest (Mk 8:31–33). The passage in Mark 10:32 sounds very realistic; according to this verse, Jesus moved up from Jericho toward Jerusalem ahead of a band of fearful disciples. Moreover, the Pharisees warned him that he was on a collision course with death. According to Luke, they advised him to be wary, because Herod Antipas was seeking ways to put him to death (Lk 13:31–33).

Again we must be sensitive both to the clear *alteration* of Jesus' traditions (only those that can reliably be traced back to him) through transmission and to the *creation* of Jesus traditions (all those that are attributed to him) in the Palestinian Jesus Movement. Jesus, like every individual, must have realized that death is the one great certainty in the life of a human being. It is unsound, however, to conclude that he feared the possibility of being crucified. The passages in which we find Jesus' proclamations that he was on the way to the cross clearly disclose the apology of the early Christians.

These are statements shaped or created after the fact of the crucifixion (*vaticinia ex eventu*). If anyone would attempt today to prove these statements are authentic, chaos would be created with other traditions that are reliable, namely Jesus' agony in Gethsemane, his quoting from Psalm 22 on the cross, the confusion of the disciples following Jesus' arrest, and the statements by the evangelists that the disciples did not understand Jesus when he spoke about his impending suffering.

A most important passage suggesting that Jesus probably knew he was facing martyrdom is a logion attributed to him and found in Q (a very early sayings source used by Matthew and Luke; see Lk 13:34 and Mt 23:37): "Oh Jerusalem, Jerusalem, she who kills the prophets and stones those sent to her. . . ." It is clear that Jesus on many occasions expressed thoughts that would connect him in some way with the prophetic tradition. It is also obvious that many reliable traditions indicate he felt compelled—or sent—to Jerusalem. Although the following verse evidences several of Luke's special concerns, it may adequately catch the intent of Jesus: "I must continue my journey, for a prophet must not perish outside (*exō,* or away from) Jerusalem" (Lk 13:33).

In favor of the option that the verse in Matthew 23:37 and Luke 13:34 —"Oh Jerusalem . . . she who . . . stones those sent to her . . ."— derives from Jesus' own words is the fact that he may well have thought he was sent to Jerusalem and was facing the possibility of being *stoned*. Why would he have thought he might be stoned in or near Jerusalem?

Jesus must have known the traditions that eventually were edited and recorded in the Mishnah *Sanhedrin*. In this tractate there are numerous offenses that would have resulted in the death penalty, including stoning. Among these that may well have been thought by some Jewish leaders to apply appropriately to Jesus are the practicing of magic, breaking the Sabbath, blaspheming God, and being a false prophet (cf. m.Sanh 7:4 and 11:1).

Secular history and Jewish literature would have confirmed for Jesus the possibility that he might be facing some form of martyrdom. John the Baptist had been beheaded just before Jesus began his public ministry; and without any doubt Jesus was in some way closely aligned with the movement set in motion by John the Baptizer. A few decades earlier than Jesus' ministry, Ḥoni Ha-Meaggel (Ḥoni the Circle Drawer), a Galilean charismatic miracle worker, was *stoned* outside *Jerusalem*.[31] Jesus' own consciousness may well have been shaped by the fate of those who had immediately preceded him. It may also have been affected by the floating traditions known to us because they are preserved in a pseudepigraphon called the Lives and Deaths of the Prophets (in *OTP* 1). This document, written probably before 70 C.E., refers to the martyrdom of some of the great prophets, including Isaiah (who is reputed to have been sawed in two by the Judahite king Manasseh [cf. MartIs]), Jeremiah (who was allegedly stoned by his own people [cf. 4Bar]), and Ezekiel (who was ostensibly murdered by the Jewish leader in Babylon).

It now becomes obvious that the core of the parable of the Wicked Tenant Farmers might ultimately derive from Jesus and reflect his premonition of a martyr's death. Jesus may have feared that, like Jeremiah and Ḥoni, he would be *stoned*. He was not stoned; the fact that he was crucified tends to anchor this logion in authentic tradition. The evangelists and their predecessors would not have created a saying that both clashes with real history and tends to portray Jesus as ignorant.

An additional factor that indicates that the Parable of the Wicked Tenant Farmers derives ultimately from Jesus is the setting reflected in the story. Even though storytellers may be inspired by prophetic traditions (here Isaiah 5), they will align a tale so that it harmonizes or reflects the contemporary situation, so that it is easy for the listener to become empathetic with it. The details in the parable reflect Jesus' time, not Mark's or that of any writer after 66 C.E., the beginning of the Great Revolt against Rome and too early a date for the composition of Mark.

Mark would have experienced or reflected back upon the destruction of vineyards and the collapse of towers by the Romans.[32] His time was much more violent than that depicted in the story.[33] Owners of vineyards would not have expected during those years to receive produce: the land was in revolt, the vineyards were unattended or burned.

Jesus' own time fits the setting quite remarkably. The story assumes that the purchase of a vineyard would be a good financial venture, that vineyards were often run by tenant farmers, that a landlord would frequently be living somewhere else (perhaps for comfort or safety), that there were abundant reasons for misunderstanding between the landlord and the tenants, that the landlord rightly expected his share of the profits, that there would be profits, and that his messengers might well be mistreated.

These assumptions amazingly and accurately portray the economic and social situation in Galilee after the time of Herod, especially after his death in 4 B.C.E.[34] The parable mirrors the agricultural reforms he introduced and that were operative during Jesus' lifetime.

The monarch Herod allowed his subjects, Jews and Gentiles, virtually no rights. Around 20 B.C.E., the year when he began to enlarge the Temple, he did indeed cancel one third of the taxes, notably the taxes on agriculture; but, according to Josephus (Ant 15.365), his motive was to win back the goodwill of the disaffected Jews and to remove the growing opportunities for revolt. He prohibited citizens to gather or even walk together (Ant 15.366). Anyone who was seen to resist this constriction, or even seemed insubordinate to him, was put to death. There were spies for Herod "in the city and on the open roads" (Ant 15.366).

Financing his massive building plans (which were monumental and successful, as we saw in the preceding chapter), his army (to fight the Nabateans), and his royal palaces (with their grandeur and foreign artisans) caused him to raise taxes to an unprecedented level. The main source of this revenue came from agricultural products (Ant 17. 205), especially from such productive regions as Galilee (some of the finest wheat came from the regions of Capernaum and Chorazin [cf. y.Taʿan 4:5]).

Herod established new forms of *tenant* farming. He habitually confiscated farms from his numerous Jewish enemies (Ant 15.5), and turned them into large royal estates, especially in the great fertile Plain of Esdraelon, just south of Nazareth. These tenant farms were owned by absentee landlords, usually Herod's own wealthy friends, who may well have lived in the sumptuous rooms in Caesarea during the winter months, and in Jerusalem in the hot summer. Because of the unusual economic prosperity, they would have demanded high returns.[35] There are sufficient reasons to imagine the many areas for misunderstanding and possible abuse of messengers: the whole area would soon explode in open revolt.

Jesus' parable entices us to imagine what a descendant of the proud Hasmonean dynasty, a wealthy landowner, would have thought when looking over his vineyards now stolen by the Idumean Herod and given to his friends. Would he see a chariot's dust rise above the harvested vineyard as a foreigner came to his home to collect the profits from the land[36] given by Yahweh to the descendants of Abraham?[37] Would a sweaty Jewish fist holding the taxes be confronted by a condescending, perhaps inebriated, intruder? Under such impossible circumstances revolt would be contemplated. The hostilities that produced the fires of 66 to 70 C.E. antedate Jesus' crucifixion in 30 C.E. and are reflected in some of his parables.

In Jesus' own time, during the rule of Herod Antipas, whom Jesus is reputed to have called "that fox" (Lk 13:32), there was prosperity, but there was essentially no middle class,[38] only the rich, usually landowners, and peasant (not necessarily poor), frequently tenant farmers. Antipas, like Herod the Great, owned large tracts of land. The Parable of the Wicked Tenant Farmers reflects Galilee precisely as Jesus would have experienced it. Galilee before 30 C.E. was significantly different from Galilee after 66 C.E. (the beginning of the war against Rome), the defeat of Josephus' Galilean "army," the subjugation of the northern territory by the Romans, and the composition of Mark. Mark's Galilee would even be subsequent to 66. The parable, therefore, in these particulars mentioned already probably derives ultimately from Jesus himself. We can now focus on the reason this parable has been chosen for examination.

The question confronting us is the reference to the son in the parable. Could Jesus have referred to himself as the son? Is that self-understanding related to his concept of God as Abba? Before pursuing these questions, it is pertinent to quote the version of the parable found in the Gospel of Thomas 65:

He (Jesus) said: A good (=Gk. chrēstos) man had a vineyard. He gave (leased) it to tenants so that (=Gk. hina) they might cultivate it and he might collect (his share of) its fruit from them. He sent (Cop. *jow* = Gk. apostellō) his *servant* (Cop. *hal* =Gk. doulos) so that the tenants might give him the fruit (=Gk. karpos) of the vineyard. They seized his *ser-*

vant; they beat him; a little longer and they would have killed him. The *servant* departed; he told it to his master (Cop. *joys* ="lord, master, and owner" =Gk. kyrios). His master said: "Perhaps he did not know them."[39] He *sent* another *servant:* the tenants beat him as well. Then the master *sent* his *son* (Cop. *shēre,* which means also "child"; it translates numerous Gk. words including *huios* [="son"]). He said: "Perhaps they will respect my *son."* Since those tenants knew that he was the heir of the vineyard, they seized him; they killed him. He who has ears let him hear.

Obviously this version of the parable is considerably distinct from the intracanonical versions. The form of the parable has three messengers: a servant, another servant, and the son. As is well known, this triadic form is found in parables ultimately deriving from Jesus.[40] It does not contain the clearly Marcan editorial words and phrases, especially "beloved son." Of all the versions of the parable, it is the one that is least developed, although it is slightly allegorical.

According to the Marcan form of the parable, the father knows that some of his servants have been murdered. He then, nevertheless, sends his own son. At this point the story ceases to be credible, and attentive listeners would have asked themselves what kind of a father is being portrayed. The father appears foolish, even unjust and cruel. Surely the heightened allusions to the death of the servants, clearly the prophets (cf. LivPro), are post-Jesus editorial expansions. They shift the realistic parable into unrealistic details. The Gospel of Thomas is impressively free from these elements;[41] in it the story is true to life in Palestine before 70 C.E. Even the parable in the Gospel of Thomas cannot be claimed to preserve the original form of the parable; because the killing of the son *within the vineyard,* which is the key to the authenticity to this saying of Jesus, is conspicuously absent and was probably dropped by the author of the Gospel of Thomas, who deemphasized the cross and passion of Jesus, elevating his eschatological and wisdom pronouncements.

Most important for us now, in the Gospel of Thomas the statement "Then the master sent his son" may be translated "Then the Lord (Yahweh) sent his son." There can be little doubt that the owner, master, or lord (Cop. *joys*) is intended to be God himself. What is then also equally clear is that Jesus is the son.

We are now confronted boldly with the key question: could Jesus have referred to himself as the son, or the son of God? Numerous scholars, representing widely differing methodologies and perceptions, have concluded that here we are obviously dealing with a parable that was created in the early Christian communities. For example, two scholars of very different perspectives, namely Hans Conzelmann[42] and Edward Schweizer,[43] conclude that "son" and "Son of God" are titles that originated within the Church. They contend that the needs of the early Christians and their celebration of Jesus as God's son confront us in the appearance of the term "son" or "Son of God" in the New Testament.

The presupposition of many New Testament specialists is simply that "Son of God" or "son" is a technical term that was coined by the preaching (kerygma) and teaching (didache) of the early Church. One of the main reasons, perhaps the most important one, specialists have concluded that the Parable of the Wicked Tenant Farmers must originate in the early Church,[44] and not with Jesus, is the appearance of the title "son" in it.[45] Obviously "son" is deeply embedded in the fabric of the story; it cannot be dismissed as an editorial addition.

Now I wish to emphasize that there are fifteen examples of this term in the literature that has been preserved *from Early Judaism*. These excerpts prove that "son" was not created in the Church. These fifteen citations represent four fairly distinct periods in Early Judaism.

The first group of texts dates from the second or early-first century B.C.E. In the Hebrew of Sirach 4:10 (in OTA) we confront the statement ". . . and God (w²l) will call you son (bn)." In the Greek version, this phrase is rendered slightly differently: "You will then be like a *son* of the Most High." The Jerusalem teacher is articulating the rewards given to those who possess wisdom and act with loving faithfulness toward those in great need, especially the poor and the orphans. In the Epistle of Enoch (in 1En; see *OTP* 1), written sometime between 125 and 75 B.C.E., God is reported to have exhorted Enoch to rejoice until "I and *my son* are united with them forever in the upright paths. . ." (1En 105:2). This passage of 1 Enoch, however, is *not* preserved in the Greek version, prompting scholars like G. Dalman, E. Lohse, and Goppelt to conclude that it is a later (perhaps Christian) interpolation. For reasons that must now be only footnoted, the arguments for questioning the Jewishness of this passage are no longer convincing.[46] If we dismiss the possibility that this verse is a Christian interpolation, we must yet confront another possibility: Enoch, not God, may be the speaker; hence the reference is to Enoch and his son Methuselah.[47] In Ezekiel the Tragedian (in *OTP* 2), Moses is called by God *"my son."* According to the Testament of Levi 4:2 (in *OTP* 1), Levi is to be, or become, a *son* to God.

In the second group are three documents that date from the late-first century B.C.E. In a Jewish writing (that probably comes from Alexandria) named the Wisdom of Solomon (in OTA), we learn that the righteous one shall be called "God's son" (2:18, cf. 2:13–16). Specifically, the author of the Wisdom of Solomon is arguing that if the righteous person is "God's *son*" then God will deliver that person from the hand of his tormenting adversaries. In a still unpublished Aramaic fragment from Qumran Cave IV, 4QpsDan A^a (= 4Q246), we learn that some human being, unfortunately not identifiable because of the fragmentary nature of the document, is called not only *"Son* of God (*brh dy ʾl*)*,"* but also *"Son* of the Most High (*wbr ʿlywn*)."*[48] In another fragment from Qumran Cave IV, labeled 4Q Florilegium, we perceive how the Qumran Essenes interpreted the prophecy of Nathan preserved in 2 Samuel 7:14. Nathan had reported to David God's promises, namely that God had said (through Nathan), "I will be his father, he shall be my *son"* (see 2Sam 7:14). In this fragment from Qumran the reference to David is transferred to David's descendant, especially the Messiah. In other words, the *Messiah* shall be *God's son.* Of course, all such references do *not* denote a physical descent of the son. They seem to express some form of legal adoption, as when, in Psalm 2, God is quoted as saying to the king, "You are my son; this day I have begotten you." The king, in other words, begins a new life on the day that he is anointed king under God.

In the third group are three documents from the first century C.E. One of them is much later than the first century; but, according to recent research, it can be traced back reliably to first-century traditions. Ḥanina ben Dosa, a Galilean miracle worker roughly contemporaneous with Jesus, is reported to have elicited approving words from above. Here is the tradition: "Every day a divine voice goes forth from Mt. Horeb and proclaims: 'The whole world is sustained for the sake of My son Hanina, and Hanina My son has to subsist on a *Kab* of carobs from one week end to the next' " (b.*Zera'im Berakot* 17a). According to the Prayer of Joseph (*OTP* 2), Jacob is not only Israel but also "an angel of God." What is significant now is that this incarnate archangel[49] is described as the supreme commander "among the *sons* of God." According to the Testament of Abraham (in *OTP* 1), which ultimately derives from the first century, Abel is depicted as one like a *son* of God.

In the final group are four documents that refer to an ideal person in Israel's history as God's son; they can be dated sometime around 100 C.E., give or take a quarter of a century. The pessimistic, but erudite and introspective, author of 4 Ezra (in *OTP* 1) describes the coming of the Messiah, whom God calls his son: "For my son the Messiah shall be revealed with those who are with him, and those who remain shall rejoice four hundred years" (4Ezra 7:28; see 7:29). Later in the narrative, Ezra is said to have received a vision of "something like the figure of a man" coming up out of the sea (4Ezra 13:3). Ezra requests an interpretation of the vision, and the Most High informs him that the man is "my son" (4Ezra 13:37). The "son" remains unseen until "his day" (4Ezra 13:52; see 14:9). All references to "son" (Lat. *filius*; Syr. *br*) or "my son" (Lat. *filius meus*; Syr. *bry*) probably derive from a Semitic *bar* or *bēn,* "son," and not, as Lohse, Goppelt, and many other scholars contend, from a Semitic *'bd,* "servant."[50] The Syriac version, which is independent of and as important as the Latin, has *bar*: "son."

Josephus describes Moses as a *son* in the likeness of God *(Ant* 2.232).[51] In Joseph and Aseneth (in *OTP* 2), which appears to be an early-second-century C.E. work of Egyptian Judaism, Joseph is presented boldly as "the *son* of God" (JosAsen 6:3, 5; cf. 13:13). Note the words of Aseneth's foster father: "At last the Lord God of heaven has chosen you as a bride for his *firstborn son, Joseph*"[52] (JosAsen 18:11; cf. 21:4 and 23:10). In the Apocalypse of Elijah (in *OTP* 1), the byways are apocalyptically personified and ask one another, "Have you heard today the voice of a man who walks who has not come to the judgment of the Son of God" (ApEl 5:25)? It is difficult to separate the Jewish from the Christian layers in this document, but this passage may well be Jewish. The Samaritan text

Memar Marqah, which in its earliest form may derive from the second century C.E. and clearly preserves much older traditions, calls Moses "the servant of God, the *son* of the house of God."[53]

We now have abundant and persuasive evidence that Jews roughly contemporaneous with Jesus did use the technical term "son" or "Son of God." They attributed this title to paradigmatic holy individuals, including the long-awaited Messiah, in God's drama of salvation. It simply will no longer suffice to attribute all references to "son" or "Son of God" to the needs and proclamations of the early Church.

While the early Church certainly interpreted these terms and titles in an unparalleled way, they nevertheless inherited them from deep and dynamic currents within Early Judaism. The appearance of the title "son" in the two earliest versions of the Parable of the Wicked Tenant Farmers (Mark and the Gospel of Thomas) does not prove, or even indicate, that it cannot derive from the Jew, Jesus of Nazareth.[54]

We have found impressive Jewish parallels to the use of the title "son," but there is a marked difference between attributing sonship to another and attributing it to oneself. Jesus, in the Parable of the Wicked Tenant Farmers, according to both Mark and Thomas, uses sonship in a *reflexive* manner, since the parable has allegorical overtones.

If this section of the parable derives ultimately from *Jesus,* it seems to follow that he *thought of himself as a son,* and perhaps, since the owner of the vineyard is none other than God, *as God's son.* This discovery is significant and momentous, but it does not clarify precisely what Jesus may have thought was denoted and connoted by the noun "son," or what he then perceived reflexively and introspectively about himself. The data that have been brought before us present us with a tantalizing possibility. It does not seem confessional, speculative, or illegitimate to suggest that Jesus considered himself "the son." But certainly this was in no way in line with the physical sonship so prominent in the ancient Near East. The physical divine sonship found no place in biblical theology or in the theology of Early Judaism. Jesus could, however, have been referring to some aspect of the biblical concept of adoption as God's son (see 2Sam 7:14, Ps 2:7; cf. Ps 89:26–27 and Isa 9:1–6). Perhaps this term indicated that he felt a special intimate relationship with God[55] and that his words and deeds were validated and sanctioned by God, the Father, Abba.

It is also clear that he did not *proclaim* himself "the son." Never in the synoptic tradition did he cut himself off from the rest of humanity. That development appears only in the thought of the early Church and is associated with the evolution of the belief that he had been born of a virgin. At first this belief said something about Jesus' uniqueness, eventually it was taken, especially in the extracanonical gospels like the Birth of Mary (=Protevangelium of James) and the Infancy Gospel of Thomas, to denote the special status of Mary, and eventually it influenced the ideas associated with her own mother, Anna.

CONCLUSION

An examination and comparison of the four versions of the Parable of the Wicked Tenant Farmers, a study of the meaning of the preredacted layers of the Gospels, and an improved understanding of the theology of Early Judaism lead cumulatively to the conclusion that ultimately the core of the tradition of this parable derives from Jesus himself. It is conceivable that Jesus was referring to himself as "the son" who would be killed. Our conclusion, therefore, confronts us not only with Jesus' intent but also with his self-understanding.

At least on one occasion, he conceived of himself as one who was sent to Jerusalem and as one who would be stoned. There is at least some prophetic consciousness in this tradition, but we must not too readily conclude that Jesus had a deep messianic self-understanding; and he did not proclaim himself the Messiah.

Some readers might wish now to conclude that Jesus considered himself "the suffering servant," or the Messiah who was to suffer and die for the people of God. Where is there convincing evidence to support this contention? Can one be relatively certain that the passages brought forward from the New Testament are not the creations of the disciples' proclamations after Easter? Certainly one cannot appeal to the theology of Early Judaism and talk about a vague Jewish expectation for or belief in a suffering servant or a suffering Messiah. Despite the impressive attempt by J. Jeremias to demonstrate the belief in a future suffering Messiah in some sectors of Early Judaism,[56] Dalman's basic insight[57] has been corroborated by the published research of numerous scholars, in particular F. Hesse, A. S. van der Woude, and M. de Jonge.[58] In his *Theology of the New Testament* Goppelt correctly states the prevailing consensus: "The concept that the promised One must suffer in accord with God's will was foreign to the milieu of Jesus. This was shown graphically by the stubborn resistance of the disciples to the path leading to Jesus' suffering. Directed at this resistance was the severe word against Peter (Mk 8:33 par.): 'Get behind me, Satan' " (vol. 1, p. 191)!

There are many other somewhat reliable Jesus traditions that confront us with Jesus' intentionality and perhaps his self-understanding. Jesus was at times rather offensive; he did apparently tell a dedicated individual that if he wanted to join his group of disciples he must not return home in order to bury his father (Mt 8:21–22; Lk 9:59–60).[59]

This shocking statement flies in the face of many precious traditions in Judaism, including the understanding of the fifth commandment.[60] Each father yearned for a son; the son would carry the name on and be the one who would ensure the father's decent burial (Sir 30:1–6).

Surely this saying of Jesus is reliable and is similar to many others, notably Jesus' charge to the rich young man (Mt 19:16–22; Mk 10:17–22; Lk 18:18–23) and the clarion call that no one who puts his hand to the plow and looks backward is worthy of God's Kingdom (Lk 9:62). Such sayings confront us, in some ways at least, with *Jesus' own self-understanding*.

Jesus also clearly broke the ancient norm for proper behavior as a guest. He frequently scolded a host before the other guests and made it clear that the host had neither acted wisely nor expressed the thoughts of one who was righteous. From many principles and methodologies, these traditions ring with a certain authenticity. If so, we are then confronted with more than a proclamation, even more than the intention of the speaker. We are finally forced to raise the question: who did Jesus really think he was? In many circles it

may be considered an impolite question. But it is one that is immediately grounded not only in the issues of intentionality,[61] but also
those of self-understanding.

Likewise, when we confront Jesus' proclamation of the nearness
of God's rule, or the Kingdom of God, it simply will no longer
suffice to report, as some scholars (including myself) have tended to
do for years, that in the Kingdom of God sayings we are confronted
only with a proclamation and not in any way with a proclaimer.
Surely, as the proclaimer, Jesus is contending also that he will play
a role in that kingdom.

The Jesus of history cannot be compared to the announcer in the
airline terminal who signals the arrival of a plane. There is much
more involvement between Jesus and his message than that simplistic analogy indicates. Bultmann and his school would have rightly
and strenuously objected to such an analogy.

As we have seen by looking at Jesus' symbolic act of choosing
twelve disciples, he had a clear intention to be involved in some way
with helping to establish a *new messianic age.* Some messianic self-
understanding may well have been part of his self-understanding.
This self-perception seems also demanded by the manner in which
he entered Jerusalem, riding on an animal and accepting salutes. He
probably also thought of himself in some way as one who was sent
to Jerusalem, presumably to die, and as the son who is portrayed in
the authentic core of the Parable of the Wicked Tenant Farmers.

The results of our research into various aspects of Early Judaism
help expose the historical setting of the earliest Christological reflections. Christology developed some aspects of Jesus' intentionality
and self-understanding.[62] By disclosing the source of Christology,
namely a minimal core such as Jesus' life and death, we must not
succumb to the unexamined claim that there is an "uninterpreted
given" that will be equally compelling to believer and agnostic. As
John McIntyre stated so brilliantly in his *The Shape of Christology,*
if "it did prove possible conceptually to reach some such minimal
historical core, it would be quite wrong to characterize it as the
given in any sense."[63] And any postulated *core* is not a pure thing-
in-itself, self-evident and obvious to all. It is always an *interpretation,* an *understanding.*

In all instances of description there is interpretation, as mentioned earlier when referring to Merleau-Ponty, Polanyi, and Käsemann. In the case of Christology, as McIntyre shows, "it is impossible even to describe the so-called uninterpreted given, the single common observable for unbeliever and believer alike; for any description involves immediate interpretation of one kind or another" (p. 22).

The proof of this insight is, again, the raw core of Christology: the cross. Historians can prove that the cross is historical, archaeologists may now be able to show us where he was crucified; but they cannot elicit a confession in a crucified Lord. It is true that Mark wants us to think that the centurion who crucified Jesus turned and faced him just after he died and confessed that he was "the Son of God" (Mk 15:39). But the overwhelming evidence is that the crucifixion was an embarrassment, a hindrance to belief in Jesus. Standing before the cross, many laughed and mocked at Jesus. Neither Peter nor Paul was moved to confession by Jesus' crucifixion. The centurion, according to Luke, only acknowledged, it seems to me, that Jesus was an admired man, because he knew how to die. The givenness of the crucifixion scarcely leads to belief in Jesus as Lord.

Behind Christology lies no myth, but an interpreted given, a life lived and died in the first third of the first century C.E., in Galilee and in Judaea. Contemporary scholars are helping us better understand how to comprehend the givens of that particular life, that particular time, and that particular society and place.

NOTES

1. R. Bultmann, *Jesus and the Word,* transl. L. P. Smith and E. H. Lantero (London, 1934; repr. 1958) p. 13.

2. E. Schillebeeckx correctly chides scholars for not attempting to master Early Judaism (a better term than "late" Judaism): "Scholars are so often inclined to make much of the Old Testament, whereas Judaism or late Judaism, particularly that of Jesus' own time, is presented in a distorted fashion. As a result, the relation between Jesus and Judaism is itself distorted; one forgets that the Old Testament was not functioning *per se* or in isolation but in the context of late Jewish piety as that had since been developing." (p. 257) *Jesus: An Experiment in Christology,* transl. H. Hoskins (New York, 1979).

3. These publications are in German; a popular English excerpt is published in J.

Jeremias, *The Prayers of Jesus,* transl. J. Bowden (SBT Second Series 6; London, 1967; repr.: Philadelphia, 1979).

4. P. Birnbaum (transl.), *Daily Prayer Book* (New York, 1977) pp. 73–76; contains Hebrew also.

5. See esp. Jub 1:24 (Deut 14:1–2, Jer 31:9), 1:28, 19:29; 1QH 9.35; Tob 13:4; Sir 51:10 (Heb.); WisSol 2:16–18, 11:10; 14:3; JosAsen 12:14–15; Sifra Lev 20:26; TargYer Lev 22:28.

6. Schillebeeckx, *Jesus,* p. 260. Also, see the important discussion by R. Hamerton-Kelly in *God the Father: Theology and Patriarchy in the Teaching of Jesus* (Overtures to Biblical Theology; Philadelphia, 1979) pp. 52–81.

7. Charlesworth, *The Old Testament Pseudepigrapha and the New Testament,* pp. 91–93.

8. Over 150 years ago that brilliant New Testament scholar who really attempted to write the first life of Jesus, namely D. F. Strauss, wisely rejected Schleiermacher's contention that the twelve somehow shaped itself. He astutely concluded: "There certainly is little doubt that this number was fixed during the life-time of Jesus; for not only does the author of the Acts represent the twelve as so compact a body immediately after the ascension of their master, that they think it incumbent on them to fill up the breach made by the apostasy of Judas by the election of a new member (i. 15 ff.); but the Apostle Paul also notices an appearance of the risen Jesus, specially to *the twelve* (I Cor. xv. 5)." *The Life of Jesus Critically Examined,* transl. G. Eliot, ed. P. C. Hodgson (Philadelphia, 1972; the original appeared in German in 1835; the English translation by Eliot dates from 1892).

9. In coming to this conclusion I realize that I have gone against the grain of much New Testament scholarship. Yet, long after preparing this chapter for a lecture at the University of Edinburgh I learned that Sanders had published a book titled *Jesus and Judaism.* In this book he concludes as "certain or virtually certain" that Jesus called into being "the twelve" (p. 326).

10. M. Dibelius, *Jesus: A Study of the Gospels and an Essay on "The Motive for Social Action in the New Testament,"* transl. C. B. Hedrick and F. C. Grant (the essay was translated by D. M. Barton) (Philadelphia, 1949; repr. London, 1963) p. 88.

11. See the arguments published by H. Conzelmann in his *An Outline of the Theology of the New Testament,* transl. J. Bowden (NTL; London, 1969) pp. 127–37.

12. Goppelt, *Theology of the New Testament,* vol. 1, p. 171.

13. For a discussion of Matthew's editorial alterations, see G. Stanton, "Matthew as a Creative Interpreter of the Sayings of Jesus," in *Das Evangelium und die Evangelien: Vorträge vom Tübinger Symposium 1982,* ed. P. Stuhlmacher (WUNT 28; Tübingen, 1983) 273–87, esp. p. 277. Also see B. M. Nolan, *The Royal Son of God: The Christology of Matthew 1–2 in the Setting of the Gospel* (OBO 23; Göttingen, 1979) pp. 184–89.

14. The best discussion of Lucan editorial alteration is by J. A. Fitzmyer in *The*

Gospel According to Luke: Introduction, Translation, and Notes, 2 vols. (AB 28 and 28a; Garden City, 1981, 1985) pp. 1276–88.

15. Many translators err by assuming the verb, which means "to leave (home) on a journey," or "be away," is connected with *eis chōran makran,* "to a distant region." The meaning may simply be that the landlord has withdrawn to another part of the same country. He could own land in Galilee and live on the coast in Caesarea or in Jerusalem. There is no reason to imagine that the landlord has left Palestine. Furthermore, we must avoid reading a parable—which is a story told usually to make one theological point—as if it were a historical narrative.

16. Bultmann claimed that the Parable of the Wicked Tenant Farmers was "a community product" (that is, it was created by the Church), because it was an allegory ("this is not a parable but an allegory"), with contents typical of the Church, and verses 10 and 11 are inserted by Mark as polemics. Bultmann, *The History of the Synoptic Tradition,* transl. J. Marsh (New York, 1963 [rev. ed.]) p. 177. Verses 10 and 11 are probably additions by Mark. As H. Anderson states, "Whatever the case may be concerning the origin of materials in the parable, there are certainly good grounds for regarding the 'stone-testimony' of verses 10–11 as a secondary addition to the story of verses 1–9" (p. 271). Anderson, *The Gospel of Mark* (New Century Bible; London, 1976).

17. A. Jülicher, *Die Gleichnisreden Jesu,* 2 vols. (Freiburg, Leipzig, Tübingen, 1899 [2d ed.]). A collection of essays on Jülicher's contribution to the study of the parables is edited by W. Harnisch: *Gleichnisse Jesu: Positionen der Auslegung von Adolf Jülicher bis zur Formgeschichte* (Wege der Forschung 366; Darmstadt, 1982).

18. Major insights regarding the meaning of allegory in the sayings of Jesus are made by Crossan and Perrin. See Crossan, *In Parables: The Challenge of the Historical Jesus* (New York, 1973) and Perrin, *Jesus and the Language of the Kingdom: Symbol and Metaphor in New Testament Interpretation* (Philadelphia, 1976) esp. pp. 156–68.

19. M. Black was one of the first scholars to point out that some of Jesus' parables were allegories. See his "The Parables as Allegory," *BJRL* 42 (1960) 273–87.

20. Anderson, *The Gospel of Mark,* p. 270. Also see the comments by Jeremias in *The Parables of Jesus,* transl. S. H. Hooke (NTL; London, 1963 [rev. ed.]) p. 70. According to Jeremias, this parable "exhibits an allegorical character which is unique among the parables of Jesus" (p. 70).

21. See the judicious comments by J. D. G. Dunn in *Jesus and the Spirit: A Study of the Religious and Charismatic Experience of Jesus and the First Christians as Reflected in the New Testament* (Philadelphia, 1975) pp. 34–35.

22. Jülicher concluded as follows: "Earliest Christianity, not Jesus himself, appears to have shaped Mark 12:1–11." Jülicher, *Die Gleichnisreden Jesu,* vol. 2, p. 406. Bultmann, *History of the Synoptic Tradition,* p. 177. W. G. Kümmel, *Promise and Fulfillment: The Eschatological Message of Jesus* (SBT 23; London, 1961 [2d ed.]) p. 83.

23. The vineyard is a symbol for Israel, and therefore for the capital city, Jerusa-

lem. The identification would have been readily apparent to Palestinian Jews versed in the Hebrew scriptures (see Ps 80:9–14 [8–13 in ET]; Isa 5:1–7 [the famous "Song of the Vineyard"], 27:2; Jer 2:21; Hos 10:1; Ezek 19:10–14). The clear allusions to Isa 5:1–2 in Mk 12:1, followed by Mt 21:33, are not found in Luke or the Gospel of Thomas. Clearly, the connection with Isa 5 has been heightened by Mark or another early follower of Jesus. It is an editorial, sermonic expansion. See note 24, which follows.

24. The so-called Garden Tomb, which most pilgrims to Jerusalem today assume (and are blatantly told) is Jesus' tomb, cannot be his tomb. It was unearthed only last century (in 1867) and was claimed to be Jesus' tomb by a military hero, General Charles George Gordon, in 1883. Excavations demonstrate that the tomb cannot even be Herodian. G. Barkay concludes a study of the Garden Tomb with these words: "On the basis of all the evidence, it seems clear that the Garden Tomb burial cave was first hewn in Iron Age II, the First Temple period, the eighth– seventh centuries B.C. It was not again used for burial purposes until the Byzantine period. So it could not have been the tomb in which Jesus was buried" (pp. 56–57). See Barkay, "The Garden Tomb: Was Jesus Buried Here?" *BAR* 12 (1986) 40–57.

25. There may be some reluctance to be firmly convinced that the vineyard represents not only Israel but also Jerusalem. Perhaps quoting Isa 5:7 will help: "Now, the vineyard of Yahweh Sabaoth is the House of Israel, and the people of Judah the plant he cherished" (NJB). Probably "the vineyard" symbolizes Israel, which through the parallelism of Semitic poetry equals "the people of Judah." The reference to "House" would certainly evoke in Early Judaism thoughts about Jerusalem and the Temple, often referred to in early Jewish literature as "the house" (e.g., PssSol 10:7–8).

26. C. H. Dodd, *The Parables of the Kingdom* (London, Glasgow, 1969 [rev. ed.]): "The most difficult of the parables referring directly to the existing situation is that of the Wicked Husbandmen (Mk. xii 1–8). For Jülicher and his followers this is an allegory constructed by the early Church with the death of Jesus in retrospect. I cannot agree. As we shall see, there is reason to think that it has suffered a certain amount of expansion, but the story in its main lines is natural and realistic in every way" (p. 93).

27. Jeremias points out that the parable cannot be attributed to the early followers of Jesus, because they would certainly have included some reference to the resurrection of Jesus; they could not have ended, as the story does, with the abrupt death of the son. "There can be no doubt that in the sending of the son Jesus himself had his own sending in mind. . . ." Jeremias, *Parables of Jesus,* pp. 72–74. Jeremias wisely draws attention to the different interpretations put on the Parable of the Wicked Tenant Farmers in Mark, Matthew, and Luke, and the rabbinic understanding that "Jacob" (who represents the people of Israel) is the "son" in a parable of the wicked tenants preserved in Sifre Deut 32.9, sec. 312. For discussions of this rabbinic parable and its importance for the Parable of the Wicked Tenant Farmers, see Billerbeck, vol. 1, pp. 874–75, which also includes the relevant parallel in LevR 11 (113a). Also see the important discussions in Flusser, *Die*

rabbinischen Gleichnisse und der Gleichniserzähler Jesus. Scholars who use Jeremias' work on the parables should consult the ninth edition of *Die Gleichnisse Jesu* (Göttingen, 1977).

28. Anderson, *The Gospel of Mark,* p. 271: "Possibly, however, there stands behind the Marcan version of the parable a simpler and less embroidered story told originally by Jesus."

29. Dunn, *Jesus and the Spirit,* p. 35: "It thus becomes quite likely that Jesus told this parable referring to his own mission under the allegorical figure of the owner's son. In which case Mark 12.6 testifies to *the unforced way in which Jesus thought of himself as God's son"* (Italics Dunn's).

30. Flusser, *Die rabbinischen Gleichnisse und der Gleichniserzähler Jesus* (Judaica et Christiana 4; Bern, Las Vegas, 1981) p. 123: "So far as I can tell, Jesus speaks about himself only in the Parable of the Wicked Tenant Farmers (Lk 20:9–19 par.)."

31. See m.Taʿan 3:8, y.Taʿan 3:9 [8], b.Taʿan 23a; *Ant* 14.22 (esp.).

32. Archaeologists surveying Yodefat (=Jotapata), the city that Josephus reported he had fortified and where he was captured by the Romans during the early years of the Great Revolt, discovered not only the remains of a defensive wall but also a tower that still lies where it collapsed under the battering by the Romans. See the photograph on p. 49 of *Explor* 3 (1977).

33. See the informed discussion by E. M. Smallwood in *The Jews Under Roman Rule: From Pompey to Diocletian* (SJLA 20; Leiden, 1976) esp. "The War of A.D. 66–70" on pp. 293–330.

34. See M. Wilcox's "Political and Economic Factors" in his "Jesus in the Light of His Jewish Environment," in *ANRW* II 25.1, pp. 131–95.

35. M. Stern writes the following significant report: "We also hear of complaints about the heavy taxes during Herod's rule and of the poverty in the country resulting from his policies *(Ant.* XVII, 308; *War* II, 85–6). It appears that these complaints were largely due to the unequal distribution of taxes, the main burden of which rested on the shoulders of the Jewish farmers and tenants of the king" (p. 97). Stern, "The Reign of Herod," in *The Herodian Period,* ed. M. Avi-Yonah, with Z. Baras (The World History of the Jewish People 1.7; Jerusalem, New Brunswick, N.J., 1975) pp. 71–123. Also see his (similar) comments in "The Reign of Herod and the Herodian Dynasty," in *The Jewish People in the First Century: Historical Geography, Political History, Social, Cultural and Religious Life and Institutions,* ed. S. Safrai and M. Stern, with D. Flusser and W. C. van Unnik (CRINT 1.1; Assen, 1974) pp. 216–307.

36. D. M. Rhoads suggests that Judas the Galilean, one of the leaders of the revolt of 6 C.E., argued for a radical interpretation of the first commandment and apparently "believed that if God's people insisted on God's rule alone in the land, then God would act to establish that rule on their behalf" (p. 49). Such beliefs would have been already harbored in Jesus' time. See Rhoads, *Israel in Revolution: 6–74 C.E.: A Political History Based on the Writings of Josephus* (Philadelphia, 1976).

37. Note the words of Stern: "It is also clear that the taxes themselves did not suffice to balance the total expenditure, and the King needed additional income. This came . . . in the main (from) the former estates of the Hasmonaean royal house which passed naturally to the possession of the new king. These embraced fertile agricultural tracts in . . . the 'Great Plain' (Esdraelon). . . . They were leased to the tenants and were a source of regular income to the royal house." *The Jewish People in the First Century,* p. 260.

38. A. N. Sherwin-White, *Roman Society and Roman Law in the New Testament* (Oxford, 1963) p. 139. H. W. Hoehner, *Herod Antipas: A Contemporary of Jesus Christ* (Grand Rapids, Mich. 1980) p. 70. The chapter on "The Economics of Antipas' Realm" is one of the many excellent sections of this important book. If there was no middle class in Jesus' time, then E. Trocmé's argument that Jesus addressed his words especially to the *"classe moyenne"* needs to be rethought. See Trocmé's important work *Jésus de Nazareth: Vu par les témoins de sa vie* (Bibliothèque Théologique; Paris, 1971) pp. 105–6. An interesting point is made by Trocmé, and he is certainly correct: "The lofty absentee landlords mentioned here and there (Lk 16:1ff; Mk 12:1–9 and par.) remain in the background; they are not the object of any particular criticism" (p. 105).

39. The brilliant linguist T. O. Lambdin emends the Coptic text so that it reads as follows: " 'Perhaps < they > did not recognize < him >.' " *The Nag Hammadi Library in English,* p. 125. This is an interesting, but not necessary, emendation.

40. See Fitzmyer, *The Gospel According to Luke,* p. 1280.

41. Crossan also points out that the "murderous activities prior to the sending of the son (in the Marcan version) render the father's action implausible and unbelievable within the conventions of a realistic narrative. This serves to underline the careful plausibility of the *Thomas* version" (p. 57). Crossan, *Four Other Gospels: Shadows on the Contours of Canon* (New York, 1985).

42. Conzelmann, *Jesus,* transl. J. R. Lord (Philadelphia, 1973), and *An Outline of the Theology of the New Testament,* pp. 127–29.

43. E. Schweizer, *Jesus,* transl. D. E. Green (London, 1971); see esp. pp. 16–17.

44. Dunn correctly argues that "the chief problem (in tracing the Marcan version of this parable back to Jesus) lies in the reference to the 'beloved son' . . . and his death, since the whole reads so much like the early church's representation of salvation-history. However, the simpler version of the parable in the Gospel of Thomas (logion 65) and the absence of *agapēton* [my transliteration] in the variant version of Matthew (21.37) strongly suggest that *an original parable of Jesus has been elaborated to some extent by the early church."* (Italics mine) I concur. See Dunn, *Jesus and the Spirit,* p. 35.

45. Conzelmann's dictum has been influential: "All [*sic*] the passages with the title 'the Son' are thus demonstrably community christology." *An Outline of the Theology of the New Testament,* p. 127. For years I tended to agree with Conzelmann; now, after over two decades of studying the theology of Early Judaism and the history of the shaping of the Jesus traditions from 30 to 70 C.E., I find his conclusion simply impossible.

46. G. Dalman, *Worte Jesu* (Leipzig, 1930 [2d ed.], ET 1902); E. Lohse's article in *TDNT,* vol. 8, pp. 360–62; Goppelt, *Theology of the New Testament,* vol.1, p. 200. It is misleading to argue, as does Lohse, that " 'my son' in Eth. En. [=1En] 105:2 . . . was added later, since it is not in Gr. En [=Gk. of 1En] and has thus to be disregarded." See Lohse's erudite discussion in *TDNT,* vol. 8, p. 361. Only portions of 1En are preserved in Greek; the relegation to Christian addition of what is not extant in Greek errs in missing passages that are added by Greek scribes, and—most important—ascribes to Christian expansion what is not pre-served in Greek, a fatal methodological flaw, as we saw earlier in the chapter on Jesus and the Pseudepigrapha when discussing 1En 37–71. Moreover, in this par-ticular instance, the preserved portions of 1 Enoch jump from 104:13 to 106:1. All of 1En 105 is missing in the Greek, and the Ethiopic texts do not support a suggestion that "son" was added (i.e., "son" is not found to be omitted in the numerous manuscripts now recovered; see *OTP* 1). Obviously no one is so foolish as to suggest that all the intervening verses were added by a Christian. The point is important: the reference to "son" in 1En 105:2 is genuinely Jewish and predates 70 C.E. For the Greek text, see M. Black (ed.), *Apocalypsis Henochi Graece* (PVTG 3; Leiden, 1970).

47. This possibility is now defended by Black; note his translation: "for I and my son (Methuselah) will be united with them for ever in the paths of uprightness in their lives. . . ." Black, *The Book of Enoch or I Enoch: A New English Edition with Commentary and Textual Notes* (SVTP 7; Leiden, 1985) p. 99; also see the important commentary on pp. 318–19.

48. For the Aramaic, an English translation, and an important discussion, see Fitzmyer, "The Contribution of Qumran Aramaic to the Study of the New Testa-ment," *NTS* 20 (1974) 382–407. Also see the judicious insights published by Hengel in *The Son of God,* pp. 44–45.

49. Elsewhere I have tried to draw attention to spiritual giants in Israel's past who have moved from elevated humanity to angelic status (or they have been revealed to have been in fact angels). See my "The Portrayal of the Righteous as an Angel," in *Ideal Figures in Ancient Judaism: Profiles and Paradigms,* ed. J. J. Collins and G. W. E. Nickelsburg (SBL SCS 12; Chico, Calif., 1980) pp. 135–51.

50. Lohse in *TDNT,* vol. 8, p. 361. Goppelt, *Theology of the New Testament,* vol. 1, p. 200.

51. See also *Ta'an.* 25a, according to which God calls Eleazar ben Pedath "my son." According to 3En 1:8, Ishmael ben Elisha is called by God "my beloved son and honored friend."

52. Chr. Burchard, the leading authority on JosAsen, cautions that these refer-ences may refer to Joseph's rank and may denote only that he is "an example of the just man in whom God can be recognized" (*OTP,* vol. 2, p. 192). In the light of the other passages from early Jewish literature now being reviewed, I find it difficult to agree with Burchard; something much more than a just man is being described.

53. For the text and translation, see J. Macdonald (ed. and transl.), *Memar Marqah: The Teaching of Marqah,* 2 vols. (BZAW 84 [and 84 again]; Berlin, 1963).

54. Kümmel, a very fine New Testament scholar, claims that this parable cannot be traced back to Jesus, because "he could not be referring to himself by introducing the 'only' son into the parable, because Judaism did not know the messianic name 'Son of God' . . ." (Promise and Fulfillment, p. 83).

55. I agree with R. E. Brown, a very careful and critical New Testament scholar, when he concludes that "the way in which Jesus speaks of God as Father certainly indicates that he claimed a special relationship to God. But it remains difficult to find in the Synoptic account of the public ministry an incontrovertible proof that he claimed a unique sonship that other men could not share." These are carefully chosen words; they reflect mastery of the complex traditions; yet Brown continues: "However, it may well be here that the quest for absolutely scientific proof causes us to miss the woods for the trees. One could argue for a convergence of probabilities that Jesus did claim to be God's unique Son." Brown, *Jesus, God and Man: Modern Biblical Reflections* (Milwaukee, 1967) p. 91. It is abundantly obvious that pursuing historical research on Jesus cannot be "purely" scientific or historical. We are working with religious traditions; it is essential to allow for the perspectives and methodologies of theology. In *Jesus and Judaism,* Sanders rails against being interested in theology (e.g., p. 2); but eventually he becomes deeply involved in theological reflection (e.g., pp. 123–56).

56. Jeremias, *TDNT,* vol. 5, pp. 686–700.

57. G. H. Dalman concluded that pre-70 Jews did not hold the belief that the Messiah would suffer. See Dalman, *Der leidende und sterbende Messias der Synagoge im ersten nachchristlichen Jahrtausend* (Berlin, 1888). To be sure, A. Wünsche had earlier struggled to find the belief in a suffering Messiah in Early Judaism: *Die Leiden des Messias* (Leipzig, 1870). J. Klausner's classic words are still authoritative: *"In the whole Jewish Messianic literature of the Tannaitic period there is no trace of the 'suffering Messiah.' "* Klausner, *The Messianic Idea in Israel: From Its Beginning to the Completion of the Mishnah,* transl. W. F. Stinespring (London, 1956) p. 405 (italics his). The Tannaitic period runs from 7 to 200 C.E.

58. See their authoritative studies in *TDNT,* vol. 9, pp. 496–527. Also see Charlesworth, "The Concept of the Messiah in the Pseudepigrapha," in *ANRW,* II.19,1, pp. 188–218.

59. This saying of Jesus is the subject of Hengel's masterful *The Charismatic Leader and His Followers,* transl. J. C. G. Greig, ed. J. Riches (Edinburgh, 1981).

60. Ex 20:12, "Honour your father and your mother so that you may live long in the land that Yahweh your God is giving you." (NJB)

61. There are numerous similarities among B. F. Meyer's *The Aims of Jesus* (London, 1979), Sanders' *Jesus and Judaism,* and my *Jesus Within Judaism*; most important, each of us uses the historical critical method, attempts to be self-critical, shuns with great disdain the distortions of Early Judaism and Jesus' place within it caused by many New Testament scholars' antipathy to early Jewish phenomena, affirms the necessity of checking hypotheses as the research proceeds through induction, struggles to place Jesus within what can be known of pre-70 Palestinian Judaism, and tries to understand Jesus' intentionality.

62. This conclusion is now developed in the works of two scholars who represent quite different understandings of the origins of Christianity. See C. F. D. Moule, *The Origin of Christology* (Cambridge, New York, 1977) and W. Marxsen, *The Beginnings of Christology,* transl. P. J. Achtemeier and L. Nieting, with an introduction by J. Reumann (Philadelphia, 1979). Each of these internationally acclaimed scholars rejects the Bultmannian claim of discontinuity between Jesus' proclamation and that of his followers.

Moule argues that we should reject the paradigm of an evolutionary leap in favor of the model of development: "When one asks, Who could Jesus have been, to affect his disciples and their successors in the ways in which he did? the 'evolutionary' type of answer, plausible though it may seem at first, seems less than adequate. More adequate is an answer which finds, from the beginning, a Person of such magnitude that, so far from pious imagination's embroidering and enlarging him, the perennial problem was, rather, how to reach any insight that would come near to fathoming him, or any description that was not pitifully inadequate" (pp. 6–7).

Marxsen hits the nail on the head: "Certainly the content of the preaching appears different at a later time than it does at the beginning, but this difference cannot be expressed by saying that the proclaimer becomes the one proclaimed. Rather, the continuity, which reaches all the way back into the time prior to Easter, exists in the fact that Jesus is always the one who is proclaimed—even when he himself appears as the proclaimer" (pp. 80–81).

I concur with each of these scholars. Incipient Christology begins with Jesus. New Testament theology commences with him. He chose and defined many of the terms that were pregnant for his followers.

63. J. McIntyre, *The Shape of Christology* (London, 1966) p. 22.

CONCLUSION

The search for the historical Jesus over the past two hundred years has been over a rocky road with many dead ends and detours. Numerous scholars have served us well; and it is now obvious that the journey is both possible and necessary. From D. F. Strauss (1835)[1] we learned about the multidimensional nature of myth and the importance of honest methodology. From M. Kähler (1896) we saw that the Gospels are post-Easter confessionals; *but* from P. Benoit (1946)[2], N. A. Dahl (1962),[3] and especially E. Käsemann (1954)[4] we perceived that pre-Easter traditions came to the post-Easter communities and shaped their redactions.

Albert Schweitzer (1906) demonstrated that the lives of Jesus produced during the nineteenth century reflected the ideals and idiosyncratic perspectives of the Victorian authors; hence, from Schweitzer we recognized that any attempt to understand Jesus must allow him to fit within Palestine of the first century.

Few perspectives are so clear as these two: the centrality of Jesus for Western culture, and the pervasive, perpetual, contemporaneous, and perennial need to portray Jesus as one of "us moderns," who embodied our own morality, cosmology, ideology, and theology. As Jaroslav Pelikan rightly emphasizes, "Regardless of what anyone may personally think . . . Jesus of Nazareth has been the dominant figure in the history of Western culture for almost twenty centuries" (p. 1)[5]. Pelikan is entirely correct to continue by claiming, in his recent *Jesus Through the Centuries,* that the intracanonical Gospels are only pictures of the historical Jesus,[6] and that the "most conspicuous feature" of the "history of images of Jesus" is the "kaleidoscopic variety" (p. 2).

Moving away from Schweitzer's exaggerated emphasis on eschatology and confused perception of apocalyptic thought, we are on the right track to stress, with E. Käsemann, G. Bornkamm, H.

Anderson, D. Flusser, M. Hengel, E. P. Sanders, and others, that we can know more of the historical Jesus than the form critics, especially R. Bultmann, had allowed. A search for reliable historical data has been fruitful; it is now clear that some facts have emerged as historical realities.

The search for Jesus' own certain and pure words (*ipsissima verba*) was often ill-conceived. It compromised the axiom that historical research, working with optimum sources and employing the finest methodologies, is capable of producing only probabilities.

To ask New Testament specialists to display with certainty Jesus' authentic words is to be deaf to the phenomenology and sociology of language: what we actually hear our closest friends say is not remembered so that it can be reproduced verbatim. Scholars work with exactitude, which must not be confused with certitude. Not even Einstein claimed such perfection, even though he is the modern paradigm for perspicacity and even though infallibility has become one of the idols of our contemporaries.

Likewise, we must not seek for *un*interpreted sayings of Jesus. If we could logically posit the possibility of discovering such sayings, they would be as lifeless and meaningless as the Hebrew disconnected consonants on ancient papyri in my filing cabinet. If we want *meaning,* we must acknowledge that it must be chosen because of some value, recognized by the one who has chosen it, and interpreted for some particular setting. History is accessible only via tradition. It is meaningful only through interpretation. Since we desire to comprehend the meaning of Jesus' words, we must focus upon the selected and interpreted Jesus traditions.

Finally, I must confess I am vitally interested in Jesus' intentionality, in what he intended to mean to those with whom he was speaking. My concern is not with the sound of his own voice (*ipsissima vox*), but with the meaning he poured forth through the words that appeared when he intended to communicate something to someone.

The question I am asking is, What is Jesus' own purpose in the alleged authentic words; what is he trying to convey to his listeners? This question is promising for future research, because, so articulated, it strives to be sensitive to Jesus' own use of language (the phenomenology of language), to the traditions he inherited (from

Ancient Israel and Early Judaism via documents and oral traditions), and the meaning of both in chaotic pre-70 Palestine (sociology).

Jesus' teaching was characterized by parables, and by the proclamation of the present dawning of God's rule (or the Kingdom of God). These two phenomena, and the Lord's Prayer itself, are deeply Jewish and paralleled abundantly in literature roughly contemporaneous with Jesus.

Certainly N. Perrin, and the large group of scholars who followed him, had the proper intention but the wrong perception of Early Judaism, and—most important—they employed a misleading methodology. By using the principle of discontinuity,[7] Jesus' authentic words were sought by using a net that released all Jesus' sayings that were paralleled either in Judaism or in the Church. By employing this methodology systematically, we begin with a tendency to portray Jesus as a non-Jew and as a leader without followers.

Yet, if two facts are unassailable today, they are Jesus' deep Jewishness—he was a Jew—and his paradigmatic effect on Jews and Gentiles. Furthermore, only those uninformed of recent research, discoveries, and thought will go on stating that Jesus is merely the presupposition of Christianity. Although Bultmann tended in that direction when he wrote his *Theology of the New Testament,*[8] after Käsemann's speech in 1953 he incorporated some of his students' insights, basically rejecting his earlier position.[9]

While it is unsatisfactory (and perhaps a reaction against Bultmann's old position) to claim that Jesus was the founder of the Church, he certainly set in motion the Palestinian Jesus Movement. Without any doubt, the origins of Christology can be traced back to Jesus' own words and the rare glimpses into his own self-understanding. But while words and terms are transported from precross to post-Easter communities, it is obvious that such terms as "covenant," "son," "Son of man," "Abba," "cross," and "Kingdom of God" received considerable development.

As we venture on ahead in Jesus Research, we would do well to listen to the pioneers before us who knew Aramaic, Greek, Coptic, Jewish history, and Jewish documents, but add to their knowledge our increased understanding of that time and our greater sensitivity to the multilayered and complex relationship between tradition and redaction in Christian writings, especially—but never again exclusively—those in the New Testament. There are many leading lights to guide us, and they are far too many to celebrate here, but some of this distinguished generation are P. Benoit, M. Hengel, H. Anderson, D. Flusser, J. Jeremias, T. W. Manson, E. Käsemann, C. H. Dodd, C. F. D. Moule, R. E. Brown, and J. A. Fitzmyer.

What is most significant in recent research on Jesus? The single most important result of "disinterested scientific" historical research is the discovery in our time of data clarifying the life of a man from another time. As the Jew Gaalyah Cornfeld, in *The Historical Jesus* (pp. 11–12), states, "Modern archaeology and scholarship have now established beyond doubt that a man known as Jesus certainly did exist in history and that the criticism of the skeptics was ill founded." This statement is possible because of amazing discoveries, especially those near Qumran, Nag Hammadi, and throughout what is now Israel. It also comes after an unparalleled barrage of charges that Jesus never existed—claims espoused especially by critics in Russia, West Germany, and England.

The monumental discoveries, however, do more than prove the polemists wrong; they help us, indeed compel us, to engage in Jesus Research. Long ago a distinguished and influential New Testament scholar at Yale, Nils Dahl, correctly argued that "we must view Jesus within the context of Palestinian Judaism. Everything which enlarges our knowledge of this environment of Jesus indirectly extends our knowledge of the historical Jesus himself."[10] Pausing long enough to stress the adverb "indirectly," let us continue to cite Dahl:

> It is still not possible to estimate what the textual findings from the Qumran caves [=Dead Sea Scrolls] may yield; in any case they impel us to resume the quest of the historical Jesus. As never before we have the possibility of tracing the trends and ideas which, both positively and negatively, form the presuppositions for his ministry.[11]

We have seen in the preceding pages how the archaeological discoveries are important not only indirectly but also on occasion directly in Jesus Research. The speculations contained in previous books are receiving significant support.[12]

Jesus did exist; and we know more about him than about almost any other Palestinian Jew before 70 C.E. He was a real person who lived in Palestine, growing up in Galilee.

The following aspects of his life are relatively trustworthy. He had some relationship with John the Baptist (who certainly baptized him), began his public ministry in Capernaum, called men and women to follow him (including a special group of twelve), performed healings (probably also exorcisms), was an itinerant preacher who proclaimed the nearness (even presence at times) of God's Kingdom, taught that God should be conceived of as a loving Father (Abba), may have had some messianic self-understanding, probably in some ways considered himself God's son, possibly faced without fear the premonition that he would be murdered (perhaps stoned), but, nevertheless, after an unknown period of public teaching in Galilee moved southward to Jerusalem, where he boldly and successfully demonstrated his disdain for the corruption in the Temple during a public confrontation with the priestly establishment, suffered through the betrayal of Judas and the denial of Peter, and eventually died ignominiously on a cross, outside the western wall of Jerusalem, in the spring of 30 C.E.

Past research and present data contain a tacit demand for a renewed dedication to Jesus Research, a request for an unbiased interconfessional exploration of Jesus and his time, and an appeal to be informed methodologically, textually, and archaeologically. We New Testament scholars work primarily with interrogatives and are faced with elusive probabilities. Because the primary documents do not present us with enough reliable historical information, we cannot write a biography of Jesus. But our primary mandate is to attempt to write a book about Jesus *within* Judaism.

We New Testament scholars are sometimes too preoccupied with the latest discoveries, although they may prove to be our best teachers, or too absorbed by methodologies, even though methods need constant refining. Sometimes we have shirked our ultimate responsibility: to focus colleagues and students on the primary sources, first the texts and then the nonliterary data.

For Christians, who seek to understand the commitment they have made, the poetic vision is becoming more firmly anchored in the Jesus who lived and died in Palestine before 70 C.E. History is part of the essence of Christian theology. The historian of Christian origins and the theologian of the New Testament share the same endeavors, which may bring us closer to the historical reality of Jesus of Nazareth and may awaken us with questions that free us to perceive more clearly the *mysterium Christi.*

EPILOGUE

Polishing these lectures given in May 1985 in New College, the University of Edinburgh, has coincided with—and at times been overwhelmed by—the flood of amazing new discoveries. In the past few months, the following discoveries have stirred debates here in Princeton. Professor Elisha Qimron arrived from Israel and presented a lecture on the discovery of 4QMMT, which may well be a letter written around 150 B.C.E. by the Righteous Teacher, the founder of the Qumran community, to the wicked priest in Jerusalem (Illus. 1). Dr. Gaudat Gabra, director of the Coptic Museum in Cairo, visited with us and showed us a slide lecture on the recovery of the earliest Coptic codex of the Davidic Psalms. And I have been overwhelmed by NBC News, the major newspapers, and National Public Radio for precise information on the oldest Syriac New Testament, which I helped the Zuckerman brothers photograph, in July 1985, using space-age technology, in St. Catherine's Monastery, which is situated at the foot of Mount Moses, in the Sinai, and which was built by order of Justinian in the sixth century (see Illus. 17).

Newton was correct. We all are but like little children, playing on the beach, running in and out among the waves, looking for attractive shells, while the great expanse of the ocean stretches unfathomed before us.

NOTES

1. For bibliographical information on the publications now being referred to, see the Selected and Annotated Bibliography, or the following notes.

2. Benoit correctly argued against some abuses and excessive claims by the form critics: "The concern for history is perhaps not *the* dominant motif which has prompted the formation of the gospel tradition; it is none the less *one* of the motifs, and it merits consideration alongside the other concerns, specifically, apologetics,

polemics, and the others" (p. 48; italics his). Benoit, "Réflexions sur la 'Formge-schichtliche Methode,' " *RB* (1946) 481–512; reprinted in Benoit, *Exégèse et Théol-ogie* (Paris, 1961) vol. 1, pp. 25–61.

3. N. A. Dahl is convinced (contra Bultmann) that "on the whole the church did not produce the traditions about Jesus, but rather reproduced them in a new form" (p. 67). Dahl, "The Problem of the Historical Jesus," in *Kerygma and History*, ed. C. E. Braaten and R. A. Harrisville (Nashville, 1962); it is reprinted in Dahl's *The Crucified Messiah and Other Essays* (Minneapolis, 1974) pp. 48–89.

4. Eschewing the possibility of writing a biography of Jesus, E. Käsemann wisely argues for "the line of the connection and tension between the preaching of Jesus and that of his community. The question of the historical Jesus is, in its legitimate form, the question of the continuity of the Gospel within the discontinuity of the times and within the variation of the kerygma" (p. 46). Käsemann's speech, deliv-ered before Bultmannians on 20 October 1953 in Jugenheim, was published in *ZTK* 51 (1954) 125–53. For the English translation see Käsemann, "The Problem of the Historical Jesus," in *Essays on New Testament Themes*, transl. W. J. Monta-gue (SBT 41; London, 1964) pp. 15–47. For me, one of the most influential sen-tences in the history of biblical research is the following: "History is only accessible to us through tradition and only comprehensible to us through interpretation" (p. 18).

5. J. Pelikan, *Jesus Through the Centuries: His Place in the History of Culture* (New Haven, 1985).

6. In *Jesus Through the Centuries* Pelikan powerfully states where, I am con-vinced, we are today in Jesus Research: "Although there is no warrant for the extreme skepticism of those who maintain that the historical figure of Jesus, if indeed there even was one, is irretrievably lost behind the smoke screen of the preaching of the early Christian church, it is necessary nevertheless to begin with the caution that every later picture of Jesus is in fact not a picture based on an unretouched Gospel original, but a picture of what in the New Testament is al-ready a picture" (p. 10). One of the skeptics is John G. Gager; yet he insightfully saw many of the methodological flaws in the so-called Quest and the "New Quest." See Gager's important "The Gospels and Jesus: Some Doubts About Method," *JR* 54 (1974) 244–71.

7. N. Perrin claimed, "the fundamental criterion for authenticity" was the crite-rion of dissimilarity, which he defined as follows: "the earliest form of a saying we can reach may be regarded as authentic if it can be shown to be dissimilar to characteristic emphases both of ancient Judaism and of the early Church, and this will particularly be the case where Christian tradition oriented towards Judaism can be shown to have modified the saying away from its original emphasis" (p. 39). *Rediscovering the Teaching of Jesus* (NTL; London, 1967).

8. *"The message of Jesus* is a presupposition for the theology of the New Testa-ment rather than a part of that theology itself." Bultmann, *Theology of the New Testament*, vol. 1, p. 3 (italics his).

9. Bultmann, "Allgemeine Wahrheit und christliche Verkündigung," *ZTK* 54

(1957) 244–54. See the excellent and classic discussion of "Bultmann's Shift in Position" by J. M. Robinson in *A New Quest of the Historical Jesus* (SBT 25; London, 1959) pp. 19–22. Also, see Bultmann's "Das Verhältnis der urchristlichen Christusbotschaft zum historischen Jesus," *Sitzungsberichte der Heidelberger Akademie der Wissenschaften, Philosophisch-historische Klasse,* 3. Abhandlung (Heidelberg, 1960) pp. 5–27; reprinted in Bultmann, *Exegetica: Aufsätze zur Erforschung des Neuen Testaments,* ed. E. Dinkler (Tübingen, 1967) pp. 445–69. Bultmann finally argued for some continuity between the Jesus of history and the Christ of the early preaching. In particular he concluded that in Jesus' deed and word the early Christian preaching was already constituted *in nuce.* See now the discussion by H. Leroy, *Jesus: Überlieferung und Deutung* (Erträge der Forschung 95; Darmstadt, 1978).

10. Dahl in *The Crucified Messiah,* pp. 68–69.

11. Ibid., p. 69 (bracketed insertion mine).

12. J. Jervell also stressed that Jesus was a Jew: "he spoke the language of the Jews, he presented his message in the forms understood by Jews. We can therefore gain indirect knowledge about him by studying the Jewish milieu in Palestine in his day. Anything we can learn about daily life in first-century Palestine is important. Knowledge of the religious, social, and political situation is indispensable to a portrayal of Jesus." Jervell, *The Continuing Search for the Historical Jesus,* transl. H. E. Kaasa (Minneapolis, 1965) p. 25. Pelikan's report is not only historically but also contemporaneously true, and must be lifted up for emphasis: "It is obvious— and yet, to judge by much of the history of later centuries, including and especially the twentieth century, it is anything but obvious—that according to the earliest portrayals Jesus was a Jew. Therefore the first attempts to understand and interpret his message took place within the context of Judaism, and it is likewise there that any attempt to understand his place in the history of human culture must begin." (Pelikan, *Jesus Through the Centuries,* p. 11)

Appendix 1

List of Documents in the Old Testament Pseudepigrapha
(With Abbreviations)

ApAb	Apocalypse of Abraham
TAb	Testament of Abraham
ApAdam	Apocalypse of Adam
TAdam	Testament of Adam
LAE	Life of Adam and Eve
Ah	Ahiqar
AnonSam	An Anonymous Samaritan Text
LetAris	Letter of Aristeas
ArisEx	Aristeas the Exegete
Aristob	Aristobulus
Art	Artapanus
2Bar	2 (Syriac Apocalypse of) Baruch
3Bar	3 (Greek Apocalypse of) Baruch
4Bar	4 Baruch
CavTr	Cave of Treasures
ClMal	Cleodemus Malchus
ApDan	Apocalypse of Daniel
Dem	Demetrius
ElMod	Eldad and Modad
ApEl	Apocalypse of Elijah
HebApEl	Hebrew Apocalypse of Elijah
1En	1 (Ethiopic Apocalypse of) Enoch
2En	2 (Slavonic Apocalypse of) Enoch
3En	3 (Hebrew Apocalypse of) Enoch
Eup	Eupolemus

Ps-Eup	Pseudo-Eupolemus
ApocEzek	Apocryphon of Ezekiel
ApEzek	Apocalypse of Ezekiel
EzekTrag	Ezekiel the Tragedian
4Ezra	4 Ezra
GkApEzra	Greek Apocalypse of Ezra
QuesEzra	Questions of Ezra
RevEzra	Revelation of Ezra
VisEzra	Vision of Ezra
HecAb	Hecataeus of Abdera
Ps-Hec	Pseudo-Hecataeus
HelSynPr	Hellenistic Synagogal Prayers
THez	Testament of Hezekiah
FrgsHistWrks	Fragments of Historical Works
TIsaac	Testament of Isaac
AscenIs	Ascension of Isaiah
MartIs	Martyrdom of Isaiah
VisIs	Vision of Isaiah
LadJac	Ladder of Jacob
PrJac	Prayer of Jacob
TJac	Testament of Jacob
JanJam	Jannes and Jambres
TJob	Testament of Job
JosAsen	Joseph and Aseneth
HistJos	History of Joseph
PrJos	Prayer of Joseph
Jub	Jubilees
LAB	*Liber Antiquitatum Biblicarum*
LosTr	The Lost Tribes
3Mac	3 Maccabees
4Mac	4 Maccabees
5Mac	5 Maccabees
PrMan	Prayer of Manasseh
SyrMen	Syriac Menander
ApMos	Apocalypse of Moses
AsMos	Assumption of Moses
PrMos	Prayer of Moses
TMos	Testament of Moses
BkNoah	Book of Noah
Ps-Orph	Pseudo-Orpheus
PJ	*Paraleipomena Jeremiou*

PhEPoet	Philo the Epic Poet
Ps-Philo	Pseudo-Philo
Ps-Phoc	Pseudo-Phocylides
FrgsPoetWrks	Fragments of Poetical Works
LivPro	Lives of the Prophets
HistRech	History of the Rechabites
ApSedr	Apocalypse of Sedrach
TrShem	Treatise of Shem
SibOr	Sibylline Oracles
OdesSol	Odes of Solomon
PssSol	Psalms of Solomon
TSol	Testament of Solomon
5ApocSyrPss	Five Apocryphal Syriac Psalms
Thal	Thallus
Theod	Theodotus
T12P	Testaments of the Twelve Patriarchs
TReu	Testament of Reuben
TSim	Testament of Simeon
TLevi	Testament of Levi
TJud	Testament of Judah
TIss	Testament of Issachar
TZeb	Testament of Zebulun
TDan	Testament of Dan
TNaph	Testament of Naphtali
TGad	Testament of Gad
TAsh	Testament of Asher
TJos	Testament of Joseph
TBenj	Testament of Benjamin
Vita	*Vita Adae et Evae*
ApZeph	Apocalypse of Zephaniah
ApZos	Apocalypse of Zosimus

Appendix 2

List of Documents in
the Apocrypha and Pseudepigrapha
of the New Testament
(With Abbreviations)

AbAng	*Abbaton, Angel of Death*
PsAb	*Pseudo-Abdias, Apostolic Histories of*
	Abgarus (Letters of Christ and Abgarus)
GosAdv	*Gospel of the Adversary of the Law and the Prophets*
AcAn	*Andrew, Acts of*
AcAnMth	*Andrew: Acts of Andrew and Matthias*
AcAnPl	*Andrew: Acts of Andrew and Paul*
	Andrew, Acts of Peter and (Peter: Acts of Peter and Andrew)
	"Andrew, Book of" (*Pseudo-Abdias*)
	Andrew: Discourse of Andrew from Prison (Acts of Andrew)
	Andrew, Fragmentary Story of (Acts of Andrew)
	"Andrew, Martyrdom of" (*Acts of Andrew*)
EpApos	*Apostles, Epistle of the*
MApos	*Apostles, Memoria of*
	"Aristodemus and the Poison Cup" (*Book of John*)
	"The Asses Colt" (*Acts of Thomas*)
	"Atticus and Eugenius" (*Book of John*)
	"The Banishment" (*Book of John*)
AcBarn	*Barnabas, Acts of*
GosBarn	*Barnabas, Gospel of*
	"Bartholomew, Book of" (*Pseudo-Abdias*)

BkBart	*Bartholomew, Book of the Resurrection of Christ by*
GosBart	*Bartholomew, Gospel of* (Questions of Bartholomew)
MartBart	*Bartholomew, Martyrdom of*
	"Book of the Cock" *(Coptic Narratives)*
	"Captain Siphor" *(Acts of Thomas)*
LetCAbg	*Christ and Abgarus, Letters of*
LetCHeav	*Christ, Letter of from Heaven*
PsCl	*Clementines, Pseudo-*
	"Cleobius and Myrte, Prophecies of" *(Acts of Paul)*
CopNar	*Coptic Narratives of the Ministry and Passion*
	Cyril of Jerusalem, Discourse of (Assumption of the Virgin)
	"Daughter of Nicocleides" *(Acts of Philip)*
	Descensus ad Inferos (Acts of Pilate)
	"The Devil and the Woman" *(Acts of Thomas)*
TDom	*Testamentum Domini (Epistle of the Apostles)*
	"The Dragon Slain" *(Acts of Philip)*
	"Drusiana, Episode of" *(Acts of John)*
GosEb	*Ebionites, Gospel of*
GosEg	*Egyptians, Gospel According to the*
BkElch	*Elchasai, Book of*
GosEv	*Eve, Gospel of*
	Evodius, Discourse of (Coptic Lives of the Virgin)
	Evodius, Narrative of (Assumption of the Virgin)
	"Fight with the Beasts at Ephesus" *(Acts of Paul)*
	"Frontina, Episode of" *(Acts of Paul)*
GosGam	*Gamaliel, Gospel of*
	"The Gardener's Daughter" *(Acts of Peter)*
	Gregory of Tours, Miracles by (Acts of Andrew)
GosHeb	*Hebrews, Gospel of the*
	"Hermocrates of Myra, Episode of" *(Acts of Paul)*
	"Hymn of the Soul" *(Acts of Thomas)*
GosInf (Arab)	*Infancy, Arabic Gospel of the*
GosInf (Arm)	*Infancy, Armenian Gospel of the*
GosInf (Lat)	*Infancy, Latin Gospel of the*
	Infantia, Liber de (Pseudo-Matthew)
	"Ireus and Aristarchus" *(Acts of Philip)*
	"Iuzanes, Baptism of" *(Acts of Thomas)*
	"Iuzanes, Son of Misdeus" *(Acts of Thomas)*
AcJas	*James (the Greater), Acts of*
AscJas	*James (the Greater), Ascent of*

	"James (the Greater), Book of" *(Pseudo-Abdias)*
	"James (the Lesser), Book of" *(Pseudo-Abdias)*
ProtJas	*James, Protevangelium of*
AcJn	*John, Acts of*
AcJnPro	*John: Acts of John by Procurus*
ApGJn	*Apocryphal Gospel of John*
BkJn	*John, Book of*
	"John, Book of" *(Pseudo-Abdias)*
	"John, Death of" *(Acts of John)*
	John, Discourse of Concerning Our Lord
	John, Narrative of (Assumption of the Virgin
1RevJn	*John, 1 Revelation of (Apokalypsis tou hagiou Iōannou tou Theologou)*
2RevJn	*John, 2 Revelation of (A Second Greek Apocryphal Apocalypse of John)*
RevJn	*John, 3 Revelation of (The Mysteries of St. John and the Holy Virgin)*
SyrHistJn	*John, Syriac History of*
	John of Thessalonica (Assumption of the Virgin)
JBCycle	*John the Baptist Cycle*
	Joseph of Arimathea *(Passing of Mary)*
JSAr	*Joseph in Arimathea, Narrative of*
	Joseph the Carpenter, Death of (History of Joseph the Carpenter)
HisJsCar	*Joseph the Carpenter, History of*
LetLen	*Lentulus, Letter of*
	"The Leopard and the Kid" *(Acts of Philip)*
	"Lycomedes, Episode of" *(Acts of John)*
AcMk	*Mark, Acts of*
BirMar	*Mary, Birth of*
GosBirMar	*Mary, Gospel of the Birth of*
	Mary, Lament of (cf. *Gospel of Gamaliel)*
PasMar	*Mary, Passing of (= Transitus Mariae* and *Dormitione Mariae)*
QuesMar	*Mary, Questions of*
	"Matthew, Book of" *(Pseudo-Abdias)*
PsMt	*Pseudo-Matthew, Gospel of*
MartMt	*Matthew, Martyrdom of*
	Matthias, Acts of Andrew and
GosTradMth	*Matthias, Gospel and Traditions of*
	Pseudo-Melito, Narrative of (Passing of Mary)

	"Mygdonia, Baptism of" *(Acts of Thomas)*
	"Mygdonia, Wife of Charisius" *(Acts of Thomas)*
GosNaz	*Nazaraeans, Gospel of the*
	"Nerkela and Ireus" *(Acts of Philip)*
GosNic	*Nicodemus, Gospel of (Acts of Pilate)*
	"The Palace in Heaven" *(Acts of Thomas)*
	"Panachares, Episode of" *(Acts of Paul)*
	"Parricide" *(Acts of John)*
	"The Partridge" *(Acts of John)*
AcPl	*Paul, Acts of*
	Paul, Acts of Andrew and (see *Acts of Andrew and Paul)*
GkAcPetPl	*Paul, Greek Acts of Peter and*
ApPl	*Paul, Apocalypse of*
	"Paul, Book of" *(Pseudo-Abdias)*
CorrPlSen	*Paul, Correspondence between Seneca and*
EpAl	*Paul: Epistle of Paul to the Alexandrians*
3Cor	*Paul, Third Epistle to the Corinthians*
EpLao	*Paul: Epistle to the Laodiceans*
MartPl	*Paul, Martyrdom of*
	Paul, Passions of Peter and (see *Passions of Peter and Paul)*
VisPl	*Paul, Vision of*
AcPet	*Peter, Acts of*
AcPet (Slav)	*Peter, (Slavonic) Acts of*
AcPetAn	*Peter, Acts of Andrew and*
ApPet	*Peter, Apocalypse of*
	"Peter, Book of" *(Pseudo-Abdias)*
GosPet	*Peter, Gospel of*
MartPet	*Peter, Martyrdom of*
PassPetPl	*Peter: Passions of Peter and Paul*
PrePet	*Peter, Preaching of*
AcPhil	*Philip, Acts of*
AcPhil (Syr)	*Philip, (Syriac) Acts of*
	"Philip at Athens" *(Acts of Philip)*
	"Philip, Book of" *(Pseudo-Abdias)*
GosPhil	*Philip, Gospel of*
MartPhil	*Philip, Martyrdom of*
	"Philip at Nicatera" *(Acts of Philip)*
	"Philip in Parthia" *(Acts of Philip)*
TransPhil	*Philip, Translation of*

	"Philip and the Widow" *(Acts of Philip)*
AcPil	*Pilate, Acts of*
DPil	*Pilate, Death of* (cf. *Report and Paradosis of Pilate*)
LetPilCl	*Pilate: Letter of Pilate to Claudius*
LetPilHer	*Pilate: Letters of Pilate and Herod*
LetPilTib	*Pilate: Letter of Pilate to Tiberius*
LetTibPil	*Pilate: Letter to Pilate from Tiberius*
RepParPil	*Pilate, Report and Paradosis of*
	"The Sale and the Wedding Feast" *(Acts of Thomas)*
AvSav	*Savior, The Avenging of the*
	"The Serpent" *(Acts of Thomas)*
SibOr	*Sibylline Oracles*
	"Sidon, Episode of" *(Acts of Paul)*
	"Simon and Jude, Book of" *(Pseudo-Abdias)*
	The Six Books (Assumption of the Virgin)
RevSte	*Stephen, Revelation of*
	"Temple of Artemis" *(Acts of John)*
	"Tertia—Wife of Misdeus" *(Acts of Thomas)*
AcThad	*Thaddeus, Acts of*
	"Thecla, Story of" *(Acts of Paul)*
	Theodosius, Discourse of (Assumption of the Virgin)
AcTh	*Thomas, Acts of*
MinAcTh	*Thomas, Minor Acts of*
ApTh	*Thomas, Apocalypse of*
	"Thomas, Book of" *(Pseudo-Abdias)*
ConTh	*Thomas, Consummation of*
GosTh	*Thomas, Gospel of*
InfGosTh	*Thomas, Infancy Gospel of*
	Thomas, Martyrdom of (Acts of Thomas 159–70)
DTimAq	*Timothy and Aquila, The Dialogue of*
EpT	*Titus, Epistle of*
	"Tyre, Episode of" *(Acts of Paul)*
GosTw	*Gospel of the Twelve Apostles (see Gospel of the Ebionites)*
	Vercelli Acts (Acts of Peter)
ApVir	*Virgin, Apocalypse of*
AVir	*Virgin, Assumption of*
CopLivVir	*Virgin, Coptic Lives of*
	Virgin, History of (see Arabic Gospel of the Infancy)

Virgin, Obsequies of (Assumption of the Virgin)
"The Wild Asses" *(Acts of Thomas)*
AcXanPol   *Xanthippe: Acts of Xanthippe and Polyxena*
ApZech   *Zechariah, Apocalypse of*

Appendix 3

List of Documents in the Nag Hammadi Codices
(With Codex and Tractate Numbers)

I,1	The Prayer of the Apostle Paul (+ colophon)
I,2	The Apocryphon of James
I,3	The Gospel of Truth
I,4	The Treatise on Resurrection
I,5	The Tripartite Tractate
II,1	The Apocryphon of John
II,2	The Gospel of Thomas
II,3	The Gospel of Philip
II,4	The Hypostasis of the Archons
II,5	On the Origin of the World
II,6	The Exegesis on the Soul
II,7	The Book of Thomas the Contender (+ colophon)
III,1	The Apocryphon of John
III,2	The (Coptic) Gospel of the Egyptians
III,3	Eugnostos the Blessed
III,4	The Sophia of Jesus Christ
III,5	The Dialogue of the Savior
IV,1	The Apocryphon of John
IV,2	The Gospel of the Egyptians
V,1	Eugnostos the Blessed
V,2	The (Coptic) Apocalypse of Paul
V,3	The First Apocalypse of James
V,4	The Second Apocalypse of James

V,5	The Apocalypse of Adam
VI,1	The (Coptic) Acts of Peter and the Twelve Apostles
VI,2	The Thunder, Perfect Mind
VI,3	Authoritative Teaching
VI,4	The Concept of Our Great Power
VI,5	Plato, Republic 588B–589B
VI,6	The Discourse on the Eighth and Ninth
VI,7	The Prayer of Thanksgiving (+ scribal note)
VI,8	Asclepius 21–29
VII,1	The Paraphrase of Shem
VII,2	The Second Treatise of the Great Seth
VII,3	The (Coptic) Apocalypse of Peter
VII,4	The Teachings of Silvanus (+ colophon)
VII,5	The Three Steles of Seth (+ colophon)
VIII,1	Zostrianos
VIII,2	The Letter of Peter to Philip
IX,1	Melchizedek
IX,2	The Thought of Norea
IX,3	The Testimony of Truth
X,1	Marsanes
XI,1	The Interpretation of Knowledge
XI,2	A Valentinian Exposition
XI,2a	On the Anointing
XI,2b	On Baptism A
XI,2c	On Baptism B
XI,2d	On the Eucharist A
XI,2e	On the Eucharist B
XI,3	Allogenes
XI,4	Hypsiphrone
XII,1	The Sentences of Sextus
XII,2	The Gospel of Truth
XII,3	Fragments
XIII,1	Trimorphic Protennoia
XIII,2	On the Origin of the World

Appendix 4

List of the Dead Sea Scrolls
(With Abbreviations)

QUMRAN RULES

1QS	Rule of the Community
1QSa	Rule of the Congregation
1QSb	Collection of Blessings
CD	The Cairo Damascus Document
5Q13	A Sectarian Rule
4Q181	The Wicked and Holy
4QOrd	Ordinances
4Q513–14	Halakah
4QMMT	The Letter to the Wicked Priest

QUMRAN HYMNS AND PRAYERS

1QH	Thanksgiving Hymns
4QPBless	Patriarchal Blessings
4QPrNab	Prayer of Nabonidus
4QŠirŠabb	Angelic Liturgy
1Q29	Liturgy of Three Tongues of Fire
3QHymn	Hymn of Praise
6QBen	Blessings
4QPssJosh	Psalms of Joshua
6QHym	Hymns
4Q504–6	Psalms
4Q507–9	Prayers for Feasts
4Q510–11	Wisdom Canticles
11QBer	Benediction
4QPsAp	Apocryphal Psalms

4QMorAb	Morning and Evening Prayers
8QHymn	A Hymn
11QPs^a	11Q Apocryphal Psalms
4Q503	Daily Prayers

QUMRAN COMMENTARIES

1QpHab	Habakkuk Pesher
4QpNah	Nahum Pesher
1QpPs68	Psalm 68 Pesher
4QpPs37	Psalm 37 Pesher
4QpPs127	Psalm 127 Pesher
4QTestim	Testimonies
4QFlor	Florilegium
4QpIsa	Isaiah Pesher 1
3QpIsa	Isaiah Pesher 2
4QpHos	Hosea Pesher
1QpMic	Micah Pesher 1
4QpMic	Micah Pesher 2
1QpZeph	Zephaniah Pesher 1
4QpZeph	Zephaniah Pesher 2
4QCatena^a	Catena A
4QCatena^b	Catena B
1QpPs	Psalm Pesher 1
4QpPs^a	Psalm Pesher 2
4QpPs^b	Psalm Pesher 3
4QapLam	Pseudo-Lamentations
4QPsDan ar	Pseudo-Daniel

QUMRAN APOCRYPHAL AND OTHER WORKS

1QM	War Scroll
11QTemple	Temple Scroll
4QPsDan A^a	Apocalypse of Pseudo-Daniel
4QAgesCreat	Ages of Creation
11QMelch	Melchizedek
1QapGen ar	Genesis Apocryphon
1QJN ar	The New Jerusalem
1QDM	Sayings of Moses
1QNoah 2	Noah Apocryphon

1QMyst	Book of the Mysteries
2QapMoses	Moses Apocryphon
2QapDavid	David Apocryphon
2QapProph	Prophetic Apocryphon
5QapMal	Malachi Apocryphon
6QapSam/Kgs	Samuel-Kings Apocryphon
6QProph	Prophetic Text
6QAllegory	Allegory of the Vine
6QapProph	Prophetic Apocryphon
6QApoc ar	Apocalyptic Text
6QPriestProph	Priestly Prophecy
6QCal	Calendar Text
4QAlpha	Alphabetic Document
4Q184	Dame Folly and Lady Wisdom
4Q'Amram	Visions of 'Amram
4Q501	Laments
4QMess ar	Elect of God Text
4QVisSamuel =	
4Q160	Vision of Samuel
4Q176	Tanḥumim
4Q185	A Sapiential Testament
4Q502	Marriage Ritual
4Q512	Purification Ritual
1Q26	A Wisdom Apocryphon
4QṬeharot B, D, etc.	Milkî-ṣedeq and Milkî-reša'

OTHER

3Q15	The Copper Scroll
1QHenGiants	Book of the Giants
4QTestuz ar	An Enochic Type Text
5QToponyms	Toponyms
5QCurses	Curses
11QtgJob	Targum on Job
4Q156	Targum on Leviticus
4Q186	Horoscopes
7Q5–19	Greek Fragments

Appendix 5

A New Trend: Jesus Research
(1980–84)

From 1980 to 1984 no fewer than thirty-eight noteworthy books dedicated to Jesus Research appeared. In 1980 five books were published.

1980

In *Jesus and the Living Past* (Oxford) Archbishop Ramsey tried to show why "historical criticism must be used honestly and rigorously in the study of the biblical writings and the origins of Christianity" (p. 4). In *The Son of Man in the Teachings of Jesus* (Cambridge) A. J. B. Higgins argued against Conzelmann and others who attribute all the Son of Man sayings to the Christian community. Against Vermes, who thinks that this phrase should not be taken as a title, Higgins contends that "Jesus envisaged his mission as destined, in no very distant future, to be validated and vindicated through his being given a status of exaltation in the presence of God, there to fulfill the functions of the 'Son of man' " (p. 126).

In *Jesus and the Transformation of Judaism* (London) John Riches perceptively attempts to show how Jesus strove to present new and penetrating theological truths by employing the terms and language of contemporary Judaism. In *Jesus* (Oxford) Humphrey Carpenter, the biographer of J. R. R. Tolkien, C. S. Lewis, and W. H. Auden, attempts a historical account of Jesus of Nazareth. In *Messiah: Six Lectures on the Ministry of Jesus* (Cambridge, 1980, repr. 1984), which were the 1975–76 Cunningham Lectures at New College, Edinburgh, J. C. O'Neill focused on Jesus' own life and thought and argued, *inter alia,* that John the Baptist did "point to Jesus as the one who was to come" (p. 12), and that Jesus did believe that the Kingdom of God was "a future event when God would establish his reign openly for all to see. . ." (p. 26). For our present purposes it is sufficient to stress that each of these four authors is trying to penetrate the obscure period that *predates Calvary.*

1981

In 1981 seven significant books disclosed a focused attention on Jesus Research. Gerd Theissen's third edition of his study of the social dimensions of the Jesus movement[1] reawakened a need for a full-scale social description of pre-70 Palestinian Judaism and evoked questions of the extent to which the early itinerant Christian prophets controlled and aborted the development of Jesus traditions. The English translation of Martin Hengel's masterpiece on Jesus, titled *The Charismatic Leader and His Followers* (Edinburgh), not only turned scholars' attention to the offensive sentence in Matthew 8:21–22, "let the dead bury their dead," but seemed also to prove that it is exceedingly problematic to attribute to Jesus either the designation "eschatological prophet" or the title "Rabbi." Likewise, he raised the whole issue of what is really meant by being charismatic in pre-70 Galilee and what "discipleship" and "following" denoted at that time. The English translation of Hengel's work justly proves his claim that "enquiry as to the historical Jesus . . . has again come to the fore. . ." (p. 1).

The 1958 Gray Lectures, at Duke University, were published in 1981 by John Marsh. In *Jesus in His Lifetime* (London) Marsh argues forcefully that unless the quest for Jesus is "found viable Christianity will become as inaccessible as Jesus in his lifetime is deemed by some to be" (p. 16). Marsh attempts nothing less than to retell the Jesus story as he, as a scholar, thinks it really happened. Regardless of the varied reviews of the success of his endeavor, Marsh has significantly attempted to flesh out the essence of what he states at the outset:

The fundamental basis of Christianity is not its doctrine, its philosophy, its worship or its morality, whether social or personal, but the story it tells about Jesus in his lifetime; from that story its doctrine, philosophy, worship and morality all derive their distinctive character. (p. 11)

Geza Vermes, in 1973, in his *Jesus the Jew* (London) argued that Jesus should be perceived among the Galilean miracle workers. In 1981, in *The Gospel of Jesus the Jew* (Newcastle-upon-Tyne) Vermes presented his first attempt to discuss the content of the message of Jesus the teacher. Significantly, many of the ideas customarily attributed with great confidence to the Church by New Testament specialists are placed by Vermes firmly within the life and thought of Jesus.

Certainly one of the major contributions in 1981 to Jesus Research is David Flusser's study of Jesus' parables in light of the rabbinic parables.[2] His goal in this first volume of work on Jesus' parables is not to study the redactional alteration of the parables; he is attempting to understand the essence of Jesus' parables and Jesus' own worldview by bringing to the fore a most neglected area of research, namely the investigation of the origin and development of Jewish parables. Shocking to many New Testament scholars is the fact of the vast amount of parables within Judaism. Those critics who had assuredly attributed Jesus' parables to authentic Jesus strata will have to rethink the method that had been employed, namely the principle of dissimilarity: the parables belong to Jesus because they are not paralleled in Early Judaism. The avenue to be explored, from my own vantage point, is the unique personality and predominance of the concept of God's Kingdom reflected in Jesus' parables.

Louis Kretz turns our attention to the humorous and witty sayings of Jesus.[3] Well-worn sayings spring forward with new life under Kretz's pen. For example, "Who has ears" is an entirely humorous way to speak to those who can hear. All humans have ears, and only through them can they hear spoken words. The artistically couched invitation "who has ears" derives directly from Jesus himself, because it is paralleled neither in the Old Testament nor in early Jewish literature (pp. 10–12). Although the book is not steeped in scholarly methods, it is a refreshing contribution to Jesus

Research.[4] The exhortation—"Who has ears let him hear"—is added sometimes by later scribes (Mk 7:16), by Matthew (11:15, contr. Lk 7:16), and by Luke (14:35, contr. Mt 5:13 and Mk 9:49–50). It is clearly early and derives from Jesus, since it is in Mark (4:9, par. Mt 13:9, Lk 8:8), the Gospel of Thomas (8, 21, 24, 63, 65, 96), special Matthew (13:43), and even in Revelation (2:7, 13:9).

In the twentieth century two major attempts to write a theology of the New Testament have been internationally celebrated. The first appeared between the two world wars and was authored by R. Bultmann. As stated earlier in the "Introduction," in *Theology of the New Testament* Bultmann claimed that Jesus' message is only the presupposition for New Testament theology; it is not part of that theology.[5]

The second highly acclaimed *Theology of the New Testament* is by L. Goppelt. It was published in two volumes, in German, in 1975 and 1976. The English translations appeared in 1981 and 1982 and deserve our attention now because of the contents of Volume 1, placarded by the subtitle *The Ministry of Jesus in Its Theological Significance.* It is eventful that half of Goppelt's *Theology of the New Testament* is devoted to an attempt to grasp the theological importance of the historical Jesus.

What is the starting point of New Testament theology? Does Goppelt agree with Bultmann? Goppelt argues wisely that "the interpretive explication of the Easter kerygma constituted the root of New Testament theology."[6] Here Bultmann would agree with Goppelt: the starting point is the forward-looking proclamation of the Easter event. But this interpretation is not at all what Goppelt intends; his next sentences are the following ones:

> Its base, however, was the recounting of the earthly ministry of Jesus. If we desire to represent New Testament theology in keeping with its intrinsic structure, then we must begin with the question of the earthly Jesus.

The break with Bultmann is obvious. He had looked forward from Easter; Goppelt also looked backward into the pre-Easter history. A new era has dawned; Jesus Research is not the sole possession of the historian.

Goppelt grants that the "purely historical" Jesus is both inaccessible and "theologically inconsequential," because of the ambiguous and incomplete nature of the data, and because of the fact that Caiphas and Pilate both knew Jesus and found him "theologically inconsequential." With these penetrating insights and freeing honesty Goppelt commences his own study of the historical Jesus.

The result is a collection of impressive theological reflections, which unfortunately are often accompanied by, though not based upon, unimpressive historical methodologies. Moreover, conclusions do not evolve out of an exegesis of individual passages in the New Testament. Synthesis tends to be posited; it is not contiguous with analysis.

Space will permit only one example.[7] In discussing "The content of faith" (vol. 1, pp. 152–53), Goppelt correctly points out that "faith had its place in the heart of Jesus' ministry" (p. 152) and that Jesus sought "faith as immediate, personal investment." The partial exegesis is unfortunately linked with verses found only in Matthew. Bultmann's argument that faith in Jesus was "faith in Jesus' power to perform miracles" is rejected without discussing the valid insights that led to Bultmann's conclusion. Most important, Goppelt's contention, "Faith had to be the break with the status quo" (p. 152), is in line with the tendency to see Jesus *against* Judaism, or an un-Jewish Jesus. It also betrays the fallacy that there was a normative status quo in Early Judaism, rather than a rich diversity of interpretations of Torah and Temple, as we now know thanks to contemporary research on the Dead Sea Scrolls and the Pseudepigrapha.

Goppelt is well trained in philosophy, referring frequently to Kant and other philosophers, and in classics, drawing attention perceptively to important parallels in Jesus' life in the stories of Romulus, cofounder of Rome, and Apollonius of Tyana (vol. 1, p. 241); but he is often misinformed about Early Judaism. He clearly strives to prove Jesus' superiority over Judaism, which moves him precariously close to anti-Semitism or anti-Judaism. These sad judgments derive from hearing him state repeatedly something like the following: "the full significance of the cleansing of the temple, like the sayings about the temple . . . do show that Jesus actually superseded Judaism at its very roots through a new dimension" (vol. 1, p. 97).

Granted that something uniquely significant for Christians happened during Jesus' life and thought, but that dimension can be exposed only through an intensive and sensitive investigation of Jewish phenomena, and even earlier Israelite traditions. In this particular instance Goppelt is wrong on both counts. Jesus' words against the excesses in the Temple cult are not only easily traced back to the prophets, he is even reported to have quoted the prophets in condemning the pollution of the holy place:

> And he (Jesus) taught, and said to them, "Is it not written (in Isa 56:7), 'My house shall be called a house of prayer for all the nations'? But you have made it a den of robbers (Jer 7:11)." (Mk 11:17)

Likewise, the opposition to the Jerusalem Temple cult is so dynamically embedded in the Dead Sea Scrolls and the Samaritan literature, as well as in other early Jewish literature, that it was one of the forces that shaped the Jewish groups that produced the documents.

The discussion of Goppelt has been more extensive than with the other authors. His influence and his arguments are so significant as to warrant these necessary caveats. New Testament theology and Jesus Research must both be built upon a thorough and appreciative examination of *all* early Jewish phenomena. This one emphasis unites all my work; it alone legitimates the integrity of my research. And it is now slowly being stressed in the leading universities and seminaries throughout the world. It is the heart of the new phase of Jesus Research.

1982

In 1982 six noteworthy books on Jesus appeared. A. E. Harvey, in *Jesus and the Constraints of History* (Philadelphia), persuasively showed how Jesus' message had to be focused so as to accommodate the limitations of his own time. Particularly fecund is the following advance in sensitivity:

> No individual, if he wishes to influence others, is totally free to choose his own style of action and persuasion: he is subject to constraints imposed by the culture in which he finds himself. (p. 6)

While reminiscent of some thoughts already encountered in Riches' discussion, these perceptions are significant advances in Jesus Research.

Volume II.25.1 of the series titled Aufstieg und Niedergang der römischen Welt (The Rise and Fall of the Roman World) was published in 1982 and is devoted to a study of Jesus' life and world. Twelve studies by recognized authorities are featured in 890 pages. A major theme running through these studies is the attempt to see Jesus in terms of our improved understanding of pre-70 Judaism. This theme is precisely the major one I am now endeavoring to develop.

After many attempts by archaeologists to align archaeology with Jesus Research, finally in 1982 a popular book appeared that highlighted the significance of recent archaeological discoveries for Jesus Research. Unfortunately it is marred by misconceptions about the complexity of the gospel tradition. In *The Historical Jesus: A Scholarly View of the Man and His World* (New York, London) Gaalyah Cornfeld shows how archaeological discoveries over the past decade have unexpectedly helped us re-create or at least reimagine the last week or so in the life of Jesus of Nazareth. Particularly poignant are the arguments that the Hanuyoth (the halls for keeping and purchasing animals, especially large ones, for sacrifices) may well have been moved to the south end of the Temple in the year Jesus was crucified, and the articulation and illustration of Coüasnon's contention that we can be relatively certain now where Jesus was crucified. This development and argumentation is discussed in Chapter 5, "The Jesus of History and the Archaeology of Palestine."

David Winter's *The Search for the Real Jesus* (London) is clearly motivated more by theological than historical concerns: "If Jesus did not live, or did not say and do what Christians believe he said and did, then it is hard to see how it [the Christian religion] can survive" (p. 8). Winter is certainly no scholar, and to phrase the "search" in such a fashion is to forfeit the credibility of an honest and disinterested study. Yet he has assessed the new shift in scholarship:

> But the last decade has seen an amazing transformation. Now, the Jesus of history seems more accessible than ever. Like archaeologists swarm-

ing over a prime location, the historians and theologians have turned with gusto to the original documents, parallel historical records and the geographical sites, and at every turn have found a clearer and clearer picture emerging of Jesus of Nazareth. (pp. 8–9)

The shift in scholarship—I must emphasize—is clearer than the picture emerging of Jesus.

The short book titled *In Quest of Jesus: A Guidebook* (Atlanta), by W. Barnes Tatum, an excellent scholar at Greensboro College, is directed to the general reader. Tatum urges his readers not to be creators of biographies or portraits of Jesus that will be personally attractive, but to "undertake a more disciplined quest for the answer" (p. 6) to the question "who was Jesus—really?" He stresses both the theological tendencies in the Gospels and the reliable tradition the evangelists received: "The dynamic but faithful character of this process is recognized" (p. 21). Particularly insightful is the reference to the "backward glance" of the Gospels, which force the reader to ask this question: "What is the relationship between Jesus as portrayed in the Gospels and Jesus as he actually lived and died" (p. 63)? Obviously Tatum strives to show that it is methodologically possible to engage in Jesus Research.

Also in 1982 William R. Farmer, a distinguished and creative New Testament scholar who teaches in the Perkins School of Theology, in Dallas, published his *Jesus and the Gospel: Tradition, Scripture, and Canon* (Philadelphia). Although his aim is to see how Jesus traditions originated and developed, Farmer clearly sides with those of us who are engaged in Jesus Research.

His book "demonstrates how it is possible to get from Jesus, as he is accessible through historical inquiry, to the Gospels, which are Scripture for the church" (p. xiii). Is it possible to say something assuredly and trustworthily about Jesus? His answer is clear:

> We have access to a large body of first-rate historical evidence that is decisive in answering important questions about Jesus, especially questions that are central for Christian faith and life. (p. 21)

Jesus and the Gospel, according to Farmer's own words,

> attempts to explicate Jesus' teachings within the context of an intrinsic development in his public career. To this extent it serves in a modest

way to demonstrate the possibility of a "story of Jesus" acceptable to historians, a story which is not essentially different from the story of Jesus familiar to us from the Gospels. (p. 21)

These words are surprising to those who have been following the work of New Testament scholars since the moratorium on the "Quest of the Historical Jesus" announced in the first decade of this century by Albert Schweitzer in his magnificent and pivotal book whose English title is *The Quest of the Historical Jesus.* Farmer's words would scarcely have been possible in the period from 1910 to 1979. They underscore my point that we are in the beginning of a new phase in the study of the historical Jesus, namely Jesus Research.

1983

In 1983 eight significant books on Jesus appeared. In that year, F. F. Bruce, in *The Hard Sayings of Jesus* (London), the first volume in a new series, The Jesus Library, attempted to explain the meaning of seventy of the most difficult sayings of Jesus. Bruce, a brilliant New Testament scholar heralded throughout the world for his skills, especially with Greek and Roman thought, intends to see Jesus "as he really was" (p. 15). It is refreshing to hear Bruce state that Jesus was "far from an inoffensive person." He gave "offence right and left" (p. 15).

Also in 1983 Paul Badham, of St. David's University College, the son of Leslie Badham, Vicar of Windsor, published the third edition of his father's apologetic work *Verdict on Jesus* (London, 1950, 1971², 1983³), in which emphasis is placed on "the fact that Christianity is based on the personality of a real and vivid historical figure" (p. 6). In the same year appeared two works centered on Jesus' sayings: Bernard B. Scott's *Jesus, Symbol-Maker for the Kingdom* (Philadelphia) and James Breech's *The Silence of Jesus: The Authentic Voice of the Historical Man* (Philadelphia).

Likewise in 1983 Gerald S. Sloyan issued his *Jesus in Focus: A Life in Its Setting* (Mystic, Conn.).[8] The significance of this book lies in its breadth—it includes the question of Jesus' place within the world's great religions—in its wise judgments, and in its attractive use of language. Arrestingly clear and convincing is Sloyan's insight that

> Jesus is exclusively concerned with the coming of God's reign. He is concerned in terms of human readiness for it. . . . He never suffers doubt that the reign of God is a future reality. It will come as surely as bread rises, as grain grows, as a crop matures to be harvested. In this certainty of the future, which for Jesus is at least in its beginnings a present reality, he has a major part. He not only has a vocation to proclaim the divine rule; he has a role in bringing it on. (p. 78)

Elisabeth Schüssler Fiorenza's *In Memory of Her* appeared in 1983, and the controversy surrounding it is related to its subtitle: *A Feminist Theological Reconstruction of Christian Origins.* Her intention is to prove that women, despite their relegated position in the Church and society for practically the entire history of Christianity, should be returned to their rightful position as *equal* partners with men. For her, "return" is the proper word, and rightly so, because she turns the spotlight directly back to Jesus and his earliest followers. One of them is most prominent in the passion narrative: "the unnamed woman who anoints Jesus. . . . The name of the betrayer is remembered, but the name of the faithful disciple is forgotten because she was a woman" (p. xiii). Here critics may veer from the topic at hand and feel that these words are not only feministic but also misanthropic (in the narrow sense). The name of the woman may have been forgotten because, unlike Judas, who was the treasurer of Jesus' group, she had not been a prominent member of that group. Essential for our present purposes is the observation that Schüssler Fiorenza is engaged in Jesus Research.

She is cognizant of the problems involved in historical reconstruction (p. 110) and perceptive of the diversities in Early Judaism (p. 112). Noteworthily insightful and informed is her discussion of Wisdom (Sophia), which includes an erudite review of the conception of Sophia in early Jewish theology, in the development of early Christology, *and in Jesus' own self-understanding:*

> The earliest Palestinian theological remembrances and interpretations of Jesus' life and death understand him as Sophia's messenger and later as Sophia herself. The earliest Christian theology is sophialogy. It was possible to understand Jesus' ministry and death in terms of God-So-

phia, because Jesus probably understood himself as the prophet and child of Sophia. As Sophia's messenger he calls "all who labor hard and are heavy laden" and promises them rest and *shalom*. He proclaims that the discipleship (the "yoke") of Sophia is easy and her load light to bear (Matt 11:28–30). (p. 134)

These are powerful words; to engage critically with them demands a mastery of early Jewish theology, the origins of Christology, and, most of all, the entire enterprise called Jesus Research.

Some critics will claim that Schüssler Fiorenza's work is vitiated by her feminist and other biases. They may tend to dismiss it like Albert B. Cleage's *The Black Messiah* (New York, 1968, 1969), which claimed that "Jesus was a revolutionary black leader, a Zealot, seeking to lead a Black Nation to freedom, so the Black Church must carefully define the nature of the revolution" (p. 4). If so, then it must be admitted that, as Cleage showed, during the racial crises of the late sixties and early seventies, Jesus was not a "whitey" and gave up his life struggling against oppression, so Schüssler Fiorenza *rightly* emphasizes (see the discussion of Witherington's book that appeared in 1984) that "Jewish women entered into the vision and movement of Jesus" (p. 107), and that the "discipleship of equals called forth by Jesus was a *Jewish* discipleship" (p. 107).

Also published in 1983 was Norman Anderson's *The Teaching of Jesus* (Downers Grove, Ill.). It was the second volume in the new series titled The Jesus Library. Anderson is a specialist in Islamic law.

Four observations help put this book into proper perspective. Firstly, analogy between the means of transmitting Jesus' sayings and Muhammad's teachings can be insightful (p. 16), but it can also be misleading (p. 17). Secondly, the discussion is sometimes uninformed of New Testament complexities (p. 17). Thirdly, the criteria for discerning Jesus' authentic sayings are unrefined (p. 21), and faith-centered judgments are sometimes intrusive: "I think, that God would not have left mankind without authoritative written testimony about the supreme revelation of himself in Jesus and the New Covenant he inaugurated" (p. 27)[9]. Even if one grants this perspective, one must acknowledge that our search is to discern the means used by Jesus' followers for hearing, preserving, transmitting, recording, and copying this message. In Jesus Research, a theological truth must be founded upon the rock of free historical inquiry.

Why, then, is Anderson's book singled out for inclusion now? The answer is found in the fourth observation. Anderson helps to demonstrate that the Jesus tradition did not begin decades after the death of Jesus, but that some "of the teaching of Jesus *may* well have been jotted down in his lifetime" (p. 18, italics mine). Anderson rightly affirms that the "assertion that the primitive Church was 'not interested' in details about the life and teaching of Jesus of Nazareth is incredible to any student of Islam" (p. 19). Finally, Anderson wisely calls for a distinction among three phenomena (p. 26): the authentic words of Jesus (*ipsissima verba*), the authentic transliterated sound (*ipsissima vox*), and the authentic intention of Jesus (*ipsissimus sensus*). It must be acknowledged, of course, that Jesus' words were frequently altered through transmission and time.

In 1983 another significant book on Jesus appeared. It is *In Fragments: The Aphorisms of Jesus* (New York, London), by John Dominic Crossan, a highly respected author and professor in the Department of Religious Studies at DePaul University. For over a decade Crossan's focus has been on the historical Jesus. Here he attempts to establish a method for distinguishing between authentic and inauthentic sayings of Jesus.

1984

In 1984 no fewer than twelve books on Jesus, worthy of mentioning, were published. Attempts to understand "Jesus' attitude to authority, both Jewish and Roman," by studying the life of Jesus "in terms of the Jewish nationalistic movements of his day" were edited by Ernst Bammel and C. F. D. Moule in a handsome book titled *Jesus and the Politics of His Day* (Cambridge, New York). Two monographs in the series Wissenschaftliche Untersuchungen zum Neuen Testament centered on the critical reevaluation of the transmission and origin of the Jesus tradition. In a book about Jesus as Teacher[10], Rainer Riesner, a brilliant young scholar in Tübingen, argued that

Jesus spoke with and claimed supreme sovereignty (Hoheitsbewuss-tseins) and appeared as the messianic teacher of wisdom. Most significantly Riesner argues that prior to the crucifixion Jesus had organized around him a "school" (Schülerkreis) of disciples (vorösterlichen Jüngerkreis) that was distinctly unlike that of his contemporaries because of his professed sovereignty and the demanded allegiance to him alone as teacher. If Riesner is correct in positing a school of Jesus that predates Easter, then there is certainly far more continuity and authenticity than any of us dared expect. What is highly significant is the impressive amount of work now being prosecuted on the pre-Easter dimension of the transmission of the Jesus tradition.

In a book on the early Christian teacher,[11] Alfred F. Zimmermann examines the meaning of teacher (*didaskalos*) in the Jesus-centered communities that date from 30 to 70 C.E. He argues that before 50 C.E. there was a Christian Rabbinate (*ein christliches Rabbinat*) which was characterized by the study and teaching of the Jesus tradition. Obviously, both Riesner and Zimmermann tend to agree more with Riesenfeld and Gerhardsson, who argue that the Jesus tradition was shaped by *a college* of Jesus' followers, than with Dibelius and Bultmann, who contended that from the very beginning Jesus' words were treated creatively. It is obvious that more and more scholars are attracted to the earliest decades of the Palestinian Jesus Movement and even to Jesus of Nazareth himself.

A decidedly different approach is brought to Jesus research by George A. Kennedy, who has established himself as one of the foremost authorities on ancient Greek and Roman rhetoric. James Muilenburg and Hans Dieter Betz have examined passages respectively in the Old Testament and Paul employing rhetorical criticism, but now for the first time an authority on this method in antiquity has brought this sensitivity to the New Testament documents. In one chapter of *New Testament Interpretation Through Rhetorical Criticism* (Chapel Hill, London) Kennedy focuses on the rhetoric of Jesus, but he readily admits, "we may initially claim no more than to be examining the rhetoric of the evangelists and seeking to see how the chapters work within an understanding of classical rhetoric" (p. 39). While it is necessary that a historian trained in the proper methodology for discerning authentic Jesus tradition follow up some of Kennedy's pregnant suggestions, the following comments seem valid and insightful:

> When a deliberative orator needs to attract the attention and goodwill of an audience as Jesus does—and in some deliberative situations that is not necessary—he begins with a formal proem. This is conventionally followed by the proposition, proposal, or thesis of the speaker, and then evidence to support his view. Sometimes narrative is required, sometimes related issues are taken up, sometimes a previous speaker is refuted. (p. 48)

The key questions for me do not concern the method of rhetorical criticism—it was a recognized art form in antiquity, is a complement to the historical approach to Christian origins, and demands we attend closely to the texts—my major concern has to do with the confusion between what Jesus said and what the evangelists thought he had said, and with the extent to which Jesus may have known about the techniques and forms of rhetoric. The evangelists portray Jesus as one of the greatest orators in antiquity, and that admission, so articulated, demands intensive investigation of the use and knowledge of rhetoric in first-century Palestine. What are the significant similarities and differences between Jesus and other famous orators, like Demosthenes and Cicero? Once again we see stress placed on the need to study the world in which Jesus actually lived.

Also in 1984 Ben Witherington III issued his *Women in the Ministry of Jesus: A Study of Jesus' Attitudes to Women and Their Roles as Reflected in His Earthly Life* (Cambridge, New York). The subtitle enunciates the piercing view into pre-Easter phenomena. Cognizant of the problems involved and the methods developed for working with the issues raised, Witherington has made a significant contribution to Jesus research. Of particular importance for a better understanding of the social setting of Jesus' ministry are the following comments:

> For a Jewish woman, the possibility of being a disciple of a great teacher, of being a travelling follower of Jesus, of remaining single "for the sake of the Kingdom," or even of being a teacher of the faith to persons other than children, were all opportunities that did not exist prior to her entrance into the community of Jesus. (p. 128)

Witherington's work is significant for historical reasons; it also seems a needed antidote to the feminist approach to the New Testament, which often seems forced and self-serving. For example, Jane Schaberg in her *The Illegitimacy of Jesus: A Feminist Theological Interpretation* argues that Jesus was illegitimate and that the truth of the good news is that God sides with a socially rejected woman and child. And Rosemary R. Ruether in *Womanguides: Reading Toward a Feminist Theology* entertains the possibility of replacing the canon and considering an exodus of women from Christianity primarily because of "the male Christ who fails to represent women." The historian needs to emphasize that one of Jesus' scandalous acts was including women within his itinerant ministry. This broad issue of feminist biblical interpretation occasioned a feature in the April 7 (1985) issue of the New York *Times Book Review* titled "Women, the Bible and Human Nature."

A religious movement emanating from South America which interprets Jesus' beatitude "blessed are the poor" in economic and social terms, namely liberation theology, influenced the study of the historical Jesus in the seventies and eighties, and especially in 1984 in Hugo Echegaray's *The Practice of Jesus* (Maryknoll, N.Y.). Echegaray claimed to focus on "the historical circumstances of his [Jesus'] time" and "to take this theology of poverty-as-solidarity-and-protest and to see it in the light of a more positive, historical approach to Jesus. How—according to the Gospels—did Jesus live poverty" (p. 1)?

An equally influential book on Jesus is Ian Wilson's *Jesus: The Evidence* (London). He wrote this book following an invitation from a London Weekend Television series executive, but Wilson is not responsible for that program. Emphasizing Jesus' "essential Jewishness," he has one objective: "not to write what I personally believe about Jesus, but rather what *anyone* can accept as reasonable and factual about him" (p. 156). In many ways this popular book is impressively erudite, informed, and interesting. The breadth and humanistic learning are impressive.

A survey of recent major contributions to Jesus research begins to close with the recognition of the great significance of this entire issue. It certainly also transcends the limits of intra-Christian dialogue. For example, the interest by Jews in Jesus has occasioned many developments, including Donald A. Hagner's *The Jewish Rec-lamation of Jesus: An Analysis and Critique of the Modern Jewish Study of Jesus* (Grand Rapids, Mich.). This book, which also appeared in 1984, argues that since Vatican II a new wind has been blowing over some hot coals. He offers the opinion that this "new climate of our modern era has brought about something that hitherto was virtually impossible: the constructive study of Jesus by Jewish scholars" (p. 24). Of central interest is not so much the final acceptance of Jesus by Jews, the so-called Heimholung Jesu, but the tendency of the triumphant Church to de-Judaize Jesus. The only means to discern the truly human Jesus and his own Jewishness is to study historically and reflectively the early Jesus traditions and the world of pre-70 Palestinian Judaism.

In 1984 Marcus J. Borg, influenced by arguments that Jesus was "a Jewish holy man and sage, in addition to being a prophet," published *Conflict, Holiness & Politics in the Teachings of Jesus* (New York, Toronto). He rightly perceives that the Jewish resistance to Rome was multiform and centered in the quest for holiness. Jesus' own life was also characterized by a concern for holiness and with struggles against other Jews, including a real conflict with the (not only some of the) Pharisees (pp. 140–41) over the concept of holiness and its actualization in daily life.

The essence of Borg's arguments is articulated in the following summary:

> In particular, Jesus' conflict with the Pharisees centered upon the adequacy of the quest for holiness as a program for Israel's national life; his choice of terrain upon which to do battle concerned those subjects (table fellowship, sabbath, Temple) important to Israel's survival and integral to her quest for holiness; . . . Jesus' ministry concerned what it meant to be Israel in the setting of Israel's conflict with Rome. (pp. 229–30)

These insights are built on impressive methodologies, in particular the importance of social understanding in the study of the origins of Christianity. He rightly sees that the conflict between Jesus and the Pharisees was heightened and given a different explication by the post-70 Christian communities. Characteristic of Borg's position is the claim that Jesus, perceiving that his nation was on a collision course with Rome, struggled "to transform the historical existence of his people so that it embodied the mercy of God, a passionate concern grounded in his own experience of God as the embracing compassionate one" (p. 263).

The year 1984 also saw the appearance of another edition of Herbert Braun's Jesus of Nazareth. The English version, *Jesus of Nazareth: The Man and His Time* (Philadelphia, 1979), was translated by Everett R. Kalin from the 1969 German edition. The new German edition, *Jesus: Der Mann aus Nazareth und seine Zeit* (Tübingen) is almost twice as long; it contains twelve new chapters.

Running through Braun's study of Jesus are the following emphases: 1) As historians we are dealing with Jesus, an actual person in the past. 2) Jesus was a Jew, and he is misunderstood if non-Jewish models are used to portray him; hence, he is neither the Greek or Persian "divine man" *(theîos anēr)* nor a savior figure like Adonis, Hercules, and Osiris. 3) The Gospel of John is of no use in Jesus research. 4) Matthew, Mark, and Luke (the Synoptics) do not contain a reliable account of Jesus' life and ministry. 5) Historical research cannot by its nature produce logical proofs. 6) Having said all this, Braun presents an impressive account of Jesus' life and thought. 7) Jesus did perform healing miracles; and the heart of his message was the proclamation of the end of the world and the appearance of God's reign (the Kingdom of God).

Two other significant books on the historical Jesus appeared in 1984. Manfred Baumotte published a study of the quest for Jesus during the eighteenth, nineteenth, and twentieth centuries.[12] Central to his study is the acknowledgment that research on the Jesus of history became possible when the study of Jesus was emancipated from the traditional Christological dogma of the Church.

In that same year, 1984, David Wenham issued his *The Rediscovery of Jesus' Eschatological Discourse* (Sheffield). This book is not focused on the Jesus of history. It is a "series of individual studies" (p. 14) on the "history of Gospel traditions" (the subtitle) pertaining to Jesus' sayings about the end of this world and time. Wenham is mentioned now because eventually he is forced to recognize the tradition lying behind the edited version of Jesus' words. In fact, the "main conclusion is that there was an elaborate presynoptic form of the eschatological discourse (or at least of major parts of the discourse), and that this was known and used independently by Matthew, Mark and Luke" (p. 365).

One concluding comment is indicative of the burgeoning fecundity of Jesus research. Although Wenham does not delve into speculations regarding the nature of the presynoptic traditions, he does admit the possibility "that there was a semiofficial form of the apostolic teaching known and taught in Jerusalem at a very early date" (p. 368). As with the arguments by Riesner and Zimmermann, in particular, we must admit that scholars have tended to caricature and demean some of the valid insights by H. Riesenfeld and B. Gerhardsson. I am convinced this *new* dimension to New Testament research, indeed the appearance of "Jesus research," is not caused by a conservative, or fundamentalist, turn in scholarship. It is caused by other factors, and these have been discussed throughout *Jesus Within Judaism.* Suffice it now to stress that Jesus research is emphatically linked with an improved view of the origins of the Gospels within first-century Judaism, thanks to pioneering explorations of the Pseudepigrapha, the Dead Sea Scrolls, the Nag Hammadi Codices, Josephus, and Palestinian archaeology.

Our review was to cover the period from 1980 to 1984. But 1985 began with the appearance of a major book contributing to our understanding of the historical Jesus. It is E. P. Sanders' *Jesus and Judaism* (London and Philadelphia). Having already eschewed the possibility of recovering any of Jesus' authentic words,[13] Sanders, by centering on facts about Jesus, now attempts to answer apparently one major question. Since Early Judaism was characteristically a religion of love and grace, how can one understand the fact of Jesus' crucifixion? His purpose in writing is twofold, to understand both Jesus' intent and his relationship to fellow Jews.

While there are major points of disagreement between us, suffice it for the present to state only three points of agreement. There is far more reliable material to assess the relationship between Jesus and Early Judaism than many critics have been willing to admit. The Sadducees are the real villains behind Jesus' arrest and death. And Jesus' own authoritative claims paved the way for conflict and possible martyrdom.

One major area in which we differ is that while I am focusing upon an understanding of Jesus within Judaism, I am also interested in the development of earliest Christologies. In passing from a glimpse of contemporary research, it is significant to observe that Sanders, who once thought that the quest for Jesus was and should be dead (we both prefer the term "Jesus research"), is *rightly* awakened and impressed by "the persuasiveness and vitality" of recent research on the Jesus of history. Sanders wisely perceives a shift in the winds: "The dominant view today seems to be that we can know pretty well what Jesus was out to accomplish, that we can know a lot about what he said, and that those two things make sense within the world of first-century Judaism" (p. 2). This insight is so significant that, although we quoted it in our "Introduction," it bears reemphasizing here.

It now seems possible to leave a far too rapid review of contemporary Jesus research with the point initially intended. A major new trend in recent study is the intensive investigation of what can be known reliably about Jesus and his world. The renewed Jesus research is placarded by two new series, one already mentioned and edited by John Riches, and the other titled The Jesus Library and edited by Michael Green. I am somewhat surprised to discover, both from working in my own study and from lecturing throughout the United States and the Continent, how clear it is now becoming that the Bultmannian moratorium on Jesus research was unperceptive and invalid.

The renewed interest in Jesus research by scholars is paralleled in contemporary society. Among some Jewish scholars there has developed a sensitivity to him. The Mary Magdalene song from *Jesus Christ Superstar* is heard in many places throughout the world. The gospel hymn "Amazing Grace" is revised, elevated to the top of the pop charts, and heard being whistled by countless numbers, including many non-Christians.

NOTES

1. G. Theissen, *Soziologie der Jesusbewegung: Ein Beitrag zur Entstehungsgeschichte des Urchristentums* (Theologische Existenz Heute 194; Munich, 1981, 3rd ed.).

2. D. Flusser, *Die rabbinischen Gleichnisse und der Gleichniserzähler Jesus: 1. Teil; Das Wesen der Gleichnisse* (Judaica et Christiana 4: Bern, Las Vegas, 1981).

3. L. Kretz, *Witz, Humor und Ironie bei Jesus* (Olten, 1981, 1982, 2d ed.).

4. Also see J. Jónsson, *Humour and Irony in the New Testament: Illuminated by Parallels in Talmud and Midrash* (BZRG 28; Leiden, 1985 [first published in 1965]). Noteworthy are some words in Krister Stendahl's Foreword: "But Jakob Jónsson helps us toward rediscovering that twinkle in Jesus' eye, that most effective device for puncturing the pomposity of those grave authority figures—from Jesus' contemporaries to our own—who claim more precision in their definitions than is good for theology."

5. R. Bultmann, *Theology of the New Testament,* 2 vols., transl. K. Grobel (New York, 1951, 1955) vol. 1, p. 3 (Bultmann's italics): *"The message of Jesus* is a presupposition for the theology of the New Testament rather than a part of that theology itself."

6. L. Goppelt, *Theology of the New Testament,* 2 vols., transl. J. E. Alsup, ed. J. Roloff (Grand Rapids, Mich., 1981 [repr. 1983], 1982) p. 7.

7. Also see the Introduction to *Jesus Within Judaism.*

8. I can imagine that some of my revered New Testament colleagues will criticize me for including in this review books on Jesus not written by members of the guild. The decision was intentional. The guild has been too preoccupied with peer pressure and the desire to be heard by fellow New Testament specialists. We must communicate to interested members of our culture, and also recognize that they are reading some pretty good books not written by New Testament specialists and not burdened by jargon.

9. The volumes in Michael Green's The Jesus Library unfortunately intermittently move from solid scholarship into Christian catechetical concerns; and that is the intention of the editor, who is rector of St. Aldate's, in Oxford. Other works in the series are S. Neill's *The Supremacy of Jesus*, M. Green's *The Empty Cross of Jesus*, and M. Griffiths' *The Example of Jesus.*

10. R. Riesner, *Jesus als Lehrer* (WUNT 2. Reihe, 7; Tübingen, 1984²).

11. A. F. Zimmermann, *Die urchristlichen Lehrer* (WUNT 2. Reihe, 12; Tübingen, 1984).

12. M. Baumotte (ed.), *Die Frage nach dem historischen Jesus: Texte aus drei Jahrhunderten* (Gütersloh, 1984).

13. E. P. Sanders, "The Search for Bedrock in the Jesus Material," *Proceedings of the Irish Biblical Association* 7 (1983) 74–86. Emphatically contrary to my own understanding, and even to many sections of his book, is the following sharp statement: "We cannot obtain enough reliable sayings by Jesus to allow us to put them together, and on the basis of them to present a portrayal of him which is convincing and which accounts for his place in history" (p. 78). In one paragraph Sanders is insightful; in the next he appears myopic. Two examples of each (in this article) are the following: Sanders brilliantly demonstrates that Bultmann erroneously thought that the Gospels had been transmitted like folk tradition. The Gospels are not like fairy tales, and there are *no* general laws governing the transmission of folk or oral tradition. Sanders, however, believes (his verb) that Jesus' message that "God's love was extended to sinners" would not have been offensive

in first-century Judaism (p. 78). This statement needs to be carefully argued. There was no "normative Judaism" in the first century. In first-century Palestine many— and not just some—Jews would have been offended by Jesus' inclusion of sinners, such as prostitutes and tax collectors, into his group. Certainly the pious Jews still living near Qumran, the Sadducees and other priests administering sacrifices in the Temple cult, the zealous ones (the forerunners of the Zealots), the strict Pharisees and even the conservative "people of the land" would have found Jesus' message of God's call to sinners to be offensive. Jesus attempted to shatter the boundaries that had been constructed by many Jewish groups to separate the pure from the impure and the righteous from the unrighteous. His movement attacked a concept of purification that was elevated after Herod increased the grandeur of the Temple.

ABBREVIATIONS

I. Modern Publications

AAR	American Academy of Religion
AcOr	*Acta orientalia*
AGAJU	Arbeiten zur Geschichte des antiken Judentums und des Urchristentums
ALBO	Analecta lovaniensia biblica et orientalia
ALGHJ	Arbeiten zur Literatur und Geschichte des hellenistischen Judentums
ALUOS	*Annual of the Leeds University Oriental Society*
ANF	Roberts, A., and J. Donaldson, eds. *The Ante-Nicene Fathers: Translations of the Writings of the Fathers Down to A.D. 325.* 10 vols. Edinburgh, 1868–72; rev. and repr. Grand Rapids, Mich., 1950–52.
ANRW	Haase, W., and H. Temporini, eds. *Aufstieg und Niedergang der römischen Welt.* Berlin, New York, 1979– .
ANT	James, M. R. *The Apocryphal New Testament.* Oxford, 1924; corrected ed., 1955.
APAT	Kautzsch, E., *Die Apokryphen und Pseudepigraphen des Alten Testaments.* 2 vols. Tübingen, 1900.
Apocrifi del NT	Erbetta, M. *Gli Apocrifi del Nuovo Testamento.* 3 vols. Turin, 1966–69.
APOT	Charles, R. H., ed. *The Apocrypha and Pseudepigrapha of the Old Testament in English.* 2 vols. Oxford, 1913.
ArOr	*Archiv orientální*
ASOR	American Schools of Oriental Research
ASTI	*Annual of the Swedish Theological Institute*
ATANT	Abhandlungen zur Theologie des Alten und Neuen Testaments

ATLA	The American Theological Library Association
ATR	*Anglican Theological Review*
AusBR	*Australian Biblical Review*
BA	*The Biblical Archeologist*
BAR	*Biblical Archaeology Review*
BASOR	*Bulletin of the American Schools of Oriental Research*
BEvT	Beiträge zur evangelischen Theologie
BHH	Reicke, B., and L. Rost, eds. *Biblisch-historisches Handwörterbuch.* 3 vols. Göttingen, 1962–66.
BHM	Jellinek, A. *Bet ha-Midrasch.* 2 vols. Jerusalem, 1967[3].
Bib	*Biblica*
Biblia Sacra	Weber, R., et al., eds. *Biblia Sacra: Iuxta Vulgatam Versionem.* 2 vols. Stuttgart, 1969.
Bibliographie	Delling, G. *Bibliographie zur jüdisch-hellenistischen und intertestamentarischen Literatur 1900–1970.* TU 106; Berlin, 1975.
BibSt	Biblische Studien
BIFAO	Bulletin de l'institut français d'archéologie orientale
BiKi	*Bibel und Kirche*
Billerbeck	H. L. Strack and P. Billerbeck. *Kommentar zum Neuen Testament aus Talmud und Midrasch.* 6 vols. Munich, 1926–28; 5th ed. of 1979 (ed. J. Jeremias with K. Adolph); 8th ed., of 1982.
BIOSCS	*Bulletin of the International Organization for Septuagint and Cognate Studies*
BJRL, BJRULM	*Bulletin of the John Rylands Library, Bulletin of the John Rylands University Library of Manchester*
BJS	Brown Judaic Studies
BLE	*Bulletin de littérature ecclésiastique*
BO	*Bibliotheca orientalis*
BSOAS	*Bulletin of the School of Oriental and African Studies*
BZ	*Biblische Zeitschrift*
BZAW	Beihefte zur Zeitschrift für die alttestamentliche Wissenschaft
BZNW	Beihefte zur Zeitschrift für die neutestamentliche

	Wissenschaft und die Kunde der älteren Kirche
BZRG	Beihefte der Zeitschrift für Religions- und Geistesgeschichte
CB	*Cultura biblica*
CBQ	*Catholic Biblical Quarterly*
CCSL	Corpus Christianorum. Series Latina.
CETEDOC	Centre de traitement électronique des documents
CG	Cairensis Gnosticus
CRINT	Compendia Rerum Iudaicarum ad Novum Testamentum
CSCO	Corpus scriptorum christianorum orientalium
CTM	*Concordia Theological Monthly*
DB	Vigouroux, F., ed. Dictionnaire de la Bible. 5 vols. Paris, 1895–1912.
DBSup	Pirot, L., et al., eds. Dictionnaire de la Bible, Suppléments. Paris, 1928– .
DJD	Discoveries in the Judaean Desert
DTT	*Dansk teologisk Tidsskrift*
EncyJud	Roth, C., et al., eds. Encyclopaedia Judaica. 16 vols. New York, 1971–72.
EOS	*Eos. Commentarii Societatis Philologae Polonorum*
ETL	*Ephemerides theologicae lovanienses*
EvT	*Evangelische Theologie*
ExpT	*Expository Times*
Falasha Anthology	Leslau, W. *Falasha Anthology.* Yale Judaica Series 6; New Haven, 1951.
FGH	Jacoby, F., ed. *Fragmente der griechischen Historiker.* 3 vols. Leiden, 1923– .
FRLANT	Forschungen zur Religion und Literatur des Alten und Neuen Testaments
GamPseud	Hammershaimb, E., et al., eds. *De Gammeltestamentlige Pseudepigrapher.* 2 vols. Copenhagen, 1953–76.
GCS	Die griechischen christlichen Schriftsteller der ersten drei Jahrhunderte
GDBL	Nielsen, E., and B. Noack, eds. *Gads Danske Bibel Leksikon.* 2 vols. Copenhagen, 1965–66.
Geschichte [Baumstark]	Baumstark, A. *Geschichte der syrischen Literatur*

	mit Ausschluss der christlichpalästinensischen Texte. Bonn, 1922.
Geschichte [Graf]	Graf, G. "Apokryphen und Pseudepigraphen," *Geschichte der christlichen arabischen Literatur.* Studi e Testi 118; Vatican, 1944; Vol. 1, pp. 196–297.
GLAJJ	Stern, M., ed. *Greek and Latin Authors on Jews and Judaism.* Vol. 1: *From Herodotus to Plutarch.* Jerusalem, 1974.
GNT	Grundrisse zum Neuen Testament
Gottesvolk	Janssen, E., ed. *Das Gottesvolk und seine Geschichte: Geschichtsbild und Selbstverständnis im palästinensischen Schrifttum von Jesus Sirach bis Jehuda ha-Nasi.* Neukirchen-Vluyn, 1971.
GTA	Göttinger Theologische Arbeiten
Gunkel Festschrift	Schmidt, H., ed. *Eucharistērion: Studien zur Religion des Alten und Neuen Testaments.* H. Gunkel Festschrift. Part 2. *Zur Religion und Literatur des Neuen Testaments.* Göttingen, 1923.
HAW	Handbuch der Altertumswissenschaft
HeyJ	*Heythrop Journal*
History [Schürer]	Schürer, E. *A History of the Jewish People in the Time of Jesus Christ.* 5 vols., plus index, trans. J. MacPherson et al. Edinburgh, 1897–98.
HNT	Handbuch zum Neuen Testament
HSW	Hennecke, E., W. Schneemelcher, and R. McL. Wilson, eds. *New Testament Apocrypha.* 2 vols. London, 1963–65.
HTKNT	Herders theologischer Kommentar zum Neuen Testament
HTR	*Harvard Theological Review*
HTS	Harvard Theological Studies
HUCA	*Hebrew Union College Annual*
ICASALS	International Center for Arid and Semi-Arid Land Studies
ICC	International Critical Commentary
IDB	Buttrick, G. A., et al., eds. The Interpreter's Dictionary of the Bible. 4 vols. New York, 1962.

IDBS	Crim, K., et al., eds. The Interpreter's Dictionary of the Bible, Supplementary Volume. Nashville, Tenn., 1976.
IEJ	*Israel Exploration Journal*
Int	*Interpretation*
Introduction	Denis, A.-M. *Introduction aux pseudépigraphes grecs d'Ancien Testament.* SVTP 1; Leiden, 1970.
ITQ	*Irish Theological Quarterly*
JA	*Journal asiatique*
JAAR	*Journal of the American Academy of Religion*
JAC	*Jahrbuch für Antike und Christentum*
JAL	Jewish Apocryphal Literature
JAOS	*Journal of the American Oriental Society*
JBC	Brown, R. E., J. A. Fitzmyer, and R. E. Murphy, eds. *The Jerome Biblical Commentary,* Englewood Cliffs, N.J., 1968.
JBL	*Journal of Biblical Literature*
JBLMS	Journal of Biblical Literature Monograph Series
JE	Singer, I., et al., eds. The Jewish Encyclopedia. 12 vols. New York, London, 1901–6.
Jewish Symbols	Goodenough, E. R. *Jewish Symbols in the Greco-Roman Period.* 13 vols. New York, 1953–68.
JJS	*Journal of Jewish Studies*
JNES	*Journal of Near Eastern Studies*
JPOS	*Journal of the Palestine Oriental Society*
JQR	*Jewish Quarterly Review*
JR	*Journal of Religion*
JRAS	*Journal of the Royal Asiatic Society*
JSHRZ	Kümmel, W. G., et al. *Jüdische Schriften aus hellenistisch-römischer Zeit.* Gütersloh, 1973–
JSJ	*Journal for the Study of Judaism*
JSS	*Journal of Semitic Studies*
JTC	*Journal of Theology and the Church*
JTS	*Journal of Theological Studies*
Judaic Tradition	Glatzer, N. N. *The Judaic Tradition: Texts Edited and Introduced.* Boston, 1969.
KS	*Kirjath Sepher*
Lampe	Lampe, G. W. H., ed. *A Patristic Greek Lexicon,* Oxford, 1961–68.

LAOT	James, M. R. *The Lost Apocrypha of the Old Testament.* TED; London, New York, 1920.
LCL	Loeb Classical Library
Legends	Ginzberg, L. *The Legends of the Jews.* 7 vols., trans. H. Szold. Philadelphia, 1909–38; repr. 1937–66.
LSJM	Liddell, H. G., and R. Scott. A Greek-English Lexicon, rev. H. S. Jones and R. McKenzie. Oxford, 1940.
LTK²	Buchberger, M., J. Höfer, and K. Rahner, eds. Lexikon für Theologie und Kirche. 11 vols. Freiburg, 1957–67.²
LUOS MS	Leeds University Oriental Society Monograph Series
MBPAR	Münchener Beiträge zur Papyrusforschung und Antiken Rechtsgeschichte
McCQ	*McCormick Quarterly*
MGWJ	*Monatsschrift für Geschichte und Wissenschaft des Judentums*
Missionsliteratur	Dalbert, P. *Die Theologie der hellenistisch-jüdischen Missionsliteratur unter Ausschluss von Philo und Josephus.* Hamburg-Volksdort, 1954.
NCE	McDonald, W. J., et al., eds. New Catholic Encyclopedia. 15 vols. New York, 1967– .
NEB	New English Bible
NHC	Nag Hammadi Codex
NHL	Nag Hammadi Library
NHS	Nag Hammadi Studies
NJB	New Jerusalem Bible
NovT	*Novum Testamentum*
NovTSup	*Novum Testamentum,* Supplements
NS	Neukirchener Studienbücher
NTL	New Testament Library
NTS	*New Testament Studies*
NTTS	New Testament Tools and Studies
OBO	Orbis Biblicus et Orientalis
OCA	*Orientalia Christiana Analeta*
Or	*Orientalia*
OrChr	*Orientalia Christiana*
OrSyr	*L'Orient syrien*
OTP	*Old Testament Pseudepigrapha,* ed. J. H.

	Charlesworth. 2 vols. Garden City, N.Y., 1983–85.
OTS	Oudtestamentische Studiën
Pauly-Wissowa	Wissowa, G., et al., eds. *Paulys Real-Encyclopädie der classischen Altertumswissenschaft,* neue Bearbeitung. Stuttgart, Munich, 1893–1972.
PCB	Peake, A. S., M. Black, and H. H. Rowley, eds. *Peake's Commentary on the Bible,* London, New York, 1962.
PEQ	*Palestine Exploration Quarterly*
PETSE	Papers of the Estonian Theological Society in Exile
Peshitta	*The Old Testament in Syriac According to the Peshitta Version,* Leiden, 1966– .
PG	Patrologiae graecae, ed. J. Migne
PIOL	Publications de l'institut orientaliste de Louvain
PL	Patrologiae latinae, ed. J. Migne
PVTG	Pseudepigrapha Veteris Testamenti Graece
RAC	Klauser, T., et al., eds. *Reallexikon für Antike und Christentum: Sachwörterbuch zur Auseinandersetzung des Christentums mit der antiken Welt.* Stuttgart, 1950– .
RB	*Revue biblique*
RBen	*Revue bénédictine*
RechBib	Recherches bibliques
REJ	*Revue des études juives*
RESl	*Revue des études slaves*
RevSem	*Revue sémitique*
RGG³	Galling, K., et al., eds. *Die Religion in Geschichte und Gegenwart.* 6 vols. plus index. Tübingen, 1957–65.³
RHPR	*Revue d'histoire et de philosophie religieuse*
RHR	*Revue de l'histoire des religions*
Riessler	Riessler, P. *Altjüdisches Schrifttum ausserhalb der Bibel.* Heidelberg, 1927; repr. 1966.
RivB	*Rivista biblica*
ROC	*Revue de l'orient chrétien*
RQ	*Revue de Qumran*
RSR	*Recherches de science religieuse*
RTP	*Revue de théologie et de philosophie*

Sacramentum Mundi	Rahner, K., et al., eds. *Sacramentum Mundi: An Encyclopedia of Theology.* 6 vols. New York, 1968–70.
SBFLA	*Studii biblici franciscani liber annuus*
SBL	Society of Biblical Literature
SBLDS	Society of Biblical Literature Dissertation Series
SBLMS	Society of Biblical Literature Monograph Series
SBL 1971 Seminar Papers	*The Society of Biblical Literature One Hundred Seventh Annual Meeting Seminar Papers—28–31 October 1971, Regency Hyatt House—Atlanta, Ga.* 2 vols. Missoula, Mont., 1971.
SBL SBS	Society of Biblical Literature Sources for Biblical Study
SBT	Studies in Biblical Theology
SC	Sources chétiennes
ScEs	*Science et esprit*
SCS	Septuagint and Cognate Studies
SEÅ	*Svensk exegetisk Årsbok*
Sem	Semitica
SHR	Studies in the History of Religions
SJLA	Studies in Judaism in Late Antiquity
SJT	*Scottish Journal of Theology*
SNTS MS	*Studiorum Novi Testamenti Societas* Monograph Series
SPB	Studia postbiblica
ST	*Studia Theologica*
StANT	Studien zum Alten und Neuen Testament
STDJ	Studies on the Texts of the Desert of Judah
Studien	Eltester, W., ed. *Studien zu den Testamenten der zwölf Patriarchen.* BZNW 36; Berlin, 1969.
SUNT	Studien zur Umwelt des Neuen Testaments
Sup *Numen*	Supplements to *Numen*
SVTP	Studia in Veteris Testamenti Pseudepigrapha
T&S	Texts and Studies
T&T	Texts and Translations
TBT	*The Bible Today*
TDNT	Kittel, G., ed. *Theological Dictionary of the New Testament.* 10 vols., trans. G. W. Bromiley. Grand Rapids, Mich., London, 1964–76.
TED	Translations of Early Documents

ThĒE	Martinos, A., ed. *Thrēskeutikē kai Ēthikē Enkuklopaideia.* 12 vols. Athens, 1962–68.
ThRu	*Theologische Rundschau*
TLZ	*Theologische Literaturzeitung*
TQ	*Theologische Quartalschrift*
TU	*Texte und Untersuchungen*
TWAT	Botterweck, G. J., and H. Ringgren, eds. *Theologisches Wörterbuch zum Alten Testament.* Stuttgart, 1970– .
TZ	*Theologische Zeitschrift*
USQR	*Union Seminary Quarterly Review*
VC	*Vigiliae christianae*
VT	*Vetus Testamentum*
WUNT	Wissenschaftliche Untersuchungen zum Neuen Testament
WZHalle	*Wissenschaftliche Zeitschrift der Martin-Luther-Universität, Halle-Wittenberg. Gesellschafts- und Sprachwissenschaftliche Reihe*
WZJena	*Wissenschaftliche Zeitschrift der Friedrich-Schiller-Universität, Jena. Gesellschafts- und Sprachwissenschaftliche Reihe*
WZKM	*Wiener Zeitschrift für die Kinde des Morgenlandes*
ZAW	*Zeitschrift für die alttestamentliche Wissenschaft*
ZDMG	*Zeitschrift der deutschen morgenländischen Gesellschaft*
ZKG	*Zeitschrift für Kirchengeschichte*
ZNW	*Zeitschrift für die neutestamentliche Wissenschaft und die Kunde der älteren Kirche*
ZPEB	Tenney, M. C., ed. *The Zondervan Pictorial Encyclopedia of the Bible.* 5 vols. Grand Rapids, Mich., 1975.
ZRGG	*Zeitschrift für Religions- und Geistesgeschichte*
ZTK	*Zeitschrift für Theologie und Kirche*
ZWT	*Zeitschrift für wissenschaftliche Theologie*

II. OTHER WRITINGS

Bible and Apocrypha

Gen	Genesis	Tob	Tobit
Ex	Exodus	Jdt	Judith

Lev	Leviticus	AddEsth	Additions to Esther
Num	Numbers	WisSol	Wisdom of Solomon
Deut	Deuteronomy	Sir	Sirach
Josh	Joshua	1Bar	1 Baruch
Judg	Judges	LetJer	Letter of Jeremiah
Ruth	Ruth	PrAzar	Prayer of Azariah
1Sam	1 Samuel	Sus	Susanna
2Sam	2 Samuel	Bel	Bel and the Dragon
1Kgs	1 Kings	1Mac	1 Maccabees
2Kgs	2 Kings	2Mac	2 Maccabees
1Chr	1 Chronicles	Mt	Matthew
2Chr	2 Chronicles	Mk	Mark
Ezra	Ezra	Lk	Luke
Neh	Nehemiah	Jn	John
Esth	Esther	Acts	Acts
Job	Job	Rom	Romans
Ps(s)	Psalms	1Cor	1 Corinthians
Prov	Proverbs	2Cor	2 Corinthians
Eccl (Qoh)	Ecclesiastes	Gal	Galatians
Song	Song of Songs	Eph	Ephesians
Isa	Isaiah	Phil	Philippians
Jer	Jeremiah	Col	Colossians
Lam	Lamentations	1Thes	1 Thessalonians
Ezek	Ezekiel	2Thes	2 Thessalonians
Dan	Daniel	1Tim	1 Timothy
Hos	Hosea	2Tim	2 Timothy
Joel	Joel	Tit	Titus
Amos	Amos	Phlm	Philemon
Obad	Obadiah	Heb	Hebrews
Jonah	Jonah	Jas	James
Micah	Micah	1Pet	1 Peter
Nah	Nahum	2Pet	2 Peter
Hab	Habakkuk	1Jn	1 John
Zeph	Zephaniah	2Jn	2 John
Hag	Haggai	3Jn	3 John
Zech	Zechariah	Jude	Jude
Mal	Malachi	Rev	Revelation
2Ezra	2 Ezra		

Old Testament
Pseudepigrapha (see Appendix 1)

New Testament
  Apocrypha and
  Pseudepigrapha (see Appendix 2)
Dead Sea Scrolls (see Appendix 4)
Philo

All abbreviations are according to *Studia Philonica* with the exception that
titles of Philonic treatises are italicized.

Josephus
Ant	*Jewish Antiquities*
Apion	*Against Apion*
Life	*Life of Josephus*
War	*Jewish Wars*

Nag Hammadi Codices (see Appendix 3)
Early Fathers
AdvHaer	Epiphanius, *Adversus Haereses*
AdvPelag	Jerome, *Dialogi adversus Pelagianos*
AposCon	Apostolic Constitutions
CommGen	Procopius of Gaza, *Commentary on Genesis,* Part I
CommIsa	Basil Caesar, *Commentary on Isaiah*
CommJn	Origen, *Commentary on the Gospel of St. John*
DialTrypho	Justin, *Dialogue with Trypho*
DivInst	Lactantius, *Divine Institutes*
ExcerPss	Origen, *Excerpta in Psalmos*
FragEv	Origen, *Fragmenta in Evangelium*
HE	Eusebius, *Historia ecclesiastica*
HebQuaestin	
LibGen	Jerome, *Hebrew Questions on the Book of Genesis*
Hom	Macarius, *Spiritual Homilies*
Paid	Clement of Alexandria, *The Tutor (Paidagōgos)*
Philoc	Origen, *Philocalia*
PrEv	Eusebius, *Praeparatio evangelica*
Princ	Origen, *De principiis*
Ref	Hippolytus, *Refutation of All Heresies*
Strom	Clement of Alexandria, *Stromata*

Rabbinics
Ab	Abot
ARN	Abot deRabbi Nathan
AZ	ʿAbodah Zarah
b. (before a	

rabbinic	Babylonian
text)	Talmud
BB	Baba Batra
Bek	Bekorot
Ber	Berakot
BHM	Bet ha-Midrasch
Bikk	Bikkurim
BM	Batei Midrashot
BMeṣ	Baba Meṣiʿa (Talmudic tractate)
DeutR	Debarim Rabbah
EcclR	Qohelet Rabbah
ʿEduy	ʿEduyyot
ʿErub	ʿErubin
ExR	Šemot Rabbah
GedMos	Gedulah Moshe
GenR	Gereʾšit Rabbah
Giṭṭ	Giṭṭin
Ḥag	Ḥagigah
Ḥall	Ḥallah
Ḥull	Ḥullin
Ker	Keritot
Kel	Kelim
Ket	Ketubot
Kid	Kiddushin
LamR	Ekah Rabbah
LevR	Wayyiqra Rabbah
m. (before a rabbinic text)	Mishnah
Makk	Makkot
Meg	Megillah
Men	Menahot
Mik	Mikwaʾot
MK	Moʿed Katan
Naz	Nazir
Ned	Nedarim
Nidd	Niddah
NumR	Bedmidbar Rabbah
OM	Ozar Midrashim
Par	Parah
Pes	Pesaḥim

PetMos	Petiroth Moshe
PR	Pesikta Rabbati
PRE	Pirke deRabbi Eliezer
RH	Rosh Hashanah
RuthR	Rut Rabbah
Sanh	Sanhedrin
SER	Seder Eliyahu Rabbah
Shab	Shabbat
SifDeut	Sifre Deuteronomy
SongR	Šir Hašširim Rabbah
Soṭ	Soṭah
Sukk	Sukkah
t. (before a rabbinic text)	Tosephta
Taʿan	Taʿanit
TargOnk	Targum Onkelos
TargYer	Targum Yerushalmi
TarJon	Targum Jonathan
Ter	Terumot
y. (before a rabbinic text)	Jerusalem Talmud
Yad	Yadayim
Yeb	Yebamot
Yom	Yoma
Zeb	Zebahim

III. ADDITIONAL ABBREVIATIONS

Ar.	Arabic
Aram.	Aramaic
Arm.	Armenian
BM	British Museum
c.	circa
cf.	compare
ch(s).	chapter(s)
col(s).	column(s)
contr.	contrast
Cop.	Coptic
ET	English translation

Eth.	Ethiopic
fol(s).	folio(s)
Gk.	Greek
GNMM	Good News for Modern Man
Heb.	Hebrew
JB	Jerusalem Bible
Kar.	Karshuni
KJV	King James Version
l. ll.	line(s)
Lat.	Latin
lit.	literally
LXX	Septuagint
MS(S)	Manuscript(s)
MT	Masoretic Text
n. nn.	note(s)
NAB	New American Bible
NEB	New English Bible
NJB	New Jerusalem Bible
NT	New Testament
OT	Old Testament
OTA	Old Testament Apocrypha
OTP	Old Testament Pseudepigrapha
par.	parallel texts
pt(s).	part(s)
rec(s).	recension(s)
RSV	Revised Standard Version
Russ.	Russian
SBL	Society of Biblical Literature
Slav.	Slavic
SV	Standard Version
Syr.	Syriac
Vat.	Vatican
vs(s).	verse(s)

SELECTED AND ANNOTATED BIBLIOGRAPHY

This bibliography on the Jesus of history, especially Jesus Research, is selected from a large group of books and focused (with some necessary exceptions) on major books published since 1980. Obviously, works in English are highlighted, because of the audience to whom the present work is directed. For reviews of scholarly publications on Jesus from 1965 through 1980 see W. G. Kümmel's articles in *ThRu* n.F. 40 (1975) 289–336; n.F. 41 (1976/1977) 198–258, 295–363; n.F. 43 (1978) 105–61, 232–65; n.F. 45 (1980) 48–84, 293–337.

Anderson, H. *Jesus and Christian Origins: A Commentary on Modern Viewpoints.* New York, 1964. [a brilliant book, informed historically and theologically, which attempts to assess the so-called "New Quest of the Historical Jesus"]

Anderson, N. *The Teaching of Jesus* (The Jesus Library). Downers Grove, Ill., 1983. [Although there are some significant insights into the methodology for discerning Jesus' authentic words, Anderson falls into some absurd positions, notably: "the suggestion that declarations made by Christian prophets in the name of Jesus as revelations from the heavenly Lord were included in the traditions as sayings of the earthly Jesus runs directly counter to the available evidence" (p. 21). Has he ever read the *ex ore Christi* sections of the OdesSol, and the *egō eimi* pronouncements in Jn?]

———. *Jesus Christ: The Witness of History.* Downers Grove, Ill., 1985. [Anderson has read widely and presents here a well-written theological book, even an apologetic statement. Unfortunately, the impression is given that it is a historical book.]

Aulén, G. *Jesus in Contemporary Historical Research,* transl. I. H. Hjelm. Philadelphia, 1976. [The former Bishop of the Church of Sweden insightfully assesses the publications on historical-critical Jesus Research from 1960 to 1975. He intends to demonstrate "that within a certain framework scholarship has arrived at a consensus which testifies to a degree of historical trustworthiness" (p. viii).]

Aune, D. E. "The Prophetic Role of Jesus" and "The Prophecies of Jesus," in *Prophecy in Early Christianity and the Ancient Mediterranean World*. Grand Rapids, Mich., 1983; pp. 153–88. [Aune, an erudite scholar, illustrates that the earliest followers of Jesus did creatively shape the Jesus traditions, and the early Christian prophets, and prophesying believers, did equate their own (inspired) words with the authentic sayings of Jesus of Nazareth, who "apparently regarded himself as a prophet" (p. 171), and who was identified as a prophet by many of his contemporaries. Aune also demonstrates that it does not appear likely "that many oracles of the risen Lord became assimilated to sayings of the historical Jesus" (p. 245).]

Baarda, T. *Early Transmission of Words of Jesus: Thomas, Tatian and the Text of the New Testament*, eds. J. Helderman and S. J. Noorda. Amsterdam, 1983. [Baarda is one of the finest NT philologians in the world; the value of the present book is the demonstration of the importance of second-century witnesses to the gospel traditions, including the Diatessaron, in evaluating authentic Jesus sayings. See esp. pp. 191–92.]

Badham, L. *Verdict on Jesus: A New Statement of Evidence*, rev. and updated by P. Badham. London, 1983. [a popular defense of "the fact that Christianity is based on the personality of a real and vivid historical figure" by the former Vicar of Windsor]

Badia, L. F. *Jesus: Introducing His Life and Teaching*. New York, 1985. [simple lucid prose, best suited for some church groups; but at times too uncritical: "Jesus was born in Bethlehem, Judea (the West Bank today) in the first century" (p. 16). Jesus may not have been born in Bethlehem (at least the debates among scholars should be mentioned); he was not born in the first century C.E.]

Bammel, E., and C. F. D. Moule, eds. *Jesus and the Politics of His Day*. Cambridge, New York, 1984. [26 magisterial essays by established scholars]

Baumbach, G. *Jesus von Nazareth im Lichte der jüdischen Gruppenbildung*. Berlin, 1971. [—an informed discussion of Jesus' possible relation with the Zealots, the Sicarii, the Sadducees, and the Pharisees (note: no Essenes)—Baumbach affirms that Jesus collided with each of these groups]

Beaude, P. M. *Jésus de Nazareth* (Bibliothèque d'histoire du Christianisme 5). Paris, 1983. [pedagogical introduction; intends to summarize the substantial results of the historical study of Jesus over 200 years]

Bell, J. B. *The Roots of Jesus: A Genealogical Investigation*, ed. R. I. Abrams. Garden City, N.Y., 1983. [The Director of the New York Historical Society, a professional genealogist, studies, from a historical point of view, the use of genealogies in the first century C.E., and attempts to trace Jesus' ancestry.]

Benoit, P. *Exégèse et théologie,* 4 vols. Paris, 1961–82. [See esp. "Réflexions sur la *Formgeschichtliche Methode,"* in vol. 1, pp. 25–61.]

————. *Jesus and the Gospel,* transl. B. Weatherhead, 2 vols. New York, 1973–74. [See esp. "Reflections on 'Formgeschichtliche Methode,' " vol. 1, pp. 11–45; there are other major studies on Jesus and first-century Jerusalem.]

Betz, O. "Jesus und Jerusalem," in *Wie Verstehen Wir das Neue Testament?* Wuppertal, 1981; pp. 23–46. [a clear, concise, informed introduction]

————. "Probleme des Prozesses Jesu," *ANRW* II, 25,1 (1984) 565–647. [a solid examination of the trial of Jesus]

————. *What Do We Know About Jesus? The Bedrock of Fact Illuminated by the Dead Sea Scrolls,* transl. M. Kohl. London, 1968. [a conservative statement by a scholar who really knows early Jewish literature]

Borg, M. J. *Conflict, Holiness & Politics in the Teachings of Jesus* (Studies in the Bible and Early Christianity 5). New York, Toronto, 1984. [Contending that Jesus was a Jewish holy man, sage, and prophet, Borg writes a seminal book on the quest for holiness by Jesus and his fellow Jews in a time of conflict.]

Bornkamm, G. *Jesus of Nazareth,* transl. I. and F. McLuskey with J. M. Robinson. New York, London, 1960. [the first and still the best post-Bultmannian attempt to write an account of Jesus' life and teaching]

Bowker, J. *Jesus and the Pharisees.* (Cambridge, 1973). [solid and insightful, claims that Jesus was a "rebellious elder" who opposed Jewish extremists (=*perushim*) and "resisted the view" that the observance of the Torah is indispensable]

Braun, H. *Jesus: Der Mann aus Nazareth und seine Zeit.* Stuttgart, 1984. [—a significantly revised and expanded work that has been popular and influential (ET: *Jesus of Nazareth: The Man and His Time,* transl. E. R. Kalin.—Philadelphia, 1979 = a translation of the German edition of 1969)]

Brown, R. E. *Jesus, God and Man: Modern Biblical Reflections.* New York, 1967. [Seeking to speak to the "widespread opposition to the humanity of Jesus" (p. ix), Brown addresses two main questions: "Does the New Testament call Jesus God?" and "How much did Jesus know?"]

Bruce, F. F. *The Hard Sayings of Jesus* (The Jesus Library). London, 1983. [a solid and honest study of Jesus' harsh sayings by one of the finest classically trained NT specialists]

————. *Jesus and Christian Origins Outside the New Testament.* Grand Rapids, Mich., 1974; London, 1984 (with some minor revisions). [an authoritative introduction to references to Jesus outside the canon]

Buchanan, D. *The Counselling of Jesus* (The Jesus Library). Downers Grove, Ill., 1985. [The principal of St. Paul's College, Grahamstown, South Africa, uses the records about Jesus' counseling to construct a model for Christian counselors; confessional, informed.]

Bultmann, R. *History of the Synoptic Tradition,* transl. J. Marsh, rev. ed. New York, London, 1963. [a classic definition of form criticism through a demonstration of how the synoptic traditions took shape]

————. *Jesus and the Word,* transl. L. P. Smith and E. H. Lantero. London, 1958. [Bultmann's work on Jesus; note these famous words: "I do indeed think that we can know almost nothing concerning the life and personality of Jesus, since the early Christian sources show no interest in either, are moreover fragmentary and often legendary; and other sources about Jesus do not exist." (p. 14)]

————. *Jesus Christ and Mythology.* New York, 1958. [—a biblical theological attempt to struggle with the contemporary meaning of Jesus' eschatology—Bultmann defines his program for demythologizing (the argument is slanted by a penchant for existentialism).]

————. *Theology of the New Testament,* transl. K. Grobel; 2 vols. New York, 1951, 1955. [Bultmann was the most influential NT scholar of this century; he denigrated the search for the historical Jesus, claiming that the *"message of Jesus* is a presupposition for the theology of the New Testament" (vol. 1, p. 3; italics his) and that the believer today is moved to follow Jesus because of existential reasons and the confrontation with him in the word preached.]

Canale, A. *Understanding the Human Jesus: A Journey in Scripture and Imagination.* New York, 1985. [Canale is neither a biblical scholar nor a theologian; he is a psychologist who portrays a Jesus who is very much alive. Critical scholars will tend to reject the book as uninformed; if so, they will miss some refreshing and imaginative thoughts (see "Sexuality," pp. 131–36).]

Capon, R. F. *The Parables of the Kingdom.* Grand Rapids, Mich., 1985. [not a historical study of Jesus]

Carpenter, H. *Jesus.* Oxford, 1980. [an interesting and thoughtful attempt to describe Jesus' life, by the biographer of J. R. R. Tolkien]

Casciaro, J. M. *Jesus and Politics,* transl. M. Adams. Dublin, 1983. [brief reflections on the meaning of Jesus' messiahship in the first century, from the view of liberation theology]

Catchpole, D. R. *The Trial of Jesus.* Leiden, 1971. [scholarly and informed, good review of research, contends that the Sanhedrin trial of Jesus is basically historical]

Charlesworth, J. H. "From Barren Mazes to Gentle Rappings: The Emergence of Jesus Research," *The Princeton Seminary Bulletin* N.S. 7 (1986) 221–30. [published more than a year after *Jesus Within Judaism* was completed; concerns the appearance of Jesus Research]

———. "The Historical Jesus in Light of Writings Contemporaneous with Him," *ANRW* II, 25,1 (1982) 451–76. [a demonstration of Jesus' Jewishness by highlighting the appearance of the concept "the Kingdom of God" in early Jewish documents]

———. "Research on the Historical Jesus," *Proceedings of the Irish Biblical Association* 9 (1985) 19–37. [clarification of the new trend to take seriously the fruitfulness of Jesus Research]

———. "Research on the Historical Jesus Today: Jesus and the Pseudepigrapha, the Dead Sea Scrolls, the Nag Hammadi Codices, Josephus, and Archaeology," *The Princeton Seminary Bulletin* N.S. 6 (1985) 98–115. [an attempt to assess the importance of the OTP, the Dead Sea Scrolls, the Nag Hammadi Codices, Josephus, and archaeological discoveries, for Jesus Research]

———. "Jesus and Jehohanan: An Archaeological Note on Crucifixion," *ExpT* 84 (1973) 147–50. [a study of the crucifixion of Jesus in light of the archaeological insights derived from the remains of a man crucified in, or near, Jerusalem before 70 C.E.]

Conzelmann, H. *Jesus*, ed. J. Reumann. Philadelphia, 1973. [a major work that is extremely skeptical about recovering Jesus' authentic words, especially any of the Son of Man sayings]

Cornfeld, G. *The Historical Jesus: A Scholarly View of the Man and His World.* New York, London, 1982. [a popular work on the new insights from archaeology on the Jesus of history; marred by a failure to observe the redactional quality of the Gospels]

Crossan, J. D. *Four Other Gospels: Shadows on the Contours of Canon.* New York, 1985. [—a study of the Gospel of Thomas, Egerton Papyrus 2, the Secret Gospel of Mark, and the Gospel of Peter—Most important for Jesus Research is Crossan's claim, and attempted illustration, that the oldest layer of the Gospel of Peter antedates and is used by the Evangelists Mark, Matthew, Luke, and John.]

———. *In Fragments: The Aphorisms of Jesus.* New York, London, 1983. [Dedicated to Jesus Research, Crossan examines Jesus' brief wisdom sayings and develops a method for distinguishing between authentic and inauthentic aphorisms.]

———. *In Parables: The Challenge of the Historical Jesus.* San Francisco, Cambridge, 1973, 1985. [scholarly, well organized, a major study]

Dahl, N. A. *The Crucified Messiah and Other Essays.* Minneapolis, 1974. [important for numerous reasons, not the least of which are the distinguished ability of the author, and his argument why the title "Christ" was transferred to Jesus]

──────. *Jesus in the Memory of the Early Church.* Minneapolis, 1976. [A significant corrective to Kähler and Bultmann is Dahl's insight that the "gospel is intended to be a witness and thereby an inspired 'commemoration' of the life and work of Jesus, in which everything radiates with the light of the resurrection." (p. 28)]

de Jonge, M. *Jesus: Inspiring and Disturbing Presence,* transl. J. E. Steely. New York, 1974. [M. de Jonge is a world-renowned scholar on Early Judaism and Early Christianity; see esp. "The Inquiry After the Man Jesus of Nazareth." (pp. 38–55)]

Derrett, J. D. M. "Law and Society in Jesus's World," *ANRW* II, 25,1 (1984) 477–564. [a brilliant work by perhaps the world's authority on first-century Palestinian law]

Dibelius, M. *Jesus,* transl. C. B. Hedrick and F. C. Grant. London, Philadelphia, 1949, 1963. [It is unfortunately often unobserved that a cofounder of form criticism wrote a book on Jesus. For me, it is a classic.]

Dodd, C. H. *The Founder of Christianity.* New York, London, 1970. [One of the foremost English NT scholars, Dodd sought to discern what can be known about Jesus.]

──────. *The Parables of the Kingdom.* London, 1935, 1961 (rev. ed.). [one of the major studies on Jesus' parables]

Duling, D. C. *Jesus Christ Through History.* New York, 1979. [a well-organized review of the study of the historical Jesus (or the lack of such a study) from the first century until the mid-seventies]

Dungan, D. L. *The Sayings of Jesus in the Churches of Paul.* Philadelphia, 1971. [a major study of Jesus sayings in Paul's authentic letters]

Dunn, J. D. G. *The Evidence for Jesus.* Philadelphia, 1985. [insightful; replies to Wilson, *Jesus: The Evidence*]

──────. *Jesus and the Spirit: A Study of the Religious and Charismatic Experience of Jesus and the First Christians as Reflected in the New Testament.* Philadelphia, 1975. [Dunn, who is rapidly becoming a widely influential thinker, writes an informed book, which, *inter alia,* demonstrates how Jesus spoke ecstatically and how early Christian prophets spoke as if they were Jesus, creating sayings of Jesus.]

Echegaray, H. *The Practice of Jesus,* transl. M. J. O'Connell. Maryknoll, N.Y., 1984. [a penetrating argument why the social setting of pre-70 Palestinian Judaism is not an empty framework but part of the essence of Jesus' life and teachings. Echegaray was a pioneer in explicating the theology of liberation, and here he asks, "How—according to the Gospels—did Jesus live poverty?"]

Eichholz, G. *Das Rätsel des historischen Jesus und die Gegenwart Jesu Christi,* ed. G. Sauter. Munich, 1984. [the publication of two lectures given in 1948 (first time, but repeated and updated) and 1966 (with minor updating to 1983)]

Falk, H. *Jesus the Pharisee: A New Look at the Jewishness of Jesus.* New York, 1985. [Rabbi Falk seeks to show that Jesus was related to the Pharisaic School of Hillel and attacked the Pharisaic School of Shammai.]

Farmer, W. R. *Jesus and the Gospel: Tradition, Scripture, and Canon.* Philadelphia, 1982. [A brilliant and creative NT scholar seeks, among other purposes, to discern how the Jesus traditions originated and developed; indicative of the new trend in the study of the historical Jesus—"Jesus Research"—is the following judgment: "We have access to a large body of first-rate historical evidence that is decisive in answering important questions about Jesus. . . ." (p. 21)]

Firpo, G. *Il problema cronologico della nascita di Gesù,* with a note by F. Fabbrini (Biblioteca di Cultura Religiosa 42). Brescia, 1983. [The convergence of astronomical data and the records regarding Quirinius' census place the date for Jesus' birth in 7/6 B.C.E.]

Flusser, D. *Bemerkungen eines Juden zur christlichen Theologie* (Abhandlungen zum christlich-jüdischen Dialog 16). Munich, 1984. [See esp. "Jesus und die Synagoge," pp. 10–34.]

———. *Jesus,* transl. R. Walls. New York, 1969. [—one of the greatest studies on Jesus by a Jew—Flusser is a brilliant linguist, and he knows the world and thought of pre-70 Palestinian Judaism.]

———. *Die rabbinischen Gleichnisse und der Gleichniserzähler Jesus. 1. Teil: Das Wesen der Gleichnisse* (Judaica et Christiana 4). Bern, 1981. [a significant corrective to NT scholars who tend to read Jesus' parables as if this literary form were not found in Early Judaism]

Gager, J. G. "The Gospels and Jesus: Some Doubts About Method," *JR* 54 (1974) 244–71. [a dated critique of the attempts of the new questers, indeed an expression of "skepticism about the possibility of the quest" (p. 272)]

Gerhardsson, B. *The Origins of the Gospel Traditions.* Philadelphia, 1979. [Gerhardsson further develops his well-known position that Jesus' sayings were studied and preserved by a group of Jews—the *collegium* of "the Twelve"—who memorized his teachings. His reflections are informed and should be carefully studied. He allows for the creative character of early Christian teaching and points out some major flaws in form criticism, but his arguments are sometimes forced, and he concentrates almost exclusively on rabbinics.]

Goppelt, L. *Theology of the New Testament,* transl. J. Alsup, ed. J. Roloff; 2 vols. Grand Rapids, Mich., 1981, 1982. [a major corrective to

Bultmann's claim that Jesus was a presupposition of NT theology; weak on the historical background of Early Christianity but full of significant theological insights]

Grant, M. *Jesus: An Historian's Review of the Gospels.* New York, 1977. [The distinguished historian of Rome steers easily through difficult passages; e.g., suggesting that while Jesus may have been born in Cana or Capernaum, he probably was born in Nazareth and certainly came from Galilee.]

Green, M. *The Empty Cross of Jesus* (The Jesus Library). Downers Grove, Ill., 1984. [a confessional and theological reflection on the death of Jesus]

Griffiths, M. *The Example of Jesus* (The Jesus Library). Downers Grove, Ill., 1985. [designed for spiritual reflection]

Guevara, H. *La Resistencia Judía Contra Roma en la Época de Jesús.* Ph.D. dissertation, Pontificio Instituto Bíblico, 1981. [—an insightful examination of the ambience of Jesus, specifically the Jewish resistance against Rome from 4 B.C.E. to 41 C.E.—Guevara shows why Jesus should not be portrayed as a Zealot]

Habermas, G. R. *Ancient Evidence for the Life of Jesus.* New York, 1984. [A presentation of the extrabiblical evidence for Jesus is vitiated somewhat by the desire to "point out another aspect of the truly exceptional historical and scientific evidence for" Jesus' resurrection.]

Hagner, D. A. *The Jewish Reclamation of Jesus: An Analysis and Critique of Modern Jewish Study of Jesus.* Grand Rapids, Mich., 1984. [a reliable discussion of why and how Jewish scholars today have taken up the study of Jesus of Nazareth]

Hamerton-Kelly, R. *God the Father: Theology and Patriarchy in the Teaching of Jesus* (Overtures to Biblical Theology). Philadelphia, 1979. [The former Dean of the Chapel in Stanford University presents a sensitive, probing, historically and theologically informed book.]

Harnisch, W. (ed.). *Gleichnisse Jesu: Positionen der Auslegung von Adolf Jülicher bis zur Formgeschichte* (Wege der Forschung 366). Darmstadt, 1982. [19 major articles on Jesus' parables are reprinted.]

Harris, H. A. *Greek Athletics and the Jews,* ed. I. M. Barton and A. J. Brothers. Cardiff, 1976. [—a major corrective to the usual portrait of first-century Jews—Harris argues that Jesus chose to frequent the cities near the Sea of Galilee, and Palestinian Jews were attracted to Greek (or Hellenistic) athletic contests.]

Harvey, A. E. *God Incarnate.* London, 1981. [Harvey argues that "in broad outline the story of Jesus as recorded in the Gospels commends itself to both literary critics and New Testament scholars as substantially true." (p. 6)]

————. *Jesus and the Constraints of History.* Philadelphia, 1982. [Harvey perceptively sees and illustrates that any great thinker such as Jesus must wed his or her message to the norms and constraints of the particular social, historical, and linguistic situation.]

Hengel, M. *Between Jesus and Paul: Studies in the Earliest History of Christianity,* transl. J. Bowden. London, 1983. [One of the most influential scholars today, Hengel contends that Jesus was eschatologically enthusiastic, was convinced of his messianic relationship with God, and was aware that God's Kingdom was dawning with his activity.]

————. *The Charismatic Leader and His Followers,* transl. J. C. G. Greig (Studies of the New Testament and Its World). Edinburgh, 1981. [—an unusually informed work—Hengel demonstrates that Jesus was neither a rabbi nor an eschatological prophet: "Jesus' 'charisma' breaks through the possibilities of categorization in terms of the phenomenology of religion. The very uniqueness of the way in which Jesus called individuals to 'follow after' him is an expression of this underivable 'messianic' authority." (p. 87)]

————. *Crucifixion: In the Ancient World and the Folly of the Message of the Cross,* transl. J. Bowden. London, 1977. [a significant study of the manner of Jesus' execution]

Higgins, A. J. B. *The Son of Man in the Teaching of Jesus* (*SNTS* MS 39). Cambridge, 1980. [Jesus' authentic Son of Man sayings are those which reflect his expectation of being vindicated after death through his exaltation before God in order to fulfill the functions of the Son of Man, specifically to judge and to bring salvation.]

Hill, D. "Jesus: 'A Prophet Mighty in Deed and Word,' " in *New Testament Prophecy* (New Foundations Theological Library). Atlanta, 1979; pp. 48–69. [Jesus is seen as a "prophet" who is also unique. Aune is critical of M. E. Boring's work (see *JBL* 91 [1972] 501–21, and *SBL Seminar Papers 1973. SBI Seminar Papers 1974,* and *SBL Seminar Papers 1976*); Hill devastates it (calling it at times cavalier and irresponsible). Both Aune and Hill argue that there are significant problems in attributing Jesus sayings to Christian prophets; they emphasize that we have no refined methodology for distinguishing between authentic and inauthentic Jesus traditions.]

Hoffmann, R. J. *Jesus Outside the Gospels.* New York, 1984. [Claiming that the intracanonical gospels are "the missionary propaganda of the cult of Christ" (p. 7), Hoffmann turns to extracanonical references to Jesus. Unfortunately much of this book is reactionary, even polemical, against the consensus of modern scholars (and of Christianity). The following statement is preposterous: "We cannot be certain whether he (Jesus) was 'crucified *under* Pontius Pilate,' . . . or was stoned as a heretic by his fellow Jews. . . ." (pp. 127–28)]

Hollenbach, P. W. "The Conversion of Jesus: From Jesus the Baptizer to Jesus the Healer," *ANRW* II, 25,1 (1984) 196–219. [an interesting, very perceptive examination of a little explored area in Jesus' life]

Horsley, R. A., and J. S. Hanson. *Bandits, Prophets, and Messiahs: Popular Movements in the Time of Jesus* (New Voices in Biblical Studies). Minneapolis, New York, 1985. [a social history of pre-70 Palestine that is a needed corrective to past studies on the Jesus of history and an impressive prolegomenon to Jesus Research]

Jeremias, J. *Abba: Studien zur neutestamentlichen Theologie und Zeitgeschichte.* Göttingen, 1966. [Jeremias argues that Jesus' uniqueness resides in his familiar address to God: Abba, "Father."]

———. *The Eucharistic Words of Jesus,* transl. N. Perrin. London, 1966. [—a seminal study on Jesus' last supper with his disciples—Jeremias contends that it was a Passover meal which was a climax to other messianic meals, and that Jesus had only one purpose in mind: "to assure the disciples of their possession of salvation." (p. 261)]

———. *New Testament Theology: The Proclamation of Jesus,* transl. J. Bowden. New York, 1971. [In many ways this unfinished work was the magnum opus of Jeremias, who—like Goppelt—wisely saw that NT theology begins with Jesus' own message (or at least an attempt to discover and understand it). Jeremias was confident that we could recover Jesus' message, even hear echoes of his voice.]

———. *The Parables of Jesus,* transl. S. H. Hooke (New Testament Library). London, 1963 (6th ed., rev.; see now the 9th ed.: po *.Die Gleichnisse Jesu.* Göttingen, 1977). [one of the major attempts to study Jesus' parables in terms of the historical setting]

———. *The Prayers of Jesus,* transl. J. Bowden, Chr. Burchard, and J. Reumann (SBT, Second Series 6). London, 1967; repr. Philadelphia, 1979. [a philological and historical study of prayer life in Jesus' time and his own prayers within that setting]

———. *Unknown Sayings of Jesus,* transl. R. H. Fuller. London, 1964 (2d ed.). [the best study of the agrapha since Resch]

Jónsson, J. *Humour and Irony in the New Testament: Illuminated by Parallels in Talmud and Midrash,* with a Foreword by K. Stendahl (BZRG 28). Leiden, 1985. [—a significant study of Jesus' use of humor—See esp. pp. 166–99.]

Kähler, M. *The So-called Historical Jesus and the Historic Biblical Christ,* transl. C. E. Braaten, with a Foreword by P. J. Tillich. Philadelphia, 1964 (first published in 1896). [—a classic work that influenced most biblical scholars and theologians (even Tillich), esp. until c. 1953—far too influential (on Dibelius, Bultmann, Schmidt, and others) is this exaggerated and misleading statement: "Every detail of the apostolic recollection of Jesus can be shown to have been preserved for the sake of its religious significance" (p. 93). Now it is widely recognized that even the earliest liturgies, embedded in Paul's early letters, are impregnated with secular, historical facts. These were considered religiously significant, because the Palestinian Jesus Movement was historically grounded, and a feeling for history was one of the characteristics of the earliest followers; indeed it was demanded by polemical encounters with other Jews. Historical significance and religious significance are not to be separated out as antithetical.]

Käsemann, E. "The Problem of the Historical Jesus," in *Essays on New Testament Themes,* transl. W. J. Montague (SBT 41). London, 1964; pp. 15–47. [This influential essay opened the "New Quest" for the historical Jesus. Käsemann perspicaciously saw that history is accessible only through tradition and understandable only through selection and interpretation.]

————. *Der Ruf der Freiheit,* 5th ed. Tübingen, 1972, 1981. (ET of 3rd ed.: *Jesus Means Freedom,* transl. F. Clarke. London, 1969; Philadelphia, 1970) [powerful and persuasive arguments that turn on many penetrating insights, notably this one: "So the problem becomes, not whether the 'liberal' man (Jesus) was devout, but, in so far as there ever was anything here to discuss, whether and why the devout man (Jesus) was 'liberal.' " (p. 19)]

Keck, L. E. *A Future for the Historical Jesus: The Place of Jesus in Preaching and Theology.* New York, 1971. [Although designed for preachers and theologians, this study by the Dean of Yale Divinity School is profoundly insightful from the historical point of view. Note, for example, Keck's warning that Jesus must not be studied in isolation from the early Church or Early Judaism, "not only from what he produced but from what produced him." (p. 33)]

Kee H. C. *Jesus in History: An Approach to the Study of the Gospels.* New York, 1977, 2d ed. [an excellent introduction to the study of the Gospels, with attention given to the search for the historical Jesus]

————. *Miracle in the Early Christian World: A Study in Sociohistorical Method.* New Haven, London, 1983. [—a mine of information—for Jesus Research see "Miracle and the Apocalyptic Tradition." (pp. 146–73)]

Kennedy, G. A. *New Testament Interpretation Through Rhetorical Criticism.* Chapel Hill, London, 1984. [The importance of this book is the application of rhetorical criticism to the NT traditions by a specialist on rhetoric in antiquity; see esp. "Deliberative Rhetoric: The Sermon on the Mount, the Sermon on the Plain, and the Rhetoric of Jesus." (pp. 39–72)]

Kesel, J. D. *Le refus décidé de l'objectivation: Une interprétation du problème du Jésus historique chez Rudolf Bultmann* (Analecta

Gregoriana 221). Rome, 1981. [—a theological reflection on presuppositions and methodologies in the study of the historical Jesus—The Christian does not believe in the historical Jesus but in a living Christ who is experienced existentially; neither God nor revelation can be objectified. To me, these philosophical and theological reflections dehistoricize Christianity, divorce it from the particularity of history, and hence from Jesus of Nazareth.]

Kissinger, W. S. *The Lives of Jesus: A History and Bibliography.* New York, London, 1985. [—the first monumental attempt to review rapidly the major attempts at a "life of Jesus" from the first harmonies in the second century to the "new quest"—Most of the works listed in the Bibliography are marred by precritical presuppositions, as Kissinger notes.]

Kretz, L. *Witz, Humor und Ironie bei Jesus.* Freiburg im Olten, 1982, 2d ed. [an informative insight into Jesus' use of humor]

Küng, H. *On Being a Christian.* Garden City, N.Y., 1976. [Küng is not a biblical scholar; his book is included in this bibliography only because of its importance in signaling the new confidence, evidenced by many scholars, in our ability to discover the historical Jesus behind the NT narratives.]

Kuhn, H.-W. "Die Kreuzesstrafe während der frühen Kaiserzeit: Ihre Wirklichkeit und Wertung in der Umwelt des Urchristentums," *ANRW* II, 25, 1 (1984) 648–793. [a superb and erudite study of crucifixion in antiquity]

Lapide, P. *Israelis, Jews, and Jesus,* transl. P. Heinegg; Foreword by S. Sandmel. Garden City, N.Y., 1979. [—a moving appeal for honest dialogue between Christians and Jews, by citing the respect for Jesus in some of the great Jewish thinkers of this century, namely C. N. Bialik (the poet laureate of modern Hebrew) and J. Klausner (who wrote *Yeshu Ha-notzri* for his students at Hebrew University)—To be honest, I must voice disagreement with Lapide's claim that all four Gospels were composed in Hebrew (they are, however, essentially based on earlier Semitic sources that were sometimes already at a written stage).]

Leenhardt, F. J. *La mort et le testament de Jésus* (Essais bibliques 6). Geneva, 1983. [a theological discussion of the meaning of Jesus' death and the Eucharist]

Leivestad, R. "Jesus—Messias—Menschensohn: Die jüdischen Heilandserwartungen zur Zeit der ersten römischen Kaiser und die Frage nach dem messianischen Selbstbewusstsein Jesu," *ANRW* II, 25,1 (1984) 220–64. [an exploration of the possible impact of Jewish messianic beliefs, defined broadly, on Jesus' self-understanding]

Leroy, H. *Jesus: Überlieferung und Deutung* (Erträge der Forschung 95). Darmstadt, 1978. [a solid review of research on "The Quest of the Historical Jesus," from Schweitzer through the late seventies]

Lindars, B. *Jesus: Son of Man; A Fresh Examination of the Son of Man Sayings in the Gospels in the Light of Recent Research.* Grand Rapids, Mich., 1983. [I can agree with Lindars, a fine NT scholar, that some of the Son of Man sayings in the Gospels are authentic and do "provide important evidence for his understanding of his mission" (p. viii). But I must lament that he misses the marked shift by experts on the OTP to recognize that the Son of Man is a pre-70 Jewish messianic, apocalyptic title in 1En.]

Lohfink, G. *Jesus and Community: The Social Dimension of Christian Faith,* transl. J. P. Galvin. London, 1985. [Among Lohfink's numerous important insights is the argument that Jesus' symbolic and prophetic action of creating twelve disciples "exemplified the awakening of Israel and its gathering in the eschatological salvific community, something beginning then through Jesus." (p. 10)]

———. *The Last Day of Jesus: An Enriching Portrayal of the Passion.* Notre Dame, Ind., 1984. [a clearly written attempt by a NT biblical theologian to show that Jesus' passion is not a play, but "an extremely concrete event that unfolded amid the play of very real power blocs which successfully pursued their interests to the end with deadly earnestness." (p. 8)]

Mackey, J. P. *Jesus the Man and the Myth: A Contemporary Christology.* 1979, 1985. [A gifted theologian addresses to a wide audience his assessment of "the central problems and the tentative solutions which have accrued in recent times to the perennial quest for the spirit of Jesus." (p. 2)]

Mackowski, R. M. *Jerusalem: City of Jesus,* photographs by G. Nalbandian. Grand Rapids, Mich., 1980. [The photographs are beautiful, the text sometimes uninformed and slanted to fundamentalist Christians.]

Maier, J. *Jesus von Nazareth in der Talmudischen Überlieferung* (Erträge der Forschung 82). Darmstadt, 1978. [—one of the major studies of Jesus in light of the Talmud, by a distinguished and careful scholar— Maier rightly claims, in light of early Jewish traditions, that the distinction between "the historical Jesus" and the "proclaimed Christ" is based on false dichotomies. He also perceptively argues that *Ant* 18 contains a Christian reworking of an authentic reference to Jesus by Josephus.]

Manson, T. W. *The Servant-Messiah: A Study of the Public Ministry of Jesus.* Grand Rapids, Mich., 1953, 1977, 1980. [This well-known book is now reissued with a Foreword by F. F. Bruce, who claims notably that Manson's arguments that Jesus interpreted the Son of Man in light of Isaiah's servant "are completely convincing."]

Marsh, J. *Jesus in His Lifetime*. London, 1981. [an attempt to tell with integrity the story of Jesus "to the typical 'twentieth century man.' "]

Marshall, I. H. *I Believe in the Historical Jesus*. Grand Rapids, Mich., 1977, 1979. [a methodological prolegomenon to any attempt to write a historical account of Jesus, by a conservative NT scholar who teaches at the University of Aberdeen]

Marxsen, W. *The Beginnings of Christology*, transl. P. J. Achtemeier and L. Nieting, with an Introduction by J. Reumann. Philadelphia, 1979. [Brilliantly and powerfully, Marxsen argues (contra Bultmann, but consonant with Moule) that "Jesus is always the one who is proclaimed—even when he himself appears as the proclaimer" (p. 81). For Marxsen, the Palestinian Jesus Movement (my term) was shaped by a Christ kerygma, which is profoundly post-Easter, and a Jesus kerygma, which is definitely pre-Easter.]

Messori, V. *Wat te zeggen van Jezus: Hyposthesen over zijn persoon en werk*, with a Foreword by M. Muggeridge. [a book by an Italian journalist, not intended for scholars; a series of theological reflections]

Meyer, B. F. *The Aims of Jesus*. London, 1979. [This Roman Catholic scholar contends that a new approach to the historical Jesus is fruitful and that Jesus intended to restore Israel. Jesus' focal point was the proclamation of the imminence of God's reign, which "meant the imminent restoration of Israel. . . ." (p. 221)]

Meyer, M. W. (transl.). *The Secret Teachings of Jesus: Four Gnostic Gospels*. New York, 1984. [translations, introductions, and notes to the Secret Book of James, the Gospel of Thomas, and the Secret Book of John]

Mitton, C. L. *Jesus: The Fact Behind the Faith*. Grand Rapids, Mich., 1974. [well-written reflections on the verifiable aspects of Jesus, for reflective Christians]

Moule, C. F. D. *The Origin of Christology*. Cambridge, New York, 1977. [In this important work, Moule argues that Christology developed out of authentic Jesus traditions, and that the genesis of Christology is found in "the impact made by him on those who knew him during his ministry . . . and the impact made by him after the resurrection . . ." (p. 5). Christology interpenetrates Jesus Research.]

Neill, S. *The Supremacy of Jesus* (The Jesus Library). Downers Grove, Ill., 1984. [The focus is on Jesus as a historic figure; confessional but informed.]

Neusner, J. *Judaism in the Beginning of Christianity*. Philadelphia, 1984. [Neusner is the most prolific author in the field of Early Judaism; although his focus is not Jesus Research, the present monograph is directly related to that area. Here Neusner correctly points to the various theologies and messianisms in Early Judaism and to the fact that "Jesus came into a world of irrepressible conflict." (p. 32)]

O'Neill, J. C. *Messiah: Six Lectures on the Ministry of Jesus: The Cunningham Lectures 1975–76.* Cambridge, 1980, 1984. [O'Neill is engaged in Jesus Research, and his thoughts are insightful and refreshingly independent.]

Pelikan, J. *Jesus Through the Centuries: His Place in the History of Culture.* New Haven, London, 1985. [—an erudite study by the Sterling Professor of History at Yale University—Pelikan rightly emphasizes that Jesus was a Jew and that the "first attempts to understand and interpret his message took place within the context of Judaism, and it is likewise there that any attempt to understand his place in the history of human culture must begin." (p. 11)]

Perkins, P. *Hearing the Parables of Jesus.* New York, 1981. [a study guide to, not a historical study of, the parables by a learned and articulate NT scholar]

Perrin, N. *Jesus and the Language of the Kingdom: Symbol and Metaphor in New Testament Interpretation.* Philadelphia, 1976. [a significant examination of Jesus' teaching; see next entry]

————. *Rediscovering the Teaching of Jesus* (New Testament Library) London, 1967. [Perrin was one of the most brilliant and influential thinkers during the sixties and seventies, during the waning years of the so-called "New Quest." Moving from under the influence of Jeremias to Bultmann, but hindered by a secondhand knowledge of first-century Palestinian Judaism, he tenaciously held to the position that one can recover Jesus' authentic words; and he developed widely influential methods to attempt this task.]

Pesce, M. "Discepolato gesuano e discepolato rabbinico: Problemie prospettive della comparazione," *ANRW* II, 25, 1 (1984) 351–89. [In the light of the oft-repeated claim that Jesus' disciples were phenomenologically different from the rabbis' disciples, it is good to see Pesce attempt a comparative study between them.]

Prophet, E. C. *The Lost Years of Jesus.* Malibu, Calif., 1984. [—the most recent, and perhaps the most elaborate, publication of the well-known claim that Jesus spent the years from thirteen to twenty-nine in northern India—Prophet looks at texts of little or no interest to most biblical scholars, who may well use biblical data to disparage such publications.]

Ramsey, M. *Jesus and the Living Past: The Hale Lectures 1978.* Oxford, New York, 1980. [The former Archbishop of Canterbury affirms the necessity of employing honest and rigorous historical criticism in the study of Christian origins and wisely evokes Bishop Lightfoot's famous dictum: "Though the gospel is capable of doctrinal exposition, and though it is eminently fertile in moral results, yet its substance is neither a dogmatic system nor an ethical code, but a person and a life" (p. 25). For Ramsey, the event of Jesus includes the precrucifixion life of Jesus, as well as the passion and resurrection, and it must be seen "not as antecedent to the event of the Church but as one event with the origin of the Church." (p. 32)]

Riches, J. *Jesus and the Transformation of Judaism.* London, 1980. [For Riches, the essential "pressing question" concerns Jesus' purpose, and for him it is that "Jesus advocated powerfully and originally the virtues of patience, forgiveness and long-suffering love" (p. x). But these virtues were characteristic of religious Jews and of the Jewish ethical writings (see *OTP,* vol. 2, and Sir). Riches tends to talk about ideas and gives us little insight into first-century intellectual history; also he sometimes exaggerates the creativity and uniqueness of Jesus without really pausing to listen to the other first-century Jews.]

Riesner, R. *Jesus als Lehrer: Eine Untersuchung zum Ursprung der Evangelien-Überlieferung,* 2d ed. (WUNT 2.7). Tübingen, 1984. [This young German NT scholar claims that the Jesus traditions were preserved and protected by a School of Jesus, which antedates the cross, since Jesus, like other Jewish teachers, gathered around himself a circle of scholars and students.]

Robinson, J. M. *A New Quest of the Historical Jesus* (SBT 25). London, 1959; repr. recently. [a penetrating, primarily theological assessment of post-Bultmannian biblical research on Jesus, with an affirmed optimism in the "New Quest"]

Ruether, R. R. *To Change the World: Christology and Cultural Criticism.* New York, 1983. [Although this little book is not a study of the historical Jesus, it is a series of incisive theological reflections, which are often impressively informed about Jesus' own life and setting by a gifted and perceptive NT theologian. See esp. "Jesus and the Revolutionaries: Political Theology and Biblical Hermeneutics," pp. 7–18.]

Sanders, E. P. *Jesus and Judaism.* Philadelphia, 1985. [Sanders is very influential today because of his work on Paul. His *Jesus and Judaism* is the most important work on Jesus published in the eighties, although he unfortunately tends to read back into first-century Palestine the "normativeness" of post-Jamnia Judaism. Also, his work is somewhat tendentious and idiosyncratic.]

———. "Jesus, Paul and Judaism," *ANRW* II, 25,1 (1984) 390–450. [a study absorbed somewhat in Sanders' *Jesus and Judaism*]

Sandmel, S. *We Jews and Jesus.* New York, 1965, 1973. [Sandmel was a dear friend and one of the most articulate spokesmen for authentic, honest Jewish and Christian dialogue. He also was a master of Early Christianity and Early Judaism.]

Schillebeeckx, E. *Jesus: An Experiment in Christology,* transl. H. Hoskins. New York, 1979. [a powerful, highly influential statement of the possibility of dialogue among the historian, the exegete, and the theologian, because behind the kerygmata lives "the concrete person Jesus of Nazareth," who is "the one and only basis for an authentic Christology." (p. 82)]

Schlatter, A. *Die Geschichte des Christus,* with a Foreword by H. Stroh and P. Stuhlmacher. Stuttgart, 1977. (This 3rd. ed. is a reprint of the 1923 version.) [Many reviews of the study of Jesus during this century fail to discuss the brilliantly independent historical work by Schlatter. Fortunately, Stuhlmacher is behind the reprinting of Schlatter's volumes. Schlatter's eyes, in the present work, are not on Bultmann, but on first-century Palestinian phenomena, especially the historical Jesus, who is portrayed as the basis for NT theology.]

————. *Jesus—der Christ,* with an Introduction by R. Riesner. Basel, 1978. [a reprinting of 8 articles]

Schürmann, H. "Zur aktuellen Situation der Leben-Jesu-Forschung," in *Geist und Leben* 46 (1973) 300–10. [argues correctly for confidence in the attempt to study the Jesus of history]

Schweitzer, A. *The Mystery of the Kingdom of God: The Secret of Jesus' Messiahship and Passion,* transl. W. Lowrie. New York, 1964, 1970. (The German original was completed in 1901 but published in 1914.) [Schweitzer attempts to understand Jesus' life, beginning from the passion; he seeks to depict Jesus as a figure of *"overwhelming heroic greatness"* (p. 274, his italics). This argument is confused, subjective, and poorly researched.]

————. *The Quest of the Historical Jesus: A Critical Study of Its Progress from Reimarus to Wrede,* with a Preface by F. C. Burkitt transl. W. Montgomery. New York, 1910, 1911[2]; repr. 1922, 1926, 1931, 1964. (The German edition dates from 1906.) [Schweitzer's masterpiece has three layers: 1) he demonstrates how the nineteenth-century lives of Jesus are mere projections of the authors' own opinions of Jesus, 2) he argues correctly that Jesus must be portrayed within his first-century Palestinian environment and that he was highly influenced by eschatology (a view far too exaggerated by Schweitzer), and 3) he waxes mystical over how Jesus comes to Christians today "as One unknown, without a name, as of old, by the lake-side" (p. 403). I doubt he was so unknown to his earliest followers. They knew his name. Schweitzer's work caused a moratorium on the "old quest" in most scholarly circles.]

Schweizer, E. *Jesus,* transl. D. E. Green (New Testament Library). London, 1971. [A gifted scholar shares his personal reflections on the Jesus of history.]

Segal, A. F. "Jesus, the Jewish Revolutionary," *Rebecca's Children: Judaism and Christianity in the Roman World.* Cambridge (Mass.), London, 1986; pp. 68–95. [an informed and sensitive attempt to show that Jesus headed an apocalyptic movement]

Segundo, J. L. *The Historical Jesus of the Synoptics,* transl. J. Drury (Jesus of Nazareth Yesterday and Today 2) Maryknoll, N.Y., London, 1985. [Liberation theologians such as Segundo are turning more and more to writing on the historical Jesus; one of the best of these works is the present volume. The work is devoted to Jesus' sayings, but there is sometimes a confusion between what the evangelists intended and what Jesus may have meant (e.g., see p. 60).]

Sloyan, G. S. *Jesus in Focus: A Life in Its Setting.* Mystic, Conn., 1983, 1984. [Sloyan sees Jesus as a mystic, an unconventional teacher, and an outsider, who taught and lived out holiness and love. The book is informed by the best in the world's great religions, is engagingly written, and is a persuasive statement why the Jesus story is possible and necessary.]

Smith, M. *Jesus the Magician.* San Francisco, Cambridge, 1978, 1981. [Unusually informed of the primary sources, including now the Jewish magical papyri, Smith focuses on magic in first-century Palestine and contends that Jesus should be understood as an "itinerant magician or holy man." (p. 109)]

Stanton, G. *Jesus of Nazareth in New Testament Preaching* (*SNTS* MS 27). Cambridge, 1974. [the Jesus of history as remembered in the earliest preaching, an emphasis on the reliability at times of this tradition]

Stauffer, E. "Jesus, Geschichte und Verkündigung," *ANRW* II, 25,1 (1984) 3–130. [virtually a book on Jesus by a distinguished scholar of Early Judaism and Jesus. Notably, Stauffer thinks that Jesus was born early in 7 B.C.E. in Bethlehem.]

Stein, R. H. *Difficult Sayings in the Gospels: Jesus' Use of Overstatement and Hyperbole.* Grand Rapids, Mich., 1985. [a good discussion of Jesus' wise use of exaggerated language: "We must be careful to distinguish between the *referent* of a verbal symbol, that is, the object to which it literally refers, and the *sense,* that is, the mental image the verbal symbol is intended to convey." (p. 99)]

———. *The Method and Message of Jesus' Teachings.* Philadelphia, 1978. [Esp. noteworthy is the discussion on the form of Jesus' teaching.]

Stewart, J. S. *The Life and Teaching of Jesus Christ.* Edinburgh, 1933, 1957 (2d ed.), 1977 (with amendments), 1981. [It is encouraging to see the Church of Scotland Committee on the Religious Instruction of

Youth endorse from 1933 through 1981 Stewart's wise statement that "the Gospels are not biographies at all. . . . What we have is a set of 'memoirs,' selected historical reminiscences." (p. 1)]

Strauss, D. F. *The Life of Jesus Critically Examined,* ed. P. C. Hodgson, transl. G. Eliot (Lives of Jesus Series). Philadelphia, 1972. [Strauss' *Das Leben Jesu,* of 1835, is the first great attempt to write a biography of Jesus. Strauss was the first one to see the importance and complexity of myth in the study of Early Judaism and Early Christianity.]

Suhl, A. (ed.). *Der Wunderbegriff im Neuen Testament* (Wege der Forschung 295). Darmstadt, 1980. [See esp. R. and M. Hengel's "Die Heilungen Jesu und medizinisches Denken." (pp. 338–73)]

Tambasco, A. J. *In the Days of Jesus: The Jewish Background and Unique Teaching of Jesus.* New York, 1983. [This little book contains the acknowledgment that the Gospels are not biographies; but it is confessional, posits false options (". . . the apostles were interested in . . . 'Who *is* Jesus, alive and present to us?' and not 'Who *was* Jesus?' " [p. 7]), is dated (p. 50), and is simplistic (even Marcionistic): "God had, as a matter of fact, come to humanity with a new kingdom and was showing himself through Jesus as 'Dad' " (p. 71). Affirmations about Jesus' unique teachings are the means for distorting his Jewish background.]

Tatum, W. B. *In Quest of Jesus: A Guidebook.* Atlanta, 1982. [a reliable introduction]

Theissen, G. *The Miracle Stories of the Early Christian Tradition,* transl. F. McDonagh, ed. J. Riches (Studies of the New Testament and its World). Edinburgh, 1983. [encyclopedic and a major improvement in cataloguing data. See esp. "Jesus' Miracles," pp. 277–80.]

———. *Sociology of Early Palestinian Christianity,* transl. J. Bowden. Philadelphia, 1978. [The book is the first attempt in the second half of this century to apply the methods and perspectives of sociology to the Jesus movement, but it is not Theissen's best work. One of the controversial claims made by Theissen is that a sociology of the Jesus movement makes a contribution to solving some of the problems in the quest for the historical Jesus because "it suggests that we should assume a continuity between Jesus and the Jesus movement and in so doing opens up the possibility of transferring insights into the Jesus movement to Jesus himself." (p. 4)]

Trocmé, E. *Jésus de Nazareth: Vu par les témoins de sa vie* (Bibliothèque Théologique). Neuchâtel, Switzerland, 1971. [an erudite but idiosyncratic study of Jesus' influence on the diverse social strata of Palestinian Jews, by a master NT scholar]

Vermes, G. *The Gospel of Jesus the Jew: The Riddell Memorial Lectures.* Newcastle-upon-Tyne, 1981. [In the late sixties this Jewish scholar began his own quest for the historical Jesus. In this book he presents a prolegomenon to Jesus' teachings. A first-century Jewish holy man (a Galilean Ḥasid), Jesus calls for repentance, announces the coming of the Kingdom of God, is "uniquely aware of his filial relation to the Father," and seeks to inculcate in others the self-same relationship.]

―――. *Jesus and the World of Judaism.* Philadelphia, 1983. [10 significant studies published earlier but now revised]

―――. *Jesus the Jew: A Historian's Reading of the Gospels.* London, 1973, 1981. [an attempt to understand Jesus and place him in history by reading the Jewish sources as well as the NT, Jesus is portrayed as one of the Galilean miracle workers, like Ḥoni and Ḥanina ben Dosa.]

Wenham, D. (ed.). *The Jesus Tradition Outside the Gospels* (Gospel Perspectives 5). Sheffield, 1984. [contains 14 important studies by scholars, significant for the study of the transmission and preservation of Jesus traditions]

―――. *The Rediscovery of Jesus' Eschatological Discourse* (Gospel Perspectives 4). Sheffield, 1984. [Wenham argues persuasively why "the onus of proof" for the authenticity of Jesus' eschatological discourse "must be on those who deny the teaching to Jesus. . . ." (p. 373)]

Wilcox, M. "Jesus in the Light of His Jewish Environment," *ANRW* II, 25,1 (1984) 131–95. [Wilcox rightly states that the basic starting point for Christianity is Jesus himself, not the early confessions. For Wilcox, Jesus is certainly a pious man, who performs miracles, cries for repentance for all Israel before the coming judgment, treads the path of a "pacifist" type of messianism, and radicalizes the love commandment.]

Wilkinson, J. *Jerusalem as Jesus Knew It: Archaeology as Evidence.* London, 1978, 1982. [an excellent, well-written, and informative guide to the remarkable amount of physical evidence of Roman Palestine, especially Jerusalem]

Wilson, I. *Jesus: The Evidence.* London, 1984, 1985. [—highly influential in unscholarly circles, because of its relation to a television series. —Wilson does try to be objective, critical, and informed: "It was in the spirit of the art restorer—a genuine, open-minded attempt to peel back the layers—that I wrote this book." (p. 156)]

Winter, D. *The Search for the Real Jesus.* London, 1982. ["But the last decade has seen an amazing transformation. Now, the Jesus of history seems more accessible than ever. Like archaeologists swarming over a prime location, the historians and theologians have turned with gusto to the original documents, parallel historical records and the geographical sites, and at every turn have found a clearer and clearer picture emerging of Jesus of Nazareth" (pp. 8–9). Hence, I call the new development "Jesus Research."]

Witherington, B. *Women in the Ministry of Jesus: A Study of Jesus' Attitudes to Women and Their Roles as Reflected in His Earthly Life* (*SNTS* MS 51). Cambridge, New York, 1984. [a careful study]

Yadin, Y. "Jesus," in *The Temple Scroll: The Hidden Law of the Dead Sea Sect,* ed. M. Pearlman. London, 1985; pp. 240–42. [Yadin was convinced that "Jesus was anti-Essene." (p. 241)]

Yaseen, L. C. *The Jesus Connection: To Triumph over Anti-Semitism.* New York, 1985. [designed for the public, intended to show that Jesus, and many other admired individuals, were Jews, and that "Jesus was a defender, not a denigrator, of Judaism." (p. 2)]

Ziesler, J. A. *The Jesus Question.* London, 1980. [an introduction to the major questions related to the historical Jesus, informed by historical methodologies, addressed primarily to Christians]

Zimmermann, A. F. *Die urchristlichen Lehre* (WUNT 2.12). Tübingen, 1984. [Against Dibelius and Bultmann, but with Riesenfeld and Gerhardsson, Zimmermann contends that the transmission of Jesus' sayings was controlled by a Christian Rabbinate.]

INDEX OF
TEXTS QUOTED

SCRIPTURE
OLD TESTAMENT
Gen 1 43
 1:28 67
Ex 20:12 154, 163*n.*60
Lev 19:18 88
 24:14 124
Deut 5:12 66
 6:4 47, 106, 133
 14:1–2 157*n.*5
2Sam 7:14 150, 152
Ezra 108, 127*n.*6
 9 49
Neh 108
 9 49
Ps(s) 38, 59
 2:7 150, 152
 22 144
 25 48
 51 48
 80:9–14 159*n.*23
 89:26–27 152
 103 48
 118 124, 125, 140
 118:22 124–25
 118:22–23 140
 118:23 125
Isa 59
 5 140, 145
 5:1–7 159*n.*23

 5:7 159*n.*25
 9:1–6 152
 11:6 35
 27:2 159*n.*23
 40:3 59
 56:7 192
Jer 145
 2:21 159*n.*23
 7:11 192
 31:9 157*n.*5
 31:31–34 59
Ezek 16, 145
 19:10–14 159*n.*23
Dan 19, 33, 34, 93
 7 40
Hos 1:10 157*n.*5
 10:1 159*n.*23
Hab 2:1–2 82
Zech 9 18

NEW TESTAMENT
Mt 12–13, 15–17, 20, 21, 28, 30,
    32, 60, 66, 70, 84–86, 87, 125,
    132, 137, 141, 157*n.*13,
    159*n.*27, 191, 203, 204
 1:16 101*n.*27
 5 39
 5:3 68
 5:13, 17 190
 5:15 19

5:31–32 72
5:37 x
5:43–44 38, 74, 88
6:7–15 13
6:9 134
6:25–33 38
7:28 42
8:14–26 109
8:20 112
8:21–22 154, 188
9:6 52n.8
10:1–4 137
10:5–6 16
10:18 17
10:23 52n.8
10:37–38 84, 87, 88
11:15 190
11:28 197
12:8 52n.8
12:11 66, 67
13:9 190
13:43 190
13:56–58 89
15:24 17
16 15
19:9 10–12, 72
19:16–22 154
19:19 88
19:29 85, 89
21:7 19
21:33 159n.23
21:33–46 139
21:37 141, 161n.44
21:39 141
21:43 17
22:1–14 89
22:39 88
23:25–26 46
23:37 144
24:14 17
28:19 17

Mk 12–13 14, 18, 21, 28, 30, 57–
58, 60, 66, 72, 84, 87, 93, 125,
132, 141, 145, 147–48, 152,
159n.27, 161n.41, 161n.44,
203, 204
1:14–15 39, 44, 71
1:22 42
1:29 109
1:29–31 115
2:1–5 112
2:24 67
2:27 65
3:13–19a 137
3:21 33–34, 89
4 18
4:9 190
6:3–6 89
6:52–53 58
7:14–23 39
7:16 190
7:37 42
8:31–33 143
8:33 154
9:1 18, 19, 39, 71, 87
9:49–50 190
10:3 39
10:21 39
10:17–22 154
10:21 70
10:23–25 39
10:29 84–85, 89
10:32 143
11:17 192
11:18 42
11:27 140
12:1 159n.23
12:1–8 159n.26
12:1–9 139–40, 142, 161n.38
12:1–12 139, 158n.16, 158n.22
12:6 141, 160n.29
12:8 141

12:10 125
12:31 88
13 18, 44
13:1 119
13:32 39, 87
14:3 73
14:36 133
14:51–52 10
15:39 156
15:44 122–23
16 125
16:18 18
Lk 12, 13, 14, 19, 21, 28, 30, 60,
    66, 70, 74, 84, 86, 87, 93, 125,
    132, 141, 157n.14, 159n.23,
    159n.27, 203, 204
1 and 2 105
1:1–4 13
2:32 42
4:16–30 115
4:25–30 89
4:32 42
4:44 115
6:5 65
6:12 50
6:12–16 137
6:20 68
6:27 38
7:16 190
8:8 190
8:16 19
8:41–56 115
9:23–24 85, 89
9:27 19, 87
9:59–60 154
9:62 154
10:27 88
11:1–4 133
11:33 19
11:39–40 46
13:15 67

13:31–33 143
13:32 147
13:33 144
13:34 144
14:5 66
14:15–24 89
14:26–27 84–85, 86, 87, 88, 89
14:35 190
16:1ff. 161n.38
17:20–22 19
18:9–14 46
18:18–23 154
19:41–44 106
19:47 42
20:9–19 139, 160n.30
20:15 141
21:20–24 106
21:33 87
23:35 52n.8
Jn 12, 13, 15, 21, 28, 30, 32, 60,
    74, 78, 87, 118, 120, 125,
    129n.20, 129n.28, 132, 203
1:25–30 10
1:42 137
2:6 108
2:14 117–18
2:15 117–18
3:22 16
3:26 16
4:1 16
4:10 79
5:1–9 120
5:2–9 120
7:38 79
7:46 42
14:2 x
19:13 122
19:41 124
21:25 13
Acts 1:11 142
1:13 137

2 105
4:11 124
9:2 86
10:36–40 14
10:36–43 13
19:9 86
22 86
22:4 86
23 86
23:35 121
24:14 86
Rom 1:1–2 30
  1:1–4 24
  1:3–4 20
  8:15 133
  8:22 43
  12:20 38
  13:9 88
1Cor 15:5 157n.8
  16:22 142
2Cor 12:1–10 37
Gal 4:6 133
  5:14 88
Phil 2:6–11 21, 24
Heb 31, 61

13:12 123
13:12–13 141
Jas 31, 57, 101n.27
  2:8 88
1Pet 2:7 124
Jude, 34
  14–15 44
Rev 19, 31, 33, 34, 36, 142
  1:13 36
  1:18 36
  2:7 190
  2:11 190
  2:17 190
  2:26 190
  3:5 36
  3:12 36
  3:21 36
  4:1 37
  7:17 79
  13:9 190
  21:6 79
  22:1 79
  22:17 79

OTHER TEXTS

OLD TESTAMENT APOCRYPHA

Sir 4:10 149 (Heb)
  30:1–6 154
  51:10 157n.5 (Heb)
Tob 13:4 157n.5
WisSol 2:13–16 150
  2:16–18 157n.5
  2:18 150
  11:10 157n.5
  14:3 157n.5

OLD TESTAMENT
  PSEUDEPIGRAPHA

ApAb 29, 34, 92

TAb 151
ApAdam 77, 79, 80
  8:16 80
  8:17 80
  84 79
TAdam 99n.10
LAE 80, 99n.9
2Bar 19, 34, 43, 44
  51:13 39
3Bar 34
4Bar 145
ApE1 34
  5:25 151
1En 30, 34, 39–40, 39, 63, 81,
  149

1:2 37
1:9 44
12:1–2 37
14:2 37
15:1 37
17 79
17:1 37
37–71 39, 40, 42, 52*n*.7, 52*n*.8,
  139, 162*n*.46
39:4*f. ix*
41:2 *ix*
46 41
48 41
48:1–10 41
53:6 41
62–63 42
69 42
81:5 49
94:8–9 39
96:4–8 39
97:8–10 39, 68
102–104 39
104:6 39
104:13 162*n*.46
105:2 149, 162*n*.46
106:1 162*n*.46
108:15 81
2En *x,* 32, 34, 35, 37, 38
1a:1[A] 35, 81
23:6[J] 35
24:3[J] 81
40:1[J] 81
42 39
44 81
45 39
45:3[J] 81
48:6–7 81
49:1[J] *ix*
52 38, 39, 81
61 39, 81
61:2[A] *ix*

63 39
65:8[J] 82
66:6[J] 35, 81
3En 1:8 162*n*.51
EzekTrag 150
4Ezra 19, 34, 38, 43, 44, 52*n*.7,
  82–83, 106, 150, 151
7:28 151
7:29 151
7:46 49
8:62 82
13:3 151
13:37 151
13:52 151
14:9 151
14:24 82
14:26 82
14:46 82
HelSynPr 31
LivPro 145, 148
MartIs 145
JosAsen 151, 162*n*.52
6:3 151
6:5 151
12:5–12 49
12:14–15 157*n*.5
13:13 151
18:11 151
21:4 151
23:10 151
PrJos 151
Jub 30, 63
1:24 157*n*.5
1:28 157*n*.5
19:29 157*n*.5
24:19 25, 79
1Mac 1:14 104
2Mac 4:7–20 104
7:23, 36
3Mac 6:3 134
6:8 134

7:20 128*n*.8

PrMan 43, 48, 49, 50, 51
  7b 50
  11–12 48

Tmos 34

SibOr 4.165 79

OdesSol 31, 38
  6:18 79
  11:7 79
  38:7–16 37

PssSol 44, 68, 105
  10:7–8, 159*n*.25
  17:23 136
  17:42 136

T12P 30, 31, 34, 63, 138

TLevi 4:2, 150

DEAD SEA SCROLLS (AND
QUMRAN FRAGMENTS)

1QS (Rule of the
Community) 49, 54, 56, 74
  3 71
  6 71

4QS 62

1QSa (Rule of the
Congregation) 56

1QSb (Collection of
Blessings) 56

CD (Cairo Damascus
Document) 56
  10.14–11.18 66
  11.13–14 67
  19.34 79

1QHab (Habakuk
Commentary) 54, 56
  7.4–5 82

1QIs (Isaiah) 54; *Illus* 5

4QpHos (Hosea Pesher) 62

11QPs (Psalms Scroll) 56

3Q15 (Copper Scroll) 56, 120

11QTemple (Temple Scroll) 56,
61, 129*n*.18
  46.13, 14 116–17
  46.16–17 72
  48.14–15 72
  57.17–18 72

1QM (The War Scroll) 44, 56,
69
  11.9 69
  11.13 69
  13.12–14 69

1QapGen (Genesis
Apocryphon) 56

11QtgJob (Targum of Job) 56

4QpsDan A (=4Q246) 150

4QFlor (Florilegium) 150

1QH (Thanksgiving Hymns) 56,
63, 69, 105
  2.32–34 70
  4 50
  4.29–33 50
  4.31 50
  5.5–6 49
  5.13–15 69
  5.16 70
  5.18 70
  5.21–22 70
  5.22 70
  8 82
  8.7, 16 79
  9.35 157*n*.5

6QpaleoLev (Leviticus), 56

11QpaleoLev (Leviticus), 56

4QMMT, 170, *Illus* 1

4QEn li (Enoch), *Illus* 3

JOSEPHUS
Ant 2.32 151
  5.224 118
  12.241 104
  14.22 160*n*.31

15.318 121
15.365 146
15.366 146
15.392 118
15.393 118
15.411–17 118
15.5 146
17.205 146
17.255 104
17.308 160*n*.35
18 93, 94, 97, 98, 101*n*.31
18.63–64 91, 92, 93, 96, 101*n*.31, 101*n*.33
20 94, 101*n*.31
20.200 94
20.252–57 106
War 1.402 121
2.44 104
2.218 116
2.277–79 106
2.8.122 68
2.8.147 67
2.85–86 160*n*.35
5.145 116
5.148 116
5.152–60 116
6.201–13 83
6.403–4 106
6.420 116
6.425 116
12.517–19 142

PHILO
Apologia pro Judaeis 11, 68

NEW TESTAMENT APOCRYPHA AND PSEUDEPIGRAPHA
GosBarn 25
BirMar 153
GosNaz 15
GosTh 12, 77, 81, 83, 84, 86, 87, 88, 89, 90, 99*n*.12, 99*n*.17, 100*n*.20, 100*n*.21, 142, 147, 148, 152, 159*n*.23, 161*n*.41
8 190
21 190
24 190
33 19
55 84, 85, 87, 88–89
63 190
64 89
65 139, 142, 147, 161*n*.44, 190
66 140
96 190
101 85, 87, 89
InfGosTh 153

OTHER EARLY CHRISTIAN WRITINGS
Didache 12, 24, 149
7:1–3 79
Eusebius
HE 3:9 90
Ignatius
Rom 7:2 79
Jerome
AdvPelag 3:2 28*n*.4
In Amos 5:23 47
Origen
FragEv 10

RABBINICS
m.Ab 1.1 104
m.Ber 5.5 8*n*.10
m.Kel 10.1 106
LevR 11 (113a) 159*n*.27
Meg 3.73d 109
m.Par 3.2 106
m.Pes 5.5–7 116
m.Sanh 6.1 124
7.4 144
11.1 144

m.Shab 1.8 66
　3.1 66
　4.1 66
　7.1 66
　7.2 66
　7.3 66
　11.2 66
　11.5 66
　11.6 66
　18.3 66
　19.2 66
SifDeut 32:9, Section
　312 159n.27
SifLev 20:26 157n.5
b.Sukk 51b 119
b.Taʿan 23a 160n.31
b.Taʿan 25a 162n.51
m.Taʿan 3:8 160n.31
y.Taʿan 3:9[8] 160n.31
　4:5 146
TargYerLev 22:28 157n.5
m.Yom 4:2 49

　8:9 134
t.Yom 1:12 73
b.Zera im Ber 17a 151

OTHER ANCIENT PASSAGES
Agapius, *Kitāb al-ʿUnwān,* 95,
　96, 97
Plato, *Republic* VI, 5, 77
Pliny the Elder, *Natural
　History* 5.15.70, 119

NAG HAMMADI CODICES
I, 3 Gospel of Truth 77
V, 2 The (Coptic) Apocalypse of
　Paul 80
V, 5 Apocalypse of Adam 77,
　79–80
VII, 1 Paraphrase of Shem 77,
　80
VIII, 1 Zostrianos 80
XIII, 1 Trimorphic
　Protennoia 80

INDEX OF NAMES

Aalen, A., 4
Achtemeier, P. J., 100n.20, 164n.62
Aland, K., 83, 87
Albright, W. F., 78, 103, 120, 126
Allegro, J., 57
Alsup, J., 7n.5
Anderson, B. W., 127, 130n.36
Anderson, H., 4, 7n.8, 10, 44, 140, 142, 158n.16, 158n.20, 160n.28, 166, 168, 223
Anderson, N., 197, 198, 223
Attridge, H. W., 100n.20
Auden, W. H., 187
Augstein, R., 25, 98
Aulén, G., 223
Aune, D. E., 11, 224
Avigad, N., 106, 119, 127n.3, 129n.22
Avi-Yonah, M., 160n.35

Baarda, T., 99n.12, 224
Bacon, B. W., 31
Badham, P. and L., 195, 224
Badia, L. F., 224
Bammel, E., 4, 101n.33, 198, 224
Baras, Z., 160n.35
Barkay, G., 159n.24
Barrett, C. K., 118

Barton, D. M., 157n.10
Barton, I. M., 127n.3
Bauer, B., 25, 97
Bauer, J. B., 83, 92
Baumbach, G., 224
Baumotte, M., 203, 206n.12
Beaude, P. M., 224
Beker, J. C., 34, 52n.3
Bell, J. B., 224
Bengel, J. A., 86
Benoit, P., 55, 103, 121, 129n.27, 165, 168, 170–71, 225
Bernard, J. H., 118, 120, 129n.26
Betz, H. D., 199
Betz, O., 101n.33, 225
Bianchi, U., 99n.7
Bienert, W., 101n.32
Billerbeck, P., 159n.27
Birnbaum, P., 157n.4
Black, M., 40, 52n.8, 53n.10, 57, 101n.31, 158n.18, 162n.46, 162n.47
Böhlig, A., 79, 80, 99n.9
Borg, M. J., 202, 225
Bornkamm, G., 1, 4, 7n.7, 29n.8, 103, 165, 225
Bousset, W., 79
Bowden, J., 7n.3, 75n.9, 130n.32, 157n.3, 157n.11
Bowker, J., 4, 225

Braaten, C. E., 171*n*.3
Brandon, S. G. F., 90
Braun, H., 4, 20, 203, 225
Breech, J., 195
Bright, J., 103
Broshi, M., 124
Brothers, A. J., 127*n*.3
Brown, R. E., 103, 118, 163*n*.55, 168, 225
Bruce, F. F., 101*n*.29, 195, 225, 226
Buchanan, D., 226
Bultmann, R., 2, 3, 5, 7*n*.1, 7*n*.4, 17, 24, 25, 42, 44, 78, 79, 98*n*.3, 103, 120, 131, 132, 141, 155, 156*n*.1, 158*n*.16, 158*n*.22, 164*n*.62, 166, 167, 171*n*.4, 171*n*.8, 171–72*n*.9, 189, 190, 191, 205, 206*n*.5, 206*n*.13, 226
Burchard, C., 162*n*.52
Burkitt, F. C., 92
Buri, F., 25

Canale, A., 226
Capon, R. F., 226
Carmignac, J., 43, 53*n*.11
Carpenter, H., 187, 226
Casciaro, J. M., 226
Catchpole, D. R., 4, 226
Cave, F. H. and C. H., 129*n*.17
Cézanne, 35
Chadwick, H., 100*n*.23
Champollion, J. F., 46
Charles, R. H., 31, 40
Charlesworth, J. H., *xi n*.1, 51*n*.1, 52*n*.6, 53*n*.9, 53*n*.14, 53*n*.15, 75*n*.2, 99*n*.8, 99*n*.10, 99*n*.16, 99*n*.17, 128*n*.12, 130*n*.29, 157*n*.7, 162*n*.49, 163*n*.58, 163*n*.61, 227
Chilton, B., 100*n*.19

Christie, P., 53*n*.13
Cleage, A. B., 197
Coleridge, S. T., 23
Collins, J. J., 79, 162*n*.49
Conzelmann, H., 4, 42, 149, 157*n*.11, 161*n*.42, 161*n*.45, 187, 227
Corbo, V., 111, 128–29
Cornfeld, G., 101–2, 111, 129*n*.19, 130*n*.31, 168, 193, 227
Cothenet, E., 11
Coüason, C., 123, 125, 130*n*.30, 130*n*.33, 193
Couchoud, P. L., 25, 97
Cross, F. M., 57, 63, 75*n*.2, 75*n*.8, 103, 105
Crossan, J. D., 100*n*.19, 158*n*.18, 161*n*.41, 198, 227

Dahl, N. A., 4, 165, 168, 171*n*.3, 172*n*.10, 227, 228
Dalman, G. H., 149, 154, 162*n*.46, 163*n*.57
Danby, H., 53*n*.16, 127*n*.1
Dautzenberg, G., 11
Davies, S. L., 87, 100*n*.20
Deissmann, A., 103
Derrett, J. D. M., 228
Dibelius, M., 138, 157*n*.10, 199, 228
Dinkler, E., 172*n*.9
Dodd, C. H., 4, 13, 28*n*.3, 71, 118, 120, 129*n*.25, 142, 159*n*.26, 168, 228
Duling, D. C., 228
Dungan, D. L., 4, 13, 28*n*.2, 228
Dunn, J. D. G., 4, 142, 158*n*.21, 160*n*.29, 161*n*.44, 228
Dupont-Sommer, A., 57, 63, 75*n*.8

Echegaray, H., 201, 228
Eichholz, G., 229
Einstein, A., 166
Eliot, G., 157*n*.8
Erbetta, M., 83
Ewing, U. C., 57, 75*n*.4

Fabricius, J. A., 30, 48, 83
Falk, H., 229
Farmer, W. R., 194, 195, 229
Feldman, L. H., 91
Filson, F. V., 60, 61, 75*n*.6,
 75*n*.11
Fiorenza, E. S., 196, 197
Firpo, G., 229
Fitzmyer, J. A., 57, 75*n*.5,
 100*n*.21, 103, 130*n*.32, 157*n*.14,
 161*n*.40, 162*n*.48, 168
Fitzmyer, S. J., 75*n*.5
Flusser, D., 4, 7*n*.9, 128*n*.6, 142,
 159*n*.27, 160*n*.30, 160*n*.35, 166,
 168, 189, 205*n*.2, 229
Forster, N., 100*n*.25
Freedman, D. N., *xi*, 57, 75*n*.2,
 75*n*.6, 103, 126, 130*n*.34
Freud, S., 38
Friedlander, M., 79
Fuller, R. G., 100*n*.22
Funk, R. W., 51*n*.2, 98*n*.5

Gabra, G., 170
Gager, J. G., 171*n*.6, 229
Galvin, J. P., 28*n*.6
Gerhardsson, B., 199, 204, 229
Glueck, N., 103
Goguel, M., 97
Goldstein, J. A., 127*n*.2
Goodenough, E. R., 120
Goppelt, L., 3, 5, 7*n*.5, 7–8*n*.10,
 24, 139, 149, 151, 154, 157*n*.12,

162*n*.46, 162*n*.50, 190–92,
 206*n*.6, 229
Gordon, C. G., 159*n*.24
Grant, F. C., 157*n*.10
Grant, R., 230
Grant, R. M., 79
Greenfield, J. C., 75*n*.6
Green, D. E., 161*n*.43
Green, M., 205, 206*n*.9, 230
Greig, J. C. G., 163*n*.59
Griffiths, M., 206*n*.9, 230
Grobel, K., 7*n*.4, 206*n*.5
Guevara, H., 230
Gunkel, H., 38
Gurev, G., 25, 97, 102*n*.40
Gutman, J., 128*n*.10

Haacker, K., 101*n*.33
Haas, N., 130*n*.29
Habermas, G. R., 230
Haenchen, E., 78, 98*n*.5
Hagner, D. A., 202, 230
Hálevy, J., 40
Hamerton-Kelly, R., 157*n*.6, 230
Hanson, J. S., 232
Hanson, P. D., 35, 52*n*.5
Harnack, A., 16, 31, 46, 96,
 102*n*.37
Harnish, W., 158*n*.17, 230
Harris, H. A., 127*n*.3, 230
Harrisville, R. A., 171*n*.3
Hartman, S. S., 99*n*.8
Harvey, A. E., 29*n*.8, 192, 230,
 231
Hedrick, C. B., 157*n*.10
Helderman, J., 99*n*.12
Heller, R., *x*
Hellholm, D., 99*n*.8
Hengel, M., 4, 75*n*.9, 101*n*.33,
 103, 130*n*.32, 162*n*.48, 163*n*.59,
 166, 168, 188, 231

Hennecke, E., 83
Hesse, F., 154
Higgins, A. J. B., 187, 231
Hill, D., 11, 231
Hodgson, P. C., 157n.8
Hoehner, H. W., 161n.38
Hoffmann, R. J., 231
Hollenbach, P. W., 232
Hooke, S. H., 158n.20
Hornschuh, M., 99n.14
Horsley, G. H. R., 128n.8
Horsley, R. A., 232
Hoskins, H., 156n.2
Hoskyns, E. C., 118
Hultgård, A., 99n.8
Hüttenmeister, F., 128n.10

James, M. R., 83
Jeremias, G., 69, 75n.10
Jeremias, J. A., 4, 7n.3, 88,
    100n.22, 103, 116, 129n.17, 132,
    142, 154, 156–57n.3, 158n.20,
    159–60, 160n.27, 163n.56, 168,
    232
Jervell, J., 172n.12
Jonge, M. de., 4, 31, 154, 228
Jongeling, B., 75n.5
Jónsson, J., 206n.4, 232
Jülicher, A., 140, 141, 158n.17,
    158n.22, 159n.26

Kaasa, H. E., 172n.12
Kähler, M., 165, 232, 233
Kalin, E. R., 203
Kando (Khalil Eskander Shahin),
    55, 56
Kant, I., 191
Käsemann, E., 1, 15, 33, 34,
    51n.2, 103, 156, 165, 167, 168,
    171n.4, 233
Katsimibinis, D., 124

Keck, L., 4, 233
Kee, H. C., 4, 31, 233
Keller, H., 126
Kennedy, G. A., 199, 200, 233
Kenyon, K. M., 103, 115, 123
Kesel, J. D., 233, 234
Kierkegaard, S., 17
Kissinger, W. J., 234
Klausner, J., 163n.57
Klijn, A. F. J., 99n.14
Klostermann, E., 83
Knibb, M. A., 40
Koester, H., 99n.11, 99n.12,
    99n.18, 100n.20
Kretz, L., 189, 206n.3, 234
Kuhn, H.-W., 234
Kümmel, W. G., 29n.8, 141,
    158n.22, 163n.54
Küng, H., 234

Lagrange, M.-J., 103
Lambdin, T. O., 161n.39
Lantero, E. H., 7n.1, 156n.1
Lapide, P., 234
LaSor, W. S., 58, 59, 60
Leenhardt, F. J., 234
Leivestad, R., 234
Leroy, H., 172n.9
Levine, L. I., 128n.10, 128n.11
Levison, Jr., 99n.10
Lewis, C. S., 187
Lichtenberger, H., 57
Lightfoot, R. H., 118
Lindars, B., 235
Lohfink, G. 16, 28n.6, 235
Lohse, E., 149, 151, 162n.46,
    162n.50
Lord, J. R., 161n.42
Lüdemann, G., 99n.13

Macdonald, J., 162n.53

McIntyre, J., 155, 156, 164*n*.63
Mackey, J. P., 21, 235
Mackowski, R. M., 235
McLuskey, I. and F., 7*n*.7
MacRae, G. W., 79, 80
Maier, J., 235
Maier, P. L., 102*n*.36
Manson, T. W., 168, 235
Marcus, R., 129*n*.21
Marsh, J., 158*n*.16, 188, 236
Marshall, I. H., 236
Marxsen, W., 164*n*.62, 236
Mazar, B., 102*n*.35, 119, 129*n*.24
Merleau-Ponty, M., 17, 156
Messori, V., 236
Meyer, B. F., 4, 163*n*.61, 236
Meyer, M. W., 236
Meyers, E. M., 112, 128*n*.10,
    128*n*.12, 129*n*.16
Migne, J.-P., 48
Milik, J. T., 39, 40, 52*n*.8,
    53*n*.12, 57
Millar, F., 101*n*.31
Mitton, C. L., 236
Moffatt, J., 102*n*.37
Montague, W. J., 171*n*.4
Moraldi, L., 83
Mother Teresa, 51
Moule, C. F. D., 164*n*.62, 168,
    198, 224, 236
Muilenburg, J., 199
Müller, U. B., 11
Murphy-O'Conner, J., 57, 111–
    12, 129*n*.14
Murray, R., 99*n*.14

Nau, F., 48
Neill, S., 206*n*.9, 236
Neugebauer, O., 53*n*.10
Neusner, J., 29*n*.9, 236, 237
Newton, I., 170

Nickelsburg, G. W. E., 162*n*.49
Nieting, L., 164*n*.62
Nolan, B. M., 157*n*.13
Noorda, S. J., 99*n*.12

O'Callaghan, J., 57, 58
O'Neill, J. C., 187, 237
Ory, G., 75*n*.7

Pagels, E., 79, 98*n*.2
Pearson, B. A., 79
Pelikan, J., 165, 171*n*.5, 171*n*.6,
    172*n*.12, 237
Perkins, P., 237
Perrin, N., 4, 5, 78, 94, 98*n*.3,
    158*n*.18, 167, 171*n*.7, 237
Pesce, M., 237
Petrie, Sir Flinders, 103
Pines, S., 95, 97, 101*n*.34,
    101*n*.35, 102*n*.39
Polanyi, M., 17, 156
Potter, C. F., 32, 75*n*.3
Prophet, E. C., 237

Qimron, E., 73, 170
Quispel, G., 79, 98*n*.4, 100*n*.20

Rad, G. von, 34, 52*n*.4
Ramsey, M., 17, 187, 237, 238
Reeg, G., 128*n*.10
Reimarus, H. S., 103
Reitzenstein, R., 79
Renan, E., 74
Reumann, J., 164*n*.62
Rhoads, D. M., 160*n*.36
Richards, G. C., 100*n*.27
Riches, J., 163*n*.59, 187, 193,
    205, 238
Riesenfeld, H., 199, 204
Riesner, R., 198, 199, 204,
    206*n*.10, 238

Ringgren, H., 99n.8
Robinson, J. M., 7n.7, 20, 78, 79,
    80, 83, 99n.11, 99n.12, 99n.15,
    172n.9, 238
Robinson, S. E., 99n.10
Roloff, J., 7n.5
Ross, J.-P. B. and C. Ross,
    130n.30
Rudolph, K., 79
Ruether, R. R., 210, 238

Safrai, S., 127n.3, 128n.8,
    160n.35
Saldarini, A. J., 108, 128n.7,
    128n.8
Saller, S., 128n.13
Sanders, E. P., 2, 5, 7n.2, 8n.11,
    16, 28–29, 44, 73, 118, 157n.9,
    163n.55, 163n.61, 166, 204, 205,
    206n.13, 238
Sanders, J. A., 57, 75n.2
Sandmel, S., 238, 239
Santos Otero, A. de, 83
Schaberg, J., 201
Schillebeeckx, E., 20, 134,
    156n.2, 157n.6, 239
Schlatter, A., 239
Schleiermacher, F., 157n.8
Schnackenburg, R., 118
Schneemelcher, W., 83
Schürer, E., 47, 53n.13, 60, 92,
    101n.31, 102n.38
Schürmann, A., 4
Schürmann, H., 239
Schweitzer, A., 71, 103, 165, 195,
    239
Schweizer, E., 4, 149, 161n.43,
    240
Scott, B. B., 195
Segal, A. F., 240
Segal, J. B., 99n.14

Segundo, J. L., 240
Sekeles, E., 130n.29
Shanks, H., 112, 128n.11,
    129n.15, 130n.29
Sherwin-White, A. N., 161n.38
Shutt, R. J. H., 100n.27
Sloyan, G. S., 195, 196, 240
Smallwood, E. M., 160n.32
Smith, D. M., 118, 129n.20
Smith, L. P., 7n.1, 156n.1
Smith, M., 4, 240
Sox, D., 25
Stalker, D. M., 52n.4
Stanton, G. N., 4, 157n.13, 240
Starowiecyki, M., 83
Stauffer, E., 240
Stein, M., 129n.23
Stein, R. H., 240
Stendahl, K., 57, 206n.4
Stern, M., 128n.6, 160n.35,
    161n.37
Stewart, J. S., 10, 240, 241
Stinespring, W. F., 163n.57
Strange, J. F., 112, 128n.10,
    129n.15, 129n.16
Strauss, D. F., 103, 157n.8, 165,
    241
Strugnell, J., 57, 73
Stuhlmacher, P., 157n.13
Suhl, A., 241
Sukenik, E. L., 55, 56
Suro, R., 128n.9

Talmon, S., 57
Tambasco, A. J., 241
Tatum, W. B., 194, 241
Taylor, S., 53n.13
Thackeray, H. St. J., 100n.25
Theissen, G., 11, 188, 205n.1,
    241
Thiede, C. P., 58

Tillich, P., 17, 25
Tolkien, J. R. R., 187
Torrey, C. C., 120
Trever, J. C., 75n.1
Trocmé, E., 161n.38, 241

Unnik, W. C. van, 128n.6, 160n.35

VanderKam, J. C., 53n.10
Vaux, R. de, 55, 57, 103
Vermes, G., 4, 57, 75n.8, 101n.31, 187, 189, 241, 242
Vermes, P., 101n.31
Vielhauer, P., 42
Vilnay, Z., 127n.3
Vincent, L. H., 103

Wallace, I., 11
Walls, R., 7n.9
Weatherhead, B., 129n.27
Weill, R., 128n.11
Wells, G. A., 25, 98
Wenham, D., 203, 204, 242

Whiston, W., 90
Widengren, G., 99n.7, 99n.8
Wikgren, A., 129n.21
Wilcox, M., 160n.34, 242
Wilkinson, J., 242
Wilson, I., 201, 242
Winter, D., 193, 242
Winter, P., 4, 97, 100n.25, 101n.31, 102n.38
Witherington, B., 197, 200, 201, 243
Woude, A. S. van der, 154
Wright, G. E., 103
Wünsche, A., 163n.57

Yadin, Y., 56, 73, 75n.12, 129n.18, 243
Yaseen, L. C., 243

Zias, J., 130n.29
Ziesler, J. A., 22, 243
Zimmermann, A. F., 199, 204, 206n.11, 243
Zuckermann, B. and K., 170

INDEX OF SUBJECTS

Adam, 36, 44, 67, 80

Adonis, 203

Agapius, 95–97, 101*n*.36

Alexander Jannaeus, 62

Angelology, 71, 82, 134, 151

ʿĀnî, 69

Anti-Jewish, 6, 137

Anti-Judaism, 45, 47, 191

Anti-Semitic, 6, 137

Anti-Semitism, 45, 47, 191

Apocalypse, apocalyptic,
    apocalypticism, *ix,* 18, 19, 33–
    39, 42, 43, 44, 45, 51*n*.2,
    52*n*.5, 52*n*.6, 59, 60, 68, 77,
    79, 80, 81, 97, 99*n*.8, 165

Apollonius of Tyana, 191

Archaeologist(s), 55, 62, 103,
    104, 106, 108, 111, 115, 116,
    117, 118, 119, 120, 121, 126,
    156, 160*n*.32, 193

Archaeology, *ix, x,* 4, 6, 9, 21,
    27, 28, 46, 52*n*.8, 61, 103, 104,
    105, 108, 115, 117–18, 119–22,
    123, 126, 127, 129*n*.16, 141,
    168, 169, 193, 204

Augustine, 127, 140

Banas, 22

Beatitude(s), 38, 39, 43, 68, 70,
    201

Belial, 59

Bruce Codex, 80

Burnt House, 106, 127*n*.5; *Illus*
    11, 12, 13

Bruta facta Jesu, 18, 27

Caesarea, 47, 105, 121, 146,
    158*n*.15; *Illus* 10

Caiphas, 191

Canon, 23, 24, 26, 45, 65, 84, 85,
    86, 140, 165, 194

Capernaum, ix, 108–12, 126,
    128*n*.13, 128*n*.15, 146, 169;
    Illus 6

Christ, 14, 15, 21, 23, 27, 36, 64,
    91, 92, 94, 95, 101–2*n*.27, 120,
    143, 172*n*.9, 201

Christology, 12, 18, 21, 29*n*.8,
    155, 156, 161*n*.45, 164*n*.62,
    167, 196, 197

Church of the Holy Sepulchre,
    123–25; *Illus* 18, 19; Map II,
    V

Cicero, 200

Codex Alexandrianus, 120

Codex Ephraemi Rescriptus, 120

Constantine, 109

Coptic Psalter, 170

Dead Sea Scrolls, *ix,* 4, 9, 25, 28, 30, 32, 39, 45, 48, 51, 54, 55–60, 61–64, 68, 69, 70, 71–72, 74, 75, 77, 78, 82, 90, 99*n.*7, 104, 126, 134, 168, 191, 192, 204
See also chapters 3 and 6; Appendix 4; Index of Texts Quoted
Demons, 59
Demosthenes, 200
Disciple(s), 12, 16, 17, 25, 50, 84, 85, 95, 119, 136–38, 139, 142, 143, 144, 153, 154, 155, 157*n.*8, 164*n.*62, 169, 188, 235
Document(s), *ix,* 3, 6, 9, 10, 15, 19, 23, 24, 25, 27, 30–33, 35, 44, 48, 56, 58, 59, 63, 64, 66, 77, 79, 80, 83, 87, 108, 120, 126, 138, 145, 150, 151, 167, 169, 192, 194, 199

ʾEbhyōn, 69, 70
Eden, 36
Egeria, 109
Egypt, 46, 49, 77, 78, 81, 151
Eighteen Benedictions, 47, 106
Ekklēsia, 15
Ephiphanius, 117
Eschatology, 3, 5, 11, 16, 17, 18, 19, 33, 34, 35, 42–44, 59, 60, 71, 138, 142, 148, 165, 203
Eusebius, 90, 117
Euthus, 18
Evagrius, 90
Evangelists, *x,* 11, 12, 14, 15, 18, 19, 20, 28*n.*7, 39, 52*n.*8, 64, 103, 117, 124, 140, 144, 145, 194, 199, 200, 227, 240

Eve, 36, 80
Ex ore Christi, 223
Eyewitnesses, 11, 19, 28*n.*7

Gamaliel, 22
Gentiles, 16, 17, 19, 41, 42, 43, 67, 98, 146
Gessius Florus, 106
Gospel(s), *x,* 3, 9, 10, 11, 12, 13, 14, 15, 18, 19, 20, 21, 22, 23, 25, 26, 30, 43, 52*n.*8, 57, 59, 61, 65, 83, 84, 85, 86, 92, 120, 121, 125, 132, 133, 135, 136, 140, 153, 165, 171*n.*4, 171*n.*6, 193, 194, 195, 201, 203, 204, 206*n.*13

Ḥanina ben Dosa, 8*n.*10, 22, 105, 150–51
Hercules, 203
Herod the Great, 104, 118, 119, 121, 142, 146–47, 160*n.*35, 161*n.*37, 207*n.*13; *Illus* 7, 8, 9, 14, 15, 16
Herod Agrippa I, 116, 123
Herod Agrippa II, 94
Herod Antipas, 143, 146, 161*n.*38
Herodium, 109, 118; *Illus* 7
Hesiod, 27
Hillel, 21, 22, 27, 29*n.*9, 66, 105
Hippocrates, 27
Homer, 27
Ḥoni ha-Meaggel, 105, 145
Hymn(s), 31, 36, 48, 49, 69, 105
Hypostatic beings, 71

Ignatius of Antioch, 79
Illiad, 11
Ipsissima verba Jesu, 18, 20, 27, 65, 166, 198

Ipsissima vox Jesu, 166, 198
Ipsissimus sensus, 198
Iranian, 78, 99*n.*8, 203

James, Jesus' brother, 94,
    101*n.*27, 117
James, son of Zebedee, 17, 137
Jehohanan, 122, 123, 130*n.*29
Jerome, 28*n.*4, 47
Jerusalem, *ix, x,* 3, 13, 18, 25,
    32, 40, 55, 61, 62, 72, 73, 83,
    94, 95, 101*n.*31, 104, 105, 106,
    109, 115–17, 119, 120, 121,
    122, 123–25, 126, 127*n.*6,
    129*n.*17, 129*n.*18, 132, 138,
    140, 141, 143, 144, 145, 146,
    149, 153, 155, 158*n.*15, 158–
    59, 159*n.*24, 159*n.*25, 169, 170,
    192, 204; *Illus* 8, 11, 12, 13,
    14, 15, 16, 18, 19
Jesus
  baptism, 14, 15, 141, 169
  birth, 105, 111, 153
  cross (crucifixion), 1, 11, 12, 14,
    17, 21, 22, 25, 90, 91, 94, 95,
    97, 116, 122–25, 143, 144, 145,
    147, 148, 156, 167, 169, 193,
    204
  healing(s), 8*n.*10, 14, 24, 115,
    120, 135, 169, 203
  Kingdom (Rule) of God, 16, 17,
    19, 24, 26, 29*n.*8, 38, 44, 68,
    70, 71–72, 135, 136, 142, 154,
    155, 160*n.*36, 167, 169, 188,
    189, 196, 200, 203
  miracle(s), 14, 39, 93, 111, 115,
    135, 189, 191, 203
  parable(s), 12, 74, 84, 89, 124–
    25, 135, 139, 140, 141, 142,
    143, 145, 146, 147, 148, 149,
    153, 155, 158*n.*15, 158*n.*16,

158*n.*17, 158*n.*19, 158*n.*20,
    159*n.*26, 159*n.*27, 159*n.*28,
    159*n.*29, 159*n.*30, 161*n.*44,
    167, 189
  resurrection, 11, 12, 14, 20, 21,
    24, 33–34, 92, 94, 125, 159*n.*27
  self-understanding, *x,* 16, 20,
    28, 40, 42, 131, 132, 134–36,
    138, 139, 143, 147, 153, 154–
    55, 166, 167, 169, 196
  teaching(s), 11, 12, 13, 24, 25,
    28*n.*7, 38, 65, 88, 92, 97, 167,
    169, 189, 198, 199
Johanan ben Zakkai, 22, 105
John, son of Zebedee, 17, 137
John Hyrcanus, 62
John the Baptist, 14, 15, 16, 42,
    61, 79, 144, 169, 188
Joseph of Arimathea, 92
Josephus, *ix,* 4, 22, 28, 60, 61,
    62, 63, 67, 68, 90, 91, 92, 93,
    94, 95, 96, 97, 98, 100*n.*24,
    100*n.*27, 101*n.*29, 101*n.*30,
    101*n.*31, 101*n.*33, 101*n.*36,
    106, 108, 109, 115, 116, 118,
    119, 121, 122, 126, 146, 147,
    160*n.*32, 204
Judas, 14, 25, 98, 136, 137,
    157*n.*8, 169
Judas the Galilean, 160*n.*36

Kerygma, 2, 3, 10, 12, 13, 20,
    24, 94, 149, 171*n.*4, 172*n.*9,
    190
Koran, 11

Lord's Prayer, 50, 167

Mary, 15, 117, 153
Mary Magdalene, 205

Masada, 109, 118; *Illus* 9; Map III

Matthias, 137

Memar Marqah, 152, 162*n*.53

Mishnah, 32, 48, 50, 51, 53*n*.16, 67, 74, 104, 106, 144
See also Index of Texts Quoted

Muhammed, 25, 197

Nag Hammadi Codices, *ix,* 4, 25, 28, 77, 78–80, 81, 83, 99–100, 104, 126, 168, 204
See also chapter 4;
Appendix 3; Index of Texts Quoted

Napoleon, 46

Near East, 11, 46, 152

Nicodemus, 22, 92

NT, 3, 5, 9, 10, 11, 13, 15, 17, 20, 21, 23, 24, 25, 26, 27, 40, 52*n*.8, 58, 59, 60, 61, 70, 72, 75*n*.6, 89, 108, 126, 131, 133, 149, 153, 154, 161*n*.45, 168, 169, 170, 171*n*.6, 201, 206*n*.5

NT Apocrypha and Pseudepigrapha, 33, 83, 99*n*.16, 99*n*.17
See also Appendix 2; Index of Texts Quoted

NT Theology, 2, 3, 7*n*.3, 21, 164*n*.62, 169, 171*n*.8, 190, 206*n*.5, 206*n*.6

Old Syriac Gospels, 170; *Illus* 17

Oral Tradition, 11, 19, 20, 42, 84, 87–88, 89, 167

Origen, 10

Osiris, 203

OT, 12, 30, 38, 54, 59, 64, 71, 79, 126, 156*n*.2, 189, 199

OT Pseudepigrapha, *ix,* 4, 25, 28, 30–31, 32, 33, 34, 38, 39, 43, 45, 48, 51, 53*n*.9, 59, 63, 74, 92, 104, 126, 134, 191, 204;
See also Chapter 2; Appendix 1; Index of Texts Quoted

Palestine, *ix,* 3, 5, 9, 21, 46, 54, 59, 61, 63, 71, 82, 86, 90, 104, 108, 119, 126, 127*n*.3, 148, 158*n*.15, 165, 167, 168, 169, 172*n*.12, 193, 200, 207*n*.13

Palestinian Jesus Movement, 13, 20, 24, 31, 59, 89, 97, 103, 124, 142, 143, 167, 199, 233, 236

Papias, 20

Parables of Enoch (1En 37–71), 39, 40, 41, 52*n*.8

Paradise, 36, 38

Paul, 13, 22, 28*n*.7, 30, 34, 37, 43, 48, 50, 61, 127*n*.3, 133, 156, 157*n*.8, 199
See also Index of Texts Quoted

Peter, 14, 15, 17, 28*n*.7, 48, 109, 115, 124, 128–29*n*.13, 136, 137, 139, 154, 156, 169

Pharisees, 29*n*.9, 45–46, 59, 66, 67, 73, 202, 207*n*.13

Philo, 22, 61, 63, 68, 105, 127*n*.3

Philo-Semitism, 7

Piety, 5, 45, 47, 48, 63, 80, 105, 156*n*.2

Plato, 77

Pliny the Elder, 63, 119

Pontius Pilate, 10, 91, 93, 95, 97, 105, 106, 121, 122, 123, 191;
Illus 10

Prayer(s), 24, 45, 47, 48, 49, 50, 51, 109, 128*n*.8, 133, 134, 192

Q, 20, 83, 84, 87, 89, 108, 132, 133, 144, 157*n*.3, 157*n*.4

Qaddish, 50

Quirinius, 105

Qumran, 32, 34, 55, 57, 60, 61, 62, 63, 64, 68, 69, 71, 73, 74, 82, 83, 168, 170, 207*n*.13; *Illus* 2, 4

Qumran Scrolls. *See* Dead Sea Scrolls

Rabbi(s), 16, 18, 66, 98, 105, 188, 189

Righteous Teacher, The (Môrēh haṣ-Ṣedek), 63, 69, 70, 73, 82, 170

Romans, *x*, 3, 55, 59, 62, 82, 90, 106, 116, 123, 124, 145, 160*n*.32

Rome, 30, 36, 44, 90, 92, 108, 112, 126, 141, 145, 147, 191, 202, 203

Romulus, 191

Sabbath, 65, 66, 67, 72, 144, 202

Sadducees, 59, 73, 204, 207*n*.13

St. Catherine's Monastery, 170; *Illus* 17

Salvation, 22, 35, 79, 81, 161*n*.44

Satan, 44, 59, 154

Shammai, 66, 105

Sin, 33, 41, 43, 44, 45, 48, 49, 50, 58, 112, 134, 206–7

Sinfulness, 48, 59

Son of God, 57, 70, 149, 150, 151, 152, 156, 160*n*.29, 162*n*.51, 163*n*.44, 169

Son of Man, 3, 36, 39, 40, 41, 42, 52*n*.7, 52*n*.8, 57, 139, 167, 187, 227, 231, 235, 236

Sozomen, 90

Synagogue(s), 16, 47, 104, 108, 109, 112, 115, 127*n*.6, 128*n*.7, 128*n*.8, 128*n*.9, 128*n*.10, 128*n*.12

Synoptic(s), 21, 100*n*.21, 118, 129*n*.20, 135, 153, 163*n*.55, 203

Syro-Phoenician woman, 16

Temple, *x*, 6, 16, 49, 63, 66, 69–70, 73, 104, 106, 115, 117–19, 121, 123, 125, 126, 127*n*.6, 128*n*.12, 138, 146, 159*n*.25, 169, 191, 192, 193, 202, 207*n*.13; *Illus* 14, 15, 16

Tertulian, 127

Testimonium Flavianum, 91, 94, 95, 96, 98, 101*n*.30

Torah, 11, 36, 43, 72, 106–8, 115, 120, 133, 191

Tradition(s), 3, 6, 10–15, 16, 18, 19, 20, 21, 22, 24, 31, 32, 41, 42, 44, 49, 52*n*.8, 59, 67, 70, 79, 80, 84, 85, 86–89, 92, 115, 120, 125, 132, 136, 137, 141, 142–44, 145, 150, 153–54, 161*n*.45, 163*n*.55, 165, 166–67, 170*n*.2, 171*n*.4, 171*n*.7, 188, 192, 193, 194, 198, 199, 202, 203, 204

Twelve. *See* Disciple(s)

Unique, uniqueness, *ix*, 5, 6, 8*n*.10, 8*n*.11, 12, 38, 58, 65, 66, 70, 74, 133, 134, 153, 158*n*.20, 163*n*.55, 189, 192

Via Dolorosa, 121, Map II

Wicked Priest, 69, 73

Woes, 39, 43, 44
WW I, 22, 31
WW II, 1, 4, 7, 60, 78, 97

Zealots, 59, 207*n.*13